Praise for
High Tension
FDR's Battle to Power America

"The little known but captivating story of electricity is at the heart of the New Deal. John A. Riggs is the perfect person to tell the tale. The battles between America's most politically astute president and a powerful industry created the hybrid, public-private electricity system that we know today. The compromises necessary to ensure equity and the public interest while unleashing the energy of private markets can inform the discussion of current issues such as telecommunications, infrastructure, and tax policy."

—Walter Isaacson, author of
The Innovators, Leonardo Da Vinci, and *Steve Jobs*

"*High Tension* vividly tells of FDR's struggle to control giant utility holding companies, build government dams, and electrify rural America. He took on powerful interests and reshaped the electricity system as a novel public-private enterprise—a legacy that continues to this day. John A. Riggs tells an important story with relevance today, from reinventing electricity regulation to accommodate new clean energy technology to offering lessons for universal broadband access."

—Ernest J. Moniz, U.S. Secretary of Energy,
2013–17; CEO Energy Futures Initiative

"Electricity was the internet of its day—and bringing it to the countryside affected more Americans than any other New Deal program. It was also the source of a bitter struggle between public and private power, full of 'high tension'—the double entendre title of John A. Riggs's lucid and compelling tale. This is a fresh angle of vision on one of the most important and underappreciated stories of the first half of the twentieth century."

—Jonathan Alter, author of
The Defining Moment: FDR's Hundred Days and the Triumph of Hope

"*High Tension* is an innovative history of the chaos and conniving that created America's transformative electricity system (judged by the *Atlantic* to be the greatest invention since the printing press). John A. Riggs has given us a compelling read. Thoroughly researched and gracefully written, it crisply covers the historical panorama of the New Deal's hard-won achievements of breaking up the giant utility holding companies and bringing light and power to the vast darkened regions of our nation."

—Martin J. Sherwin, Pulitzer Prize-winning co-author of
American Prometheus: The Triumph and Tragedy of J. Robert Oppenheimer

"Narrative history at its best. Riggs brings FDR to life as he gathers a team of brilliant and eccentric New Dealers to battle for public power, rural electrification, and the abolition of holding companies. The industry fights back with a coalition of stock manipulators and free enterprise proponents led by a remarkable advocate named Wendell Willkie."

—Bruce Babbitt, U.S. Secretary of the Interior, 1992–2000

"The story of electrification is the story we must return to, over and over again, to understand what it really means to build a public utility. Our age, like every age, has its essential services, and as John A. Riggs demonstrates, getting it right does not happen by accident, nor without a fight, but demands great political courage."
—**Tim Wu, Professor, Columbia Law School;** *New York Times* **contributing opinion writer; and author of** *The Curse of Bigness: Antitrust in the New Gilded Age*

"Electric utilities are fascinating combinations of economics, technology, and politics. Somehow all three have to be kept in harness for utility companies to succeed. Mr. Riggs explores the interplay of these factors in one of the most complex periods in the history of the industry. Good reading for anyone who likes the lights to come on and the computer to work."
—**John Rowe, former CEO of Commonwealth Edison and Exelon**

"A valuable resource dealing with a largely—and undeservedly—ignored slice of FDR's New Deal agenda, but also of American history and, indeed, of all human progress."
—**David Pietrusza, author of** *1948: Harry Truman's Improbable Victory and the Year That Transformed America*

"John A. Riggs gives us a fresh look at the people and politics that brought electricity to virtually all Americans, shaped today's economy, and powered the Arsenal of Democracy that led to victory in World War II. *High Tension* is a strong reminder of Edmund Burke's eighteenth-century admonition that 'politics ought to be adjusted, not to human reasoning, but to human nature, of which the reason is a part.'"
—**Charles B. Curtis, Chairman, Federal Energy Regulatory Commission, 1977–81**

"The US electric system not only underpins our economy, but also our way of life. Yet most Americans know nothing about its history. This story of a critical era in the development of the US power sector is a riveting tale of inventors, entrepreneurs, politics, legal battles, and shenanigans. The reader will come away with a new appreciation for what we take for granted."
—**Elizabeth Moler, Federal Energy Regulatory Commissioner, 1988–97, Chair, 1993–97; Deputy US Energy Secretary 1997–98, Acting Secretary, 1998**

"In an engaging narrative, *High Tension* captures a transformative time in American history with titanic characters, exploring some of the most compelling battles of the early twentieth century with scintillating detail. It's also a book with powerful relevance today, reminding us that the conflict between corporate concentration of power and public interests is ongoing, unresolved, and demands our attention."
—**John F. Wasik, author of** *The Merchant of Power: Thomas Edison, Samuel Insull and the Creation of the Modern Metropolis*

HIGH TENSION

FDR'S BATTLE TO POWER AMERICA

JOHN A. RIGGS

DIVERSION
BOOKS

Copyright © 2020 by John A. Riggs

All rights reserved, including the right to reproduce this book
or portions thereof in any form whatsoever.

For more information, email info@diversionbooks.com

Diversion Books
A division of Diversion Publishing Corp.
www.diversionbooks.com

First Diversion Books edition, November 2020
Paperback ISBN: 978-1-63576-732-2
eBook ISBN: 978-1-63576-733-9

Printed in The United States of America

1 3 5 7 9 10 8 6 4 2

Library of Congress cataloging-in-publication data is available on file.

To Judy,
for lighting my life

CONTENTS

For nearly forty years my vocation has been energy policy, and for even longer my avocation has been history and politics. In late 1990, I read *The Prize: The Epic Quest for Oil, Money & Power*, the Pulitzer Prize-winning history of the oil industry by renowned energy expert and author Daniel Yergin. It was one of the most informative energy books and one of the most fascinating histories I have ever read.

Upon finishing the book, I invited Yergin to be the initial, scene-setting witness in a two-year series of hearings in the House of Representatives Energy and Power subcommittee, of which I was then the staff director, hearings that led to the comprehensive Energy Policy Act of 1992. I also looked for a similarly informative and readable history of the electricity industry in the United States. I didn't find one, but a seed was planted. Could I "unite my avocation and my vocation," as Robert Frost yearned to do, by writing such a book?

Over time, the topic seemed to grow in importance as the industry faced new regulatory and environmental challenges and national politics became more contentious. In addition, by November 2013, a group of prominent historians, scientists, and engineers judged the electricity system to be the greatest invention since the printing press.[1] The poet and essayist Paul Valéry once lamented that historians neglected stories such as "the conquest of the earth by electricity" that have "more meaning . . . than all the political events combined," and the historian Marc Bloch wrote in 1941 that "this vast subject had still received no serious treatment." But in the United States, as elsewhere, the development of the electricity system was political as well as technological, and historians for at least the last sixty years have, in fact, explored aspects of this intersection.[2]

The industry passed through its technological and entrepreneurial

infancy in the age of Edison in the late nineteenth century—a story
that has been told often and well. After the industry's less well known
adolescence in the first quarter of the twentieth century, when it
spawned state-regulated utility monopolies and largely unregulated
interstate utility holding companies, it faced a critical fork in the road
when Franklin Roosevelt took office in the depths of the Depression.

Roosevelt's historic presidency has been even more extensively
written about than the Edison era, but none of the Roosevelt
biographies or histories of the New Deal describe in depth, or for a
general audience, the fierce, linked political battles over electricity—the
Tennessee Valley Authority, the Public Utility Holding Company Act,
the Rural Electrification Administration, and the Bonneville Power
Administration—and their importance to his administration and to
the future shape of the industry.

The focus of *High Tension* is on these battles.

Perhaps the nation's most politically astute president, Roosevelt
took on an array of powerful and sometimes corrupt antagonists—
captains of an industry led by a formidable and honest champion,
Wendell Willkie, whose role in the battle propelled him to national
fame and a bid to unseat Roosevelt in 1940. The high-tension power
lines that marched across America in the first quarter of the twentieth
century foretold a high-tension political struggle in the second, which
played out in Congress and the courts, including the court of public
opinion.

FDR and Willkie, each endowed with outstanding personal
magnetism, wound up in direct opposition over one of the most fiercely
contested issues of the day. They jousted over the right balance of
government intervention and private market forces in the electricity
system, and the enduring hybrid industry that resulted from their
struggle brought affordable electricity to almost all Americans and
powered the industrial might that won World War II. The model they
established, of hard fought political compromise and public-private
solutions, may suggest a path forward today in areas such as infrastructure, internet access, and health care.

MAJOR CHARACTERS

M. H. Aylesworth directed the National Electric Light Association in the 1920s. The utility organization became the Edison Electric Institute early in the next decade.

Hugo Black, a Democratic senator from Alabama from 1927 to 1937, New Deal supporter, and subsequently associate justice of the Supreme Court, chaired influential hearings on utility lobbying efforts on the Holding Company Act.

James Bonbright, a Columbia University finance professor, advised Governor Roosevelt on utility issues, served on his St. Lawrence Seaway Commission, and later chaired the New York Power Authority.

William Borah, a progressive Republican senator from Utah from 1907 to 1940, actively opposed Roosevelt's Court-packing proposal.

William Jennings Bryan, a progressive leader from Nebraska and strong opponent of trusts, was the Democratic nominee for President in 1896, 1900, and 1908.

John Carmody directed the Rural Electrification Administration from 1937 to 1939. Subsequently he was head of the Federal Works Agency and a member of the U.S. Maritime Commission.

B. C. Cobb founded and chaired the Commonwealth & Southern holding company, hired Wendell Willkie as its attorney, and designated him as president and his successor.

Charles Coffin was the president of the Thomson-Houston Company, which merged with the Edison General Electric Company in 1892. He became president of General Electric, the merged company, and in 1905 founded Electric Bond and Share, the first electric utility holding company and one of the largest.

Benjamin Cohen, a protégé of Felix Frankfurter, helped draft, along with Thomas Corcoran, the TVA Act, the REA Act, and the Public Utility Holding Company Act.

Morris Llewellyn Cooke carried out Pennsylvania Governor Gifford Pinchot's Giant Power Survey in 1923, served on Governor Franklin Roosevelt's commission that recommended the New York Power Authority in 1931, and designed and served as first administrator of President Roosevelt's Rural Electrification Administration from 1935 to 1937.

Calvin Coolidge, vice president under President Warren G. Harding, succeeded to the presidency upon Harding's death in 1923 and served through 1928. He did not support an expanded federal government role in power generation, but he signed the legislation authorizing Boulder Dam at the end of his term. At about the same time, he killed Senator Norris's Muscle Shoals bill with a pocket veto.

Thomas Corcoran, a former law student of Felix Frankfurter, was a co-draftsman, with Benjamin Cohen, of the TVA Act, the REA Act, and the Public Utility Holding Company Act. He also actively lobbied Congress for New Deal legislation.

James M. Cox, former Congressman and governor of Ohio and Democratic nominee for President in 1920, chose Roosevelt as his vice-presidential running mate sight unseen. He campaigned for Roosevelt in all four of his presidential elections.

Arthur Powell Davis, director of the Bureau of Reclamation, opposed a 1919 bill to build a massive dam on the Colorado River to provide water to southern California without a comprehensive study of the entire river basin. He then supported building a dam "at or near" Boulder Canyon.

John W. Davis was the compromise Democratic nominee for president on the 103rd ballot in 1924 but lost to President Coolidge. In 1935 he represented Alabama Power shareholders in the *Ashwander v. TVA* case.

Clarence Dill, a Democratic senator from Washington, supported federal dams on the Columbia River and in particular a high dam with great power potential at Grand Coulee.

William O. Douglas was commissioner of the Securities and Exchange Commission in 1936 and chairman from 1937 to 1939. He opposed Wendell Willkie's suggestion that the SEC set a price for the sale of Tennessee Electric Power to TVA. In 1940, Roosevelt appointed him to the Supreme Court, the second youngest nominee in history, and he retired in 1975 after thirty-six years, the longest serving justice in history.

Cyrus Eaton was a Cleveland financier who founded Republic Steel in 1927. In 1928, he purchased a large volume of stock in Samuel Insull's companies, frightening Insull into defensive actions that helped lead to the insolvency of his holding companies. Eaton also lost most of his wealth in the Depression but later rebuilt it. In the 1950s, he sought better relations between the U.S. and the Soviet Union and won the Lenin Peace Prize in 1960.

Thomas Edison opened the first central station for electric power in 1882, improving the incandescent light and most of the other components along the way. He was already famous for his phonograph and other inventions, and J. P. Morgan and other prominent financiers backed his nascent Edison Electric Company. Nine years later, as Edison continued to defend his direct-current system while other manufacturers were advancing alternating current, his competition-averse investors arranged a merger with his largest competitor and forced him out of the merged company, General Electric.

James Farley was campaign manager for three of Al Smith's gubernatorial campaigns as well as Roosevelt's two gubernatorial campaigns and first two presidential campaigns. He was chairman of the New York and national Democratic committees, was Postmaster General during Roosevelt's first two administrations, and hoped to be the nominee for president if Roosevelt chose not to run in 1940.

Henry Ford developed an inexpensive, mass-produced automobile that revolutionized American transportation. He was a pacifist during the early years of World War I and promoted anti-Semitism through his newspaper. He sought unsuccessfully to buy the dam at Muscle Shoals when it was offered for sale in the early 1920s.

Felix Frankfurter was a public utilities expert who taught law at Harvard, including to Franklin Roosevelt, and recommended many of his students for jobs in the Roosevelt administration. He proposed the strategy that achieved passage of the Holding Company Act in 1935 and was appointed to the Supreme Court in 1939.

John Nance Garner was a congressman from Texas from 1903 to 1933, Speaker of the House from 1931 to 1933, and a conservative presidential candidate in 1932. He accepted the vice-presidential nomination in a deal to secure the California and Texas delegates for Roosevelt. As vice president he served as a valuable liaison to Congress, but his opposition helped doom Roosevelt's Court-packing proposal.

John J. Gore, a U.S. district court judge from Eastern Tennessee and a distant relative of Vice President Al Gore, issued an injunction in *Tennessee Electric Power Co. v. TVA* blocking TVA's territorial expansion. After a circuit court voided the injunction and remanded the case to the district court for trial, Congress inserted a provision in the eviscerated Court-packing bill that required three judges to hear such an application for injunctive relief, and Gore was outvoted.

C. F. Groesbeck was chief executive of Electric Bond and Share Co., the utility holding company created by General Electric that was the nation's largest by the mid-1920s.

Warren Harding, president from 1921 until his death in 1923, supported public operation of the dam at Muscle Shoals but opposed government transmission of its power. The Teapot Dome scandal, in which his appointees accepted bribes by oil companies for leases of government reserves, made it difficult for government to continue the generous one hundred-year leases of hydropower sites to private companies.

William Randolph Hearst, developer of the nation's largest newspaper chain, served in Congress and ran twice for mayor of New York, once as candidate of the Municipal Ownership League. His feud with Al Smith led him to help block Smith and deliver the presidential nomination to Roosevelt at the 1932 Democratic convention. After 1934, he turned against Roosevelt and became one of his most prominent critics on the right.

Herbert Hoover, as secretary of commerce in the Harding administration, negotiated the water rights compromise among Colorado River states that eventually made possible the construction of Boulder Dam, later named Hoover Dam. President from 1929 to 1933, his perceived inaction in response to the beginning of the Great Depression caused his landslide defeat to Roosevelt in 1932.

Harry Hopkins, a social worker, headed the Civil Works Administration, the Federal Emergency Relief Administration, the Works Progress Administration, and the Commerce Department in the Roosevelt administration, and he was a key foreign policy advisor early in World War II. Roosevelt considered him a potential successor until Hopkins' declining health intervened.

Howard Hopson was chief executive of Associated Gas and Electric, a large holding company pyramid. A Senate investigation of his lobbying activities, which included thousands of forged telegrams, helped turn public opinion against holding companies and in favor of the Holding Company Act. After his retirement he was sentenced to seven years in prison for fraud and income tax evasion.

Louis Howe was a reporter in New York who attached himself to Franklin Roosevelt and became his closest aide and political advisor on his road to the White House. He died before the end of Roosevelt's first term.

Charles Evans Hughes was counsel for a state senate committee that exposed wrongdoing by New York utilities, leading to his election as governor in 1906 and his establishment of the first state utility regulatory commission in 1907. He was associate justice of the Supreme Court from 1910 to 1916, Republican nominee for President in 1916, Secretary of State from 1921 to 1925, and chief justice from 1930 to 1941.

Harold Ickes was a progressive Republican attorney in Chicago, where he fought several legal battles with Samuel Insull. He campaigned for Theodore Roosevelt in 1912 and Hughes in 1916. He served as secretary of the interior from 1933 to 1946 and concurrently as head of the Public Works Administration until 1944. He was a supporter of public power and played an active role in government energy policy.

Martin Insull, Samuel Insull's younger brother, was president of his holding company, Middle West Utilities. He was active in the publicity efforts of the National Electric Light Association.

Samuel Insull was the personal assistant and business manager for Thomas Edison. He became president of Chicago Edison in 1892 and turned it into a monopoly and a model for growth-oriented utilities. He founded one of the early utility holding companies and by the early 1920s was second only to the GE group in national market share. Acknowledged as the leader of the utility industry, he became its villain after his overextended holding companies went into receivership following the Great Crash.

Robert H. Jackson was assistant attorney general, solicitor general, attorney general, associate justice of the Supreme Court, and chief U.S. prosecutor at the Nuremberg Trials after World War II. Before deciding to run for a third term himself, Roosevelt considered supporting Jackson.

Hiram Johnson, a progressive Republican from California, served as governor from 1911 to 1917 and U.S. senator from 1917 to 1945. He ran for vice president on Theodore Roosevelt's Bull Moose ticket in 1912 and sought the Republican nomination for president in 1920 and 1924. He supported Franklin Roosevelt in the 1932 election and was an ally of Senator George Norris on most utility issues, sponsoring the bill to build Boulder Dam in 1922 and subsequent years.

Louis A. Johnson, a former corporate lawyer and national commander of the American Legion, was assistant secretary of war from 1937 to 1940 and chaired an interagency National Defense Power Committee in anticipation of war. President Harry Truman appointed him secretary of war in 1949 but replaced him with George Marshall after the start of the Korean War.

Jesse Jones, a Texas businessman, was chair of the Reconstruction Finance Corporation from 1933 to 1939 and secretary of commerce from 1940 to 1945. He was more pro-business and fiscally conservative than most New Dealers.

Joseph P. Kennedy, first chair of the Securities and Exchange Commission, established in 1934, provided Roosevelt with information about holding companies to build the case for the Holding Company Act. He subsequently served as first chair of the U.S. Maritime Commission and as ambassador to Great Britain.

Philip La Follette, son of Governor and Senator Robert M. La Follette Sr. and brother of Senator Robert M. La Follette Jr., was governor of Wisconsin from 1931 to 1933 and 1935 to 1939. He appointed David Lilienthal to the Wisconsin utility regulatory commission.

David E. Lilienthal was appointed to the Wisconsin regulatory commission in 1931. In 1933, Arthur Morgan recommended him and Roosevelt appointed him as a director of TVA, where he supervised legal and utility issues and was the negotiator with Wendell Willkie over TVA's territory and the purchase of Commonwealth & Southern utilities. He became chair of TVA in 1941 and of the Atomic Energy Commission in 1948.

Basil Manly served on the Federal Power Commission from 1933 to 1945 and was a member of the interagency National Defense Power Committee in advance of and during World War II.

Joseph Martin was a congressman from Massachusetts from 1925 to 1967 and served as House Republican leader from 1939 to 1959, including two terms as Speaker. He chaired the Republican national conventions from 1940 to 1956, was instrumental in the selection of Senator Charles McNary as Wendell Willkie's running mate in 1940, and was selected by Willkie to be chairman of the national committee after the 1940 convention.

William B. McKinley, owner of several electric utilities and streetcar companies in southern Illinois, served in the U.S. Senate from 1921 to 1926. Large contributions by Samuel Insull in the 1926 Republican primary to McKinley's opponent, the chair of the state regulatory commission, led to a widely publicized Senate investigation of utility contributions in the Illinois and Pennsylvania Republican primaries.

Charles McNary of Oregon served in the Senate from 1917 to 1944, was Republican Minority leader from 1933 to 1944, and ran for vice president on Wendell Willkie's ticket in 1940. He supported many New Deal initiatives during the Depression, including Bonneville and Grand Coulee dams.

Frank R. McNinch, a Democrat who supported Herbert Hoover in the 1928 election, was appointed by Hoover to the Federal Power

Commission and elevated to the chairmanship by President Roosevelt in 1933. He subsequently served as chairman of the Federal Communications Commission from 1937 to 1939.

James C. McReynolds was appointed by Woodrow Wilson as U.S. attorney general in 1913 and as associate justice of the Supreme Court in 1914, where he served until 1941. He was best known for his opposition to New Deal legislation and for his overt anti-Semitism.

Arthur E. Morgan, a civil engineer, was president of Antioch College and former head of planning and dam construction for the Miami River flood control district in Ohio when President Roosevelt asked him to chair TVA's board of directors in 1933. He clashed with David Lilienthal over the degree of cooperation with private utilities and was fired by Roosevelt for "contumacious behavior" in 1938.

Harcourt A. Morgan was president and former dean of agriculture at the University of Tennessee when Arthur Morgan recommended him and Roosevelt appointed him as a TVA director in 1933, where he served until 1948. In the division of responsibility among the original directors, he oversaw agriculture and forestry. He sided with David Lilienthal in most disagreements with Arthur Morgan and was named chair for three years after Morgan was fired.

James Pierpont (J. P.) Morgan Sr., the pre-eminent Wall Street financier from the late nineteenth century until his death in 1913, spurred the consolidation of U.S. industry. He funded Thomas Edison's early electrical work and orchestrated the merger of his company and the Thomson-Houston Company into General Electric in 1892.

Henry Morgenthau Jr., Roosevelt's neighbor in the Hudson Valley, was secretary of the treasury from 1934 to 1945. He helped design financing for major aspects of the New Deal and was instrumental in devising the Lend-Lease plan to provide assistance to England early in World War II.

George W. Norris of Nebraska served as a member of the U.S. House from 1903 to 1913 and of the Senate from 1913 to 1943. A progressive, often insurgent, Republican, he is best known for leading the battle in the House to reduce the power of the Speaker in 1910 and for helping develop and champion TVA in the Senate.

John J. O'Connor of New York, a Democratic member of the House of Representatives from 1923 to 1939 and chair of its Rules Committee from 1935 to 1939, was one of the few conservative Democrats targeted by Franklin Roosevelt in the 1938 primaries to lose his seat.

Francis S. Peabody founded Peabody Coal, later Peabody Energy, the largest private sector coal company in the world. Samuel Insull provided him with credit to acquire his first mines in Illinois, and Peabody signed a contract with him to provide coal indefinitely at cost plus a reasonable profit, a factor in Insull's relatively low electricity rates.

Frances Perkins, the first woman U.S. cabinet member, was secretary of labor from 1933 to 1945. She had known Roosevelt when he was in the New York Senate and had been appointed by him as New York industrial commissioner in 1929. Her memoir, *The Roosevelt I Knew,* covers her history with Roosevelt from 1910 to his death.

Gifford Pinchot, a progressive Republican, was the first director of the U.S. Forest Service, appointed by Theodore Roosevelt, and governor of Pennsylvania from 1923 to 1927 and from 1931 to 1935. With the help of Morris Cooke, he developed his Great Power Survey in his first term, recommending building power plants near coal mines to save transportation costs, stricter regulation of utilities, and greater rural electrification.

James P. Pope was a Democratic senator from Idaho from 1933 to 1939 and a strong supporter of New Deal programs, including the Columbia River dams. President Roosevelt appointed him a director of TVA in 1939, and he served until 1951.

John E. Rankin was a Democratic member of the U.S. House of Representatives from Mississippi from 1921 to 1953. He supported New Deal programs from 1933 to 1936 and introduced the TVA bill in the House in 1933, but from 1937 onward he was a member of the conservative coalition that increasingly dominated domestic policy. He openly supported racial segregation and white supremacy and helped establish the House Un-American Activities Committee.

Sam Rayburn, a Democratic congressman from Texas from 1913 to 1961, was a strong supporter of rural electrification and the House sponsor of the Holding Company Act. From 1940 to 1961, he was either Speaker or House Minority Leader.

James Reed served as a Democratic Senator from Missouri from 1911 to 1929. In 1926, he chaired the committee to investigate the excessive spending in Senate primary elections in Illinois and Pennsylvania.

Donald Richberg was a labor, railroad, and utilities attorney who practiced with Harold Ickes and David Lilienthal in Chicago and litigated against Samuel Insull's Chicago Gas Company. He supported Roosevelt's election, helped draft New Deal legislation during the transition and the First Hundred Days, and served as general counsel of the National Recovery Administration.

William Z. Ripley was a political economist, a critic of the financial practices of corporations, and the author of the 1927 best-selling book *Main Street and Wall Street*. At Harvard, Franklin Roosevelt took Ripley's course on corporate concentration.

Owen Roberts was an associate justice of the Supreme Court from 1930 to 1946 and early in the New Deal was often a swing vote between the conservative and liberal justices. After several New Deal measures had been declared unconstitutional, his vote with the liberals to uphold a state minimum wage law while Roosevelt was attempting to expand the size of the Court was called "the switch in time that saved nine."

Joe T. Robinson was a Democratic senator from Arkansas from 1913 to 1937, serving as Minority Leader from 1923 to 1933 and Majority Leader from 1933 to 1937. Widely believed to have been promised Roosevelt's first Supreme Court nomination, he supported the President's Court-packing bill but died while it was being debated.

Will Rogers was a popular humorist whose syndicated daily columns and radio monologues from 1926 until his death in 1935 offered a running commentary on the issues of the day.

Eleanor Roosevelt, wife of Franklin Roosevelt, helped develop his social conscience and kept alive his political prospects while he was working to rehabilitate his polio-ravaged legs. A niece of Theodore Roosevelt, in 1924 she campaigned for Al Smith when her cousin, Theodore Roosevelt Jr., challenged Smith in his race for New York governor.

Franklin D. Roosevelt was a state senator in New York from 1911 to 1913, assistant secretary of the Navy from 1913 to 1920, governor of New York from 1929 to 1932, and president from 1933 until his death in 1945.

Theodore Roosevelt served as assistant secretary of the Navy from 1897 to 1898, won a two-year term as governor in 1898, was elected to the vice presidency on William McKinley's ticket in 1900, and succeeded him when he was assassinated in 1901. He signed the Reclamation Act in 1902 that authorized the construction of irrigation projects in arid Western states. When turbines were added to the dams, he became the first president to establish a major federal role in power generation.

Theodore Roosevelt Jr. was assistant secretary of the Navy in Warren Harding's administration, where he oversaw the national petroleum reserves but was absolved of blame for the Teapot Dome scandal by a Senate committee. He ran for governor of New York in 1924, and

Eleanor Roosevelt campaigned against him because of his campaigning against the James Cox—Franklin Roosevelt ticket in 1920. He died of a heart attack in France during World War II after a heroic role in the Normandy invasion.

James D. (J. D.) Ross was administrator of the Bonneville Project Administration from 1937 to 1939. He was superintendent of Seattle City Light—a municipal utility—for thirty-six years, and served as a Securities and Exchange Commissioner from 1935 to 1937. At BPA he increased markets for BPA power, accelerated the completion of high-voltage transmission lines, and planned for the rapid expansion of capacity in anticipation of increased wartime demand for electricity.

Alexander Sachs was a banker at the Lehman Brothers investment company before serving in the National Recovery Administration. He originated the power pooling proposal that Roosevelt floated by Wendell Willkie late in 1936. In 1939, he brought to Roosevelt and argued in support of Albert Einstein's letter recommending that the U.S. undertake nuclear fission research for nuclear weapons.

Al Smith, a New York City politician, served four terms as governor between 1919 and 1928. He initiated some of the electricity policies that Roosevelt carried forward, including state dams on the St. Lawrence River and a New York State Power Authority. He was the Democratic nominee for president in 1928, losing to Herbert Hoover in a landslide. He sought the presidential nomination in 1932, losing to Roosevelt in the convention, and he became a public opponent during the New Deal.

Frank Smith was chairman of the Illinois utilities commission when he ran in the 1926 Republican primary against U.S. Senator William B. McKinley. His campaign contribution from Samuel Insull triggered a Senate investigation because of the huge size of the contribution and the apparent conflict of interest. He lost the primary, but McKinley died after winning the November election. The governor appointed Smith to fill McKinley's seat for the remainder of the term, but the Senate refused to seat him.

Phil Swing was chief counsel of the Imperial (Valley) Irrigation District from 1916 to 1919 and served in the U.S. House of Representatives as a Republican from 1921 to 1933. An advocate of obtaining Colorado River water for the Imperial Valley and San Diego, he sponsored the bill to authorize Boulder Dam, which passed in 1928.

Nicola Tesla, a Serbian-American inventor and engineer, developed an alternating current motor that, along with his polyphase AC, made possible the modern AC supply system. He licensed his patents to Westinghouse Electric, which pioneered the AC system in competition with Edison's DC system.

William S. Vare, the Philadelphia Republican boss, won a three-way U.S. Senate primary against incumbent George Pepper and Governor Gifford Pinchot in 1926. Lavish contributions to his campaign, some from utilities, led to a senatorial investigation of campaign fundraising and expenditures that also included Illinois candidate Frank Smith. Like Smith, Vare was not seated.

Frank P. Walsh, a former chair of President Wilson's Commission on Industrial Relations, was appointed in 1929 by Governor Roosevelt to a commission to review the New York Public Service Commission. In 1931 Roosevelt appointed him to chair the New York Power Authority. Walsh was an Irish nationalist and chaired the American Commission on Irish Independence.

Thomas Walsh was a senator from Montana from 1913 to 1933. From 1922 to 1924 he led the Teapot Dome investigation, and he chaired the Democratic national conventions in 1924 and 1932. In 1927 he introduced a bill for a senate investigation of the utility industry, but it was amended to transfer the investigation to the Federal Trade

Commission. The voluminous FTC reports that followed damaged the utility industry's public reputation.

Louis B. Wehle was a nephew of Justice Louis Brandeis and a friend of Franklin Roosevelt from Harvard. He participated in Roosevelt's White House Conference on power pooling in 1936 and later served as Ambassador to the Netherlands.

George Westinghouse, an engineer and entrepreneur who made a fortune with a railway air brake, founded the Westinghouse Electric Company. With patents purchased from Nikola Tesla, he developed an AC distribution system and won contracts to light the World's Columbian Exposition in Chicago in 1893 and to build the generating system at Niagara Falls in 1895.

Burton Wheeler was a Democratic senator from Montana from 1923 to 1947. He ran for vice president on the Progressive ticket with Robert La Follette Sr. in 1924 and sponsored Roosevelt's Holding Company Act in the Senate. He broke with Roosevelt on the Court-packing issue in 1937 and opposed entry into World War II until the Pearl Harbor attack.

Wendell Willkie was president of Commonwealth & Southern Co. from 1933 until he received the Republican nomination for president in 1940. He was the principal adversary of David Lilienthal in the fight against TVA's takeover of C&S territory, and he became the utility industry's most effective spokesperson in the fight against the Holding Company Act.

Woodrow Wilson was president of Princeton University, governor of New Jersey, and president of the United States from 1913 to 1921. He appointed Franklin Roosevelt as assistant secretary of the Navy in 1913, and during World War I oversaw an effort to expand and consolidate the electricity industry to support the war effort.

Owen D. Young co-authored the Dawes plan to reduce German reparations after World War I and counseled five presidents, from Wilson to Franklin Roosevelt. He was chairman of General Electric from 1922 to 1939, chaired the committee representing Samuel Insull's creditors that forced him out of his companies in 1932, and participated in Roosevelt's White House conference on power pooling in 1936. He was put forward as a Democratic candidate for president in 1932 but did not campaign.

September 4, 1882—Thomas Edison successfully tests his Pearl Street Station in Manhattan, the first central power station.

1887—George Westinghouse purchases Nicola Tesla's patent for an alternating-current motor and hires him, making it possible for alternating current to compete with direct current, which was used by Edison's company.

April 15, 1892—The Edison General Electric and Thompson-Houston companies merge to create General Electric.

July 1, 1892—Samuel Insull leaves Edison General Electric to become president of the Chicago Edison Company.

November 14, 1896—The first long distance transmission of power for commercial purposes begins from Niagara Falls to Buffalo.

June 17, 1902—President Theodore Roosevelt signs the Reclamation Act, authorizing the construction of irrigation dams in arid western states. A turbine is added to the first dam, on the Salt River in Arizona, and it becomes the first federal hydroelectric dam.

March 1905—GE creates Electric Bond and Share, the first utility holding company.

1907—Governors Charles Evans Hughes of New York and Robert La Follette Sr. of Wisconsin establish the first state utility regulatory commissions.

May 1912—Insull creates his first holding company, Middle West Utilities.

March 17, 1913—Franklin Roosevelt becomes assistant secretary of the Navy.

1917-18—Insull chairs Illinois Council of Defense.

July 6, 1920—Roosevelt is nominated for the vice presidency on the ticket headed by Ohio Governor James M. Cox.

April 10, 1922—Senator George Norris introduces his first bill for permanent government operation of the power plant at Muscle Shoals on the Tennessee River in Alabama.

Summer, 1926—Hearings on lavish expenditures in U.S. Senate primary elections in Illinois and Pennsylvania discredit Insull and other utility interests.

November 6, 1928—Franklin D. Roosevelt is elected governor of New York.

December 21, 1928—President Calvin Coolidge signs a bill authorizing construction of Boulder Dam, later Hoover Dam, on the Colorado River.

October 1929—The Wall Street Crash begins the severe stock market decline that bankrupts some overextended utility holding companies.

April 27, 1931—Governor Roosevelt signs a bill establishing the New York Power Authority to develop hydropower on the St. Lawrence River.

June 6, 1932—·After Middle West Utilities goes into receivership, bankers and outside directors force Insull out of his companies.

September 21, 1932—Roosevelt delivers a campaign speech in Portland, Oregon, outlining his electricity agenda.

January 24, 1933—Wendell Willkie becomes president of Commonwealth & Southern Company, a utility holding company in the Midwest and South.

March 4, 1933—Chief Justice Charles Evans Hughes swears in Roosevelt as president.

May 18, 1933—Roosevelt signs the bill creating the Tennessee Valley Authority (TVA).

July 28 and October 29, 1933—The Public Works Administration announces grants to start construction of Grand Coulee and Bonneville dams on the Columbia River.

August 24, 1933—Director David Lilienthal issues a press statement outlining the territorial goals of TVA.

November 11, 1933—TVA signs its first power sales agreement, with the Tupelo, Mississippi, municipal utility.

January 4, 1934—Lilienthal and Willkie renew a contract for the sale of power from Muscle Shoals to Alabama Power, a subsidiary of Commonwealth & Southern. The contract had been transferred to TVA from the War Department when TVA was established.

June 1, 1934—The first member-owned electric cooperative, in Alcorn County, Mississippi, signs an agreement to buy TVA power.

November 24, 1934—A Chicago jury acquits Insull of using the mails to defraud.

January 1935—Several stockholders of Alabama Power file suit challenging government transmission of power from TVA dams (*Ashwander v. TVA*).

February 6, 1935—Senator Burton Wheeler and Congressman Sam Rayburn introduce the Public Utility Holding Company Act, Roosevelt's proposal to break up utility holding companies and to allow federal regulation of interstate power sales.

May 11, 1935—Roosevelt establishes the Rural Electrification Administration by executive order and subsequently appoints Morris Cooke as director.

July 12, 1935—An investigative committee chaired by Senator Hugo Black begins hearings on excessive lobbying related to the Holding Company Act.

August 25, 1935—Roosevelt signs the Holding Company Act.

February 17, 1936—The Supreme Court rules in the *Ashwander* case that TVA may transmit and sell power from Muscle Shoals, but it does not rule on the constitutionality of the TVA Act.

May 29, 1936—Willkie's Tennessee Electric Power Co. and 18 other utilities file a suit, *Tennessee Electric Power Co. v. TVA*, challenging the constitutionality of the TVA Act.

May 20, 1936—Roosevelt signs the Rural Electrification Act, giving more permanence to the Rural Electrification Administration.

August 1, 1936—Norris Dam, the first built by TVA, begins power production, triggering the expiration ninety days later of the contract with Willkie limiting TVA's expansion.

December 1936—Judge John J. Gore of the District Court in Tennessee issues an injunction in *Tennessee Electric Power Co. v. TVA* blocking TVA expansion for six months.

January 1937—Roosevelt appoints an interagency Committee on National Power Policy, chaired by Interior Secretary Harold Ickes, to develop legislation on the distribution of power from Bonneville Dam.

February 5, 1937—Senator Norris introduces a "Seven Little TVAs" bill drafted in collaboration with the administration.

February 5, 1937—Roosevelt proposes a court reform bill that would give him the opportunity to appoint up to six new justices to the Supreme Court.

August 20, 1937—Roosevelt signs the Bonneville Project Act, giving the Army Corps of Engineers responsibility for operating the dam and giving a new Bonneville Project Administration in the Interior Department authority to market the power.

September 28, 1937—Roosevelt dedicates Bonneville Dam.

March 1938—Roosevelt directs the War Department and the Federal Power Commission to review the readiness of the nation's power system for a possible war.

March 23, 1938—Roosevelt fires TVA Chairman Arthur Morgan after a long-running feud between Morgan and Director David Lilienthal.

March 28, 1938—The Supreme Court decides *Electric Bond & Share v. SEC*, upholding the Holding Company Act's requirement for companies to register but not ruling on the "death sentence" provision abolishing certain types of holding companies.

September 1938—Roosevelt creates an interagency National Defense Power Committee and appoints Assistant Secretary of War Louis Johnson as its chair.

January 31, 1939—The Supreme Court rules in *Tennessee Electric Power Co. v. TVA* that utilities do not have standing to challenge the Act's constitutionality. Willkie begins negotiations with Lilienthal to sell TEPCO to TVA.

May 1939—Roosevelt decides to move REA into the Agriculture Department. REA Administrator John Carmody resigns soon after.

July 1939—Roosevelt merges the National Power Policy Committee with the National Defense Power Committee and appoints Ickes as chair.

August 15, 1939—Lilienthal presents Willkie with a check for the purchase of Tennessee Electric Power Co. by TVA.

September 1, 1939—Germany invades Poland, starting World War II.

June 28, 1940—The Republican Party nominates Willkie for president, and he resigns from Commonwealth & Southern on July 8.

July 1940—The high-tension transmission line from Bonneville to Grand Coulee is completed.

August 1940—Roosevelt renames the Bonneville *Project* Administration the Bonneville *Power* Administration and makes it the transmission and marketing agency for power from Grand Coulee as well as Bonneville.

January-February 1941—Willkie represents Roosevelt on visits to world leaders.

March 1941—The first two generators at Grand Coulee begin producing power.

March 1941—Lend-Lease legislation to provide war materials to England passes, and Roosevelt credits Willkie's help.

March 1941—The SEC presents Commonwealth & Southern with three options for dissolution.

1942—Nearly forty percent of American farms have been electrified.

July 1944—Three months after Willkie loses a critical primary and withdraws from the presidential race, Roosevelt sends him a message that he would like to talk with him about joining in a new political party in "the somewhat distant future."

October 8, 1944—Willkie dies.

April 12, 1945—Roosevelt dies.

1945—TVA produces 11.9 billion kilowatt hours, triple its pre-war production. The Bonneville Power Administration sells 3.4 billion kwh from Bonneville Dam and 5.7 billion from Grand Coulee.

August 6 and 9, 1945—The United States bombs Hiroshima and Nagasaki with weapons using enriched uranium produced with TVA power and plutonium produced with BPA power.

April 1, 1946—The Supreme Court upholds the constitutionality of the Holding Company Act in *North American Co. v. SEC*.

1949—Southern Company, a contiguous holding company consisting of several of Commonwealth & Southern's operating utilities, commences operation.

1949—The number of electrified farms in the United States reaches 78 percent, up from 11 percent in 1935.

ABBREVIATIONS

AC	alternating current
AG&E	Associated Gas and Electric Company
Bond and Share	Electric Bond and Share Company
BPA	Bonneville *Project* Administration until 1937, Bonneville *Power* Administration thereafter
C&S	Commonwealth & Southern Corporation
CIPSCo	Central Illinois Public Service Company
Corp	Corporation Securities Company of Chicago
DC	direct current
FPC	Federal Power Commission
IUI	Insull Utility Investments
NELA	National Electric Light Association
OPM	Office of Production Management
PUD	public utility district
PWA	Public Works Administration

RFC   Reconstruction Finance Corporation

REA   Rural Electrification Administration

SEC   Securities and Exchange Commission

TEPCO   Tennessee Electric Power Company

TVA   Tennessee Valley Authority

CHAPTER 1

THROWING DOWN THE GAUNTLET

In the midst of the economic crisis that would come to be called the Great Depression, a crowd of two thousand thronged to Portland's Union Station on September 21, 1932, to greet presidential candidate Franklin Roosevelt's campaign train. The American Legion's national-champion drum and bugle corps from nearby Salem stood by, ramrod straight, the morning sun glinting off their blue and gold uniforms. Police struggled to hold the crowd at bay as the train approached. The next morning's *Oregonian* would describe the clamorous welcome as merely "cordial." No fan of Roosevelt, the paper had recently editorialized in support of President Herbert Hoover: "As the result of Hoover's policy and leadership confidence is restored, industry is reviving, closed banks are reopening . . . . Let Hoover go on and complete his program."[1]

Roosevelt and his swelling ranks of supporters saw the state of the nation, and Hoover's job performance, quite differently. The Hoover administration, Roosevelt had declared, had "attempted to minimize the crash and mislead the people as to its gravity, . . . refused to recognize and correct the evils, . . . delayed relief and forgot reform."[2]

As station workers rushed to attach a gangplank to Roosevelt's car at the back of the train, the candidate emerged, leaning on the arm of his son James. The crowd roared as drums beat in vigorous welcome, with the frenetic clicking of photographers' cameras adding to the percussive fanfare. Roosevelt swung one and then the other of his iron-braced legs forward to "walk" down the gangplank, his famous broad smile betraying not the slightest notion of effort.

When National Democratic Chairman James Farley, waiting on the platform, introduced Roosevelt to a reporter from *The Oregonian*, the candidate exclaimed, "*The Oregonian*?! Should I talk to *The Oregonian* after all the things it has said about me?" He then extended his hand and laughed so cheerfully that the reporter and everyone within earshot joined in. "Come to the hotel," Roosevelt urged the reporter, "I want to have a chat." He modeled his relations with the press, like so much in his political career, after those of his late cousin Theodore Roosevelt, who was the first president to hold informal press conferences at the White House. [3]

The candidate was ten days into his first western campaign trip since winning the Democratic presidential nomination. A speech to the Multnomah County Grange, a farmers' association, was the day's first event. The caravan headed east over the Willamette River, with majestic Mt. Hood commanding the horizon, to the Gresham fair grounds, where Roosevelt spoke from the back of his convertible to about six thousand people crowded into the grandstand and bleachers. The patrician candidate sought to identify with the struggling farmers by describing the difficulty of making ends meet on his "family farm" in upstate New York and his struggle to raise peaches and cotton near Warm Springs, Georgia. "Your problems are the same," he said, "for in my trip across the country I cannot find any farmer making money." [4]

The main event of the stop would be a nationally broadcast radio address in the evening. Back in Portland, along the banks of the Columbia River, Roosevelt spoke about the greed and corruption of the electric power industry. The address, which *The Oregonian* labeled the next morning "an indictment against private power utilities," became known as "the Portland speech." [5]

Americans had sharply divided opinions about the utility industry. Denounced by critics as the "Power Trust," it was dominated by nine holding companies, the largest controlled by J. P. Morgan & Company.

By the beginning of the decade, those nine companies managed about three-quarters of the nation's power resources.[6] Holding companies were elaborately structured financial mechanisms adopted by utilities early in the century to provide desperately needed capital to the industry, which was perpetually starved for funds due to the high cost of equipment needed to boost production. Their supporters credited the holding companies with the explosive growth of the industry and the rapid electrification of much of the country. But they had also charged higher rates than their critics thought were justified and, rather than reinvesting the resulting profits, funneled the vast share to the owners of the holding companies that owned the utilities.

Whether motivated primarily by greed, a zeal for growth, or both, holding company owners had also borrowed recklessly to expand their empires during the Roaring Twenties. As long as the stock prices of the companies were rising, they could cover those debts. But in the stock market crash of 1929, many less wealthy investors, who had been encouraged to purchase utility stock with promises of safety and rapid growth, lost their life's savings.

Rural Americans, most of whom were too poor to have invested in the companies, were angry for a different reason. While the industry had dramatically improved the lives of many citizens by bringing them the wonders of electric lighting and labor-saving appliances, rural residents had been left behind. Companies refused to run lines to sparsely populated areas or, if they did, charged impossibly high rates. In some cases, they built "snake lines" that twisted hither and yon through rural areas to pick off only the few clusters of profitable customers. The contrast between the often harsh way of life in the vast swaths of agricultural territory and the growing conveniences in the cities and burgeoning suburbs was glaring, and to farmers, galling.

By the time Roosevelt spoke to the Oregon farmers in 1932, about 70 percent of American homes were electrified. Chicago, where Thomas Edison's protégé and longtime business manager, Samuel Insull, invented the modern electric utility in the 1890s, was the most electrified city in the world, with service to about 90 percent of homes.[7] Electric lighting had lengthened the day by several hours. Electric streetcars coursed through most large cities by the beginning of the century, easing travel to central department stores and encouraging the growth of "streetcar suburbs." A bevy of ingenious inventions were taking some of the drudgery out of housework. Small appliances that were initially luxuries had quickly become necessities. Electric fans, irons, and toasters were almost immediate must-haves, while more expensive washing machines, vacuum cleaners, electric stoves, and refrigerators spread more slowly but were transformative.

The improvements were not only matters of convenience. Educational attainment was enhanced as lights brightened classrooms and allowed children to more easily do homework in the evenings. The electrification of factories allowed machinery to take over much of the back-breaking physical labor, as well as raising the quality of manufactured goods and making the workplace cleaner, brighter, and safer. Motors on individual machines eliminated the dangerous belts and pulleys that had brought power from a factory's centrally located steam engine, and traveling overhead cranes now did most of the heavy lifting. Electric motors also powered assembly-line mechanization, improving industrial productivity.

Leisure activities grew more varied and exciting. Radios had become almost universal in electrified homes, tying most of the nation together through national news broadcasts, as well as through music and comedy shows and real-time sports events. Chicago's WGN began broadcasting the first soap opera in 1930. Almost 60 percent of Americans attended a movie at least once a week, and some new theaters were air-conditioned.[8] Thanks largely to electric trolleys, amusement parks flourished on the outskirts of many larger cities.

Farm families enjoyed none of this boon, and their lives were becoming increasingly difficult. Crop prices and farm income fell precipitously in the 1920s, well before the Depression crippled the rest of the economy. Most families struggled to pay the rent or their taxes and mortgage, and thousands lost their farms. Many lived in conditions little different from those their pioneering grandparents had endured.

With only kerosene lanterns for artificial light, the sun still governed their daily rhythms. The grueling work of pumping and hauling water was matched by the arduous cutting and toting of firewood for heat as well as cooking and washing. Wood-burning stoves required on average a staggering fifty pounds of wood a day. Subsistence farming was common, as many families struggled to grow most of their own food. A few chickens, a hog or two, and sometimes a cow supplemented cornmeal, wheat flour, and homegrown produce. Hunting, mostly of squirrels or rabbits, growing a few fruit trees, and bartering with neighbors might provide a little variety. Only a root cellar and perhaps an icebox kept food fresh.

Rugs had to be taken outdoors and beaten. The "washing machine" was a large iron pot, and clothes were cleaned with lye soap, a rub board, and women's muscle power. Ironing was an especially onerous chore, particularly in hot weather. Flatirons were heavy and could readily scorch clothing or fingers.[9] In many homes, Saturday was often the one bath night, and even a large family might make do with only two or three tubsful of water heated at the wood-burning stove.

The primary leisure activity for adults was reading, which was often limited to the Bible, an old newspaper passed on by someone who had recently visited town, and the painfully tantalizing Sears, Roebuck catalogue with its drawings and descriptions of electrical wonders. Imagining what life would be like with water pumps and heaters, lamps and irons, refrigerators, stoves and radios, if only the utilities would charge less to run lines to their farms, had discouraged rural residents. The divide between electricity haves and have-nots had become one of the most vexing national issues, and Roosevelt was well aware of farmers' discontent.

His interest in agriculture and his advocacy for widespread rural electrification were largely responsible for his winning the governorship of New York in 1928, pulling many traditional Republican rural voters into the Democratic column. Diving deeply into a study of regulating the electrical industry, he had learned that private utilities in New York State were charging much higher residential rates than Canada's publicly owned utility Ontario Hydro, that ratemaking methods used by state commissions usually favored utilities, and that dividends alone gave the owners at the top of holding company pyramids rates of return ranging from 19 to 55 percent.[10] Emboldened with this newfound knowledge, Roosevelt lambasted pro-utility regulators, attacked Republican efforts to privatize dam sites, and championed building a large public hydropower plant on the St. Lawrence River. In his Portland speech he applied the lessons he'd learned in New York to the national stage.

In the Portland Public Auditorium, Roosevelt threw down the gauntlet to the industry. "The question of power, of electrical development and distribution, is primarily a national problem," he asserted, proceeding to pillory the industry's "systematic, subtle, deliberate and unprincipled campaign of misinformation," which had flooded newspapers and even schools with unattributed columns and lesson plans justifying higher rates and associating government-owned utilities with socialism. He attacked the giant holding companies for charging exorbitant rates due to their "selfish purposes." He excoriated them for denying farmers the rightful benefits of electrification, and he referred with pride to his fights against the industry in New York as, his voice rising to a stirring climax, he intoned, "My friends, judge me by the enemies I have made." The crowd roared its approval.[11]

The centerpiece of the speech was a bold proposal. The waters of the nation belong to the people, he argued, and therefore the government, not the private sector, should harness the enormous power to be generated on the country's many large rivers. He called for "four great Government power developments"—on the St. Lawrence River, the Tennessee River, the Colorado River, and the Columbia River. "Each one of these," he said, "in each of the four quarters of the United States, will be forever a national yardstick to prevent extortion against the public."[12]

Roosevelt proposed to wage battle with the industry on three fronts—the unraveling of the holding companies; the construction of massive government dams; and a great push for rural electrification. But he was a reformer, not a revolutionary. Anticipating the charge that he was promoting socialism, he added, "I do not hold with those who advocate Government ownership or Government operation of all utilities. I state to you categorically that as a broad general rule the development of utilities should remain, with certain exceptions, a function for private initiative and private capital."[13]

Franklin Roosevelt campaigning with his daughter Anna on September 22, 1932, the day after his Portland speech. (*Courtesy of the Franklin D. Roosevelt Library.*)

Two days later, in a fiery San Francisco speech, he set his sights on Samuel Insull, the most notorious—if far from the guiltiest—of the industry's leaders. Insull had been the architect of the expanded electric utility industry in its second and third decades, rising with astonishing speed from a position as a mere clerk to Thomas Edison in the 1880s to become by far the most influential, and one of the wealthiest, of its captains. His business innovations not only supercharged the industry's growth but helped shape the entire landscape of American business, pioneering, for example, the concept of mass production to lower costs and prices, as well as advancing the practice of public relations— newspaper columns, speakers for schools and service clubs, paid advertising, selling utility stock to small buyers—at which he excelled.[14]

Insull had been the public face of the industry for two decades, but after winning recognition as an innovator, he had become better known for financial legerdemain. He expanded too rapidly in the 1920s, relying too heavily on borrowed money, and his badly bloated empire was one of those that collapsed in the wake of the 1929 Crash, eviscerating the savings of tens of thousands of small investors. In the San Francisco speech, Roosevelt deplored the depredations of "the lone wolf, the unethical competitor, the reckless promoter, the Ishmael or Insull whose hand is against every man's," signaling that in his crusade against bad actors in the electric utility industry he would hit hard and low.[15]

The story of the electrification of the United States in the first quarter of the twentieth century is one of triumph, of brilliant inventors, public-spirited entrepreneurs, and financial innovators who unleashed unprecedented economic growth and in many ways invented modern America. But it is also one of greed, abuse of power, and betrayal. Roosevelt singled out Insull, but a larger cast of characters had brought the country to this juncture.

The cash-flush and well-organized forces of private enterprise had waged war for decades against a public role in the electric utility industry. The very technological and financial innovations that had transformed the daily life of so many Americans, though, had produced an industry laced with corruption that, many felt, had callously turned its back on millions of hard-pressed families. Through its concentration of power, it had also come to pose serious threats to cornerstone principles of American democracy. Franklin Roosevelt was now fighting back, not only against the excesses of an industry, but in support of a new vision of private and public partnership that was to lay the foundation for unprecedented prosperity for many decades to come.

CHAPTER 2

THE FIRST WAVE OF ELECTRIFICATION

"When Edison . . . snatched up the spark of Prometheus in his little pear-shaped glass bulb," wrote the German historian Emil Ludwig, "fire had been discovered for the second time."[1] The irrepressibly optimistic Thomas Edison predicted many of the twentieth century's technical advances in electricity, but not the political conflicts they would provoke.

A few weeks after he began working on electric lighting in 1879, well in advance of any actual discoveries, he told a *New York Sun* reporter, "When the brilliancy and cheapness of the lights are made known to the public—which will be in a few weeks, or just as soon as I can thoroughly protect the process—illumination by . . . gas will be discarded." Only a month later he announced that electric current from one source could be dispersed to many small lights, "subdivided so that it could be brought into private houses."[2] This was big news. Other electrical pioneers were developing a very different type of system, planning to sell dynamos (soon to be called generators) to factories, hotels, department stores, and city streetlight departments, with which each would generate its own electricity. But Edison seemed to be proposing that electricity could instead be transmitted to customers from a central location.

Thomas Edison in about 1880, soon after he began working on electricity.
(*Library of Congress.*)

He was already America's most famous inventor, and when he spoke, markets listened. Gas shares on the New York and London exchanges tumbled 25 to 50 percent on Edison's boast that electricity would replace gas.[3] Within days, J. P. Morgan, William H. Vanderbilt, and several other of the country's most powerful investors joined forces with Edison to establish the Edison Electric Light Company, an early harbinger of the influential role bankers would play in the growth of the new industry. Morgan alerted his partners in London to "a matter which is likely to prove most important . . . to the world at large [and] to us in particular in a pecuniary point of view."[4]

In 1882, Edison opened the Pearl Street Station in lower Manhattan, the progenitor of all utility power plants. In a torrent of creative genius at his laboratory in Menlo Park, New Jersey, he and his team had invented or improved on all the components of the centralized system he had envisioned. The Edison Electric Light Company retained ownership of the dynamos and owned the distribution lines, selling only the current itself, mimicking the successful sales model of the gas lighting system. This structure still defines electric service for most Americans to this day. But his system had a major flaw: it used direct current (DC), which could transmit power for only about a half-mile because current passing through a wire encounters resistance and gives off heat, wasting energy. A solution would be to increase either the diameter of the wire or the voltage, also known then as tension or pressure, the force that moves current through a wire, but either would be uneconomic. Higher voltage would also be dangerous. Despite his initial technological triumph, Edison was in an bind.

In 1885, George Westinghouse, a Pittsburgh engineer and entrepreneur who had made a fortune by inventing and marketing the air brake for trains, read an article in an English engineering journal about an alternating current (AC) system that used transformers to raise or lower the voltage of electricity as it was transmitted. He intuited that AC could be generated economically at low voltage, converted to high voltage for long-distance transmission with less energy loss, and then converted back to low voltage for safer delivery to customers. AC could supersede Edison's DC and enable larger, more cost-effective dynamos, which would provide more power that could be transmitted over longer distances. Power could even be generated cheaply at dams on distant rivers and brought to cities. AC transmission lines could also make large regional grids and great economies of scale possible.

Yet Westinghouse's idea, visionary as it was, was also hobbled by a major flaw. Since the market for electrical lighting alone was not sufficient to make most power plants profitable, they also needed to sell power to factories to run industrial motors. But an efficient AC motor had not been invented. That problem was solved two years later by Nicola Tesla, who patented such a motor. Tesla had briefly worked for Edison, but the inventor he initially idolized had adamantly refused to entertain using AC. Westinghouse, who needed no convincing, bought Tesla's patent.

The battle between DC and AC systems, personified by Edison and Westinghouse, was joined. While other inventors and utility investors saw the potential advantage of AC and expected it to prevail,

Edison stood stubbornly behind DC. One of the most innovative thinkers in history, who had created a stunningly inventive system a few short years earlier, had turned conservative.

Edison, whom one biographer noted "could be a good hater,"[5] launched a ghoulish campaign warning about the risk of death from the high-voltage current in AC power lines. His tactics included promoting the use of AC for capital punishment and secretly funding "research" that demonstrated to the press how painful death by AC electrocution (using dogs as subjects) could be.[6]

While most of Edison's charges were trumped up, a cat's cradle of wires that had been strung above the streets of downtown Manhattan by several companies—for telephones, telegraphs, burglar alarms, and stock tickers, as well as AC electricity—did pose a serious safety hazard. (Edison, in contrast, had buried his DC distribution wires for safety reasons, at great cost.) Largely unregulated, many of the overhead wires were attached to the same poles, some of which had dozens of cross-arms. Others were strung from rooftop to rooftop. Companies frequently neglected to cut down wires no longer in service, and sagging wires rubbed against each other, wearing off the insulation.

In the spring of 1888, several disasters occurred in rapid succession. In April, a boy grabbed a dangling telegraph wire on East Broadway, swinging it back and forth until it made contact with a poorly insulated, high-voltage wire. As horrified crowds watched, he was electrocuted in a shower of sparks. Later that month, a young clerk touched a low-hanging wire outside his uncle's store and was instantly killed. In May, a lineman was cutting away old wires above West Houston Street without wearing rubber gloves. He died instantly when he cut into a live wire. Each tragedy involved AC.

A Western Union lineman suffered, in October 1889, the most gruesome electrical death anyone had yet seen. Above a lunchtime crowd a few blocks from City Hall, the *New York Times* reported, John Feeks was reaching through a maze of wires, "when he was suddenly seen to shiver and tremble as though he had received a violent shock. He seized a wire as though to steady himself, and immediately there was a flash of flame under his hand. His hand slipped from the wire and he fell forward across a network of wires which caught him across the throat and face and held him suspended some forty feet above the ground. The man appeared to be all on fire. Then blood began to drop down from the body and a great pool formed on the sidewalk beneath."[7] One of the telegraph wires had come in contact with an AC wire a few blocks away and rubbed through its insulation, sending high-voltage AC current coursing back to the lineman.

The newspapers had a field day. Nellie Bly, an investigative reporter for Joseph Pulitzer's sensationalist *New York World*, luridly described the scene. "A dark-red stream gushes from the wrist. Now it springs from the throat, spotting the pole and dripping down on the heads of the fleeing crowd." More important, she identified the villain as a utility: Feeks had been "roasted, not by heathens, but by a monopoly."[8]

The next day the Board of Electrical Control ordered all unsafe wires taken down immediately. Two Westinghouse subsidiaries owned most of the lines in the worst condition, and before the order could be implemented, Westinghouse lawyers secured an injunction blocking it. The press hinted at bribery, and public outrage grew. The caricature that Edison had been peddling of a callous Westinghouse risking lives for profits suddenly seemed all too plausible. On December 13, the New York Supreme Court ordered the wires removed, harshly rebuking the Westinghouse-owned companies.

AC's reputation worsened further after New York State approved the creation of an alternating-current electric chair powered by Westinghouse dynamos. The first execution, of an ax murderer, was conducted in August 1890. After current was administered for seventeen seconds, the prison doctor declared the man dead. But then his chest began rising and falling, and horrified witnesses shouted for the job to be finished. As current was again administered, flames burst from his head and his clothes caught fire. The *Times* headline the next day read, "Far Worse Than Hanging." Edison, however, predicted that the next electrocution "will be accomplished instantly and without the scene at Auburn today." Westinghouse said, "They could have done it better with an axe."[9]

Yet the competition for dominance over the industry remained unresolved. Three companies led the pack—Edison, Westinghouse, and

Thomson-Houston, run by Charles Coffin. There was no love lost between the would-be titans. One biographer said, "Edison and Thomson disliked each other as much as competitors with hearty egos could." Edison ridiculed the "amateurs" at Thomson-Houston who "boldly appropriated and infringed every patent we use." For his part, Coffin bemoaned Westinghouse's "attitude of bitter and hostile competition." Westinghouse retorted that Coffin had "a very swelled head." Edison disparaged Westinghouse's business methods, saying, "The man . . . is flying a kite that will land him sooner or later in the mud," and a Thomson banker agreed, adding, "He irritates his rivals beyond endurance." The bankers who were funding the expansion of all three companies weren't amused. Their concern was to create an efficient industry, and the rivalry was standing in the way, with both Westinghouse and Edison ardently resisting all proposals to cooperate or merge.[10]

The two leading banks with investments in Edison General Electric and Thomson-Houston finally prevailed in 1891, forcing a merger of the two. They chose Coffin as president, and three of the other four top officers appointed were from Thomson-Houston, which had better management, higher profits, and a product line that used both DC and AC.[11] Edison was forced out of the new company, which was rechristened as General Electric. "Something had died in Edison's heart," his secretary recalled. "He had a deep-seated, enduring pride in his name. And this name had been violated, torn from the title of the great industry created by his genius."[12]

The stage was now set for a new struggle, pitting the greatly empowered merged firm against the smaller Westinghouse. The most important line of battle would be over the contract to harness the mighty waters of Niagara Falls and build the world's largest power plant.

The staggering force of Niagara Falls had long tantalized engineers. With 210,000 cubic feet of water surging over a 164-foot precipice every second, and a reservoir of four Great Lakes to ensure constant flow, the falls presented a tremendous potential source of energy. Yet they had thus far inspired only small plans. That changed dramatically in 1886 when a former Erie Canal engineer proposed building a mile-long canal to divert water from the falls to 238 waterwheels. When a local consortium was unable to raise sufficient capital, J. P. Morgan and an associate of William Vanderbilt stepped in, founding Cataract Construction Company in 1890 to buy the rights to build and manage the project.

After consideration of the original plan, Cataract's chief engineer dropped it for an even more ambitious one. He proposed contracting with two Swiss companies for turbines of unprecedented size, to be housed in two central stations with equally massive dynamos that would transmit power to nearby factories and to the industrial city of Buffalo twenty miles away. Cataract sought bids for design and construction in 1891 from the most eminent electrical manufacturing companies in the world. (Edison General Electric and Thompson-Houston had not yet merged.) A 40 percent tariff and an estimated 10 percent freight charge on European equipment effectively eliminated foreign competition, and the merger reduced the Niagara competition to a head-to-head battle between GE and Westinghouse. Whether the current produced would be AC or DC was an open question, and the project became a proving ground in the "War of the Currents."[13]

The archrivals had two years to develop their plans. Prospects brightened for Westinghouse when, in 1891, an experimental AC transmission line in Germany carried power from a mountain waterfall all the way to Frankfurt, 108 miles away.[14] Long-distance transmission now appeared much less theoretical. AC also dazzled the industry when the Columbian Exposition opened in Chicago in March 1893. The fair grounds were illuminated with an awe-inspiring display of 92,000 outdoor lights, more than had been assembled in any location before, and all powered by AC provided by Westinghouse.

By the time proposals were due, the Cataract Construction Company had placed a thumb on the scale in favor of AC, and both companies submitted proposals including three five thousand-horsepower AC generators. Changes in the initial GE proposal, bringing it more closely in line with the Westinghouse design, raised suspicions of industrial espionage, and private investigators reported that GE had arranged for a draftsman to be hired at the Westinghouse plant, paid a monthly fee by GE, provided with a fund to bribe others for confidential papers, and given a code to telegraph information to GE. A search warrant for GE's Lynn, Massachusetts, plant turned up drawings and financial information on the Chicago and Niagara projects, but GE claimed they were obtained through normal channels and were only used to seek evidence of Westinghouse infringement of GE patents. The Pittsburgh district attorney indicted Coffin, but the GE president denied any knowledge of the affair, calling it "part of the bitter and vituperative work of the Westinghouse people." The trial resulted in a hung jury in September, disappointing both sides but allowing the incident to fade from prominence.[15]

Despite Cataract's backing from Morgan and other GE investors, its management seemed persuaded that they must deal with Westinghouse because of his control of key patents. In October they signed the AC generator contract with Westinghouse, and the "War of the Currents" was won. Government had no role in planning or financing the largest electricity project to date.[16]

The transition to an all AC system proceeded slowly because so much money had been invested in DC systems, but by the turn of the century the transformation of the country through electrification shifted into high gear with the replacement of steam turbines and the introduction of turbogenerators—steam turbines coupled to generators on a single frame—which were smaller, faster, quieter, and cheaper. They facilitated the construction of more compact but more powerful central stations, which could serve larger areas at lower cost. Prices fell and many more homes were wired. Electric streetcars rapidly replaced horse-drawn buses, and electric streetlights replaced dimmer gas lamps. Stores and offices were wired, and grand exhibitions in Buffalo in 1901 and St. Louis in 1904 showcased an abundance of novel appliances, including a tabletop stove, a coffeemaker, a bread machine, a dishwasher, and an electric typewriter. A popular song invited, "Meet me in St. Louis, Louis. Meet me at the Fair. Don't tell me the lights are shining, any place but there."[17]

The booming demand for electricity drove more and more utility expansion and increasing economies of scale, and the larger companies reduced costs further still. Seizing the day in driving growth was Edison's former secretary and business manager, Samuel Insull.

When Thomas Edison had sought a new private secretary in 1881, Samuel Insull was working in London as a secretary and bookkeeper for Colonel George E. Gouraud, who was overseeing the sales of Edison's inventions—primarily improved telephones—on the continent. A visiting Edison Company vice president found that Insull knew more about the business than Gouraud and advised a colleague that Insull was "the kind of young man that Mr. Edison should have as private secretary."[18]

Edison invited Insull to New York for a meeting. Insull's Cockney accent and Edison's Midwestern drawl and deafness initially made communication difficult, and the two were day and night in their personal appearance and manners. Insull had a formal bearing and was impeccably groomed and dressed, while the casual Edison wore a large sombrero, a dirty white shirt, a carelessly knotted tie, baggy trousers, and a seedy black coat and waistcoat sprinkled with cigar ash. Nonetheless, the meeting proceeded well enough that the two ended up talking all night, and by morning Insull had the job.[19]

Edison soon expanded Insull's duties from answering letters and keeping the books to arranging financing for various ventures and conveying orders to more senior employees. Insull "loved power and gloried in the exercise of authority," one of Edison's "boys" wrote, and "he seemed to think that sustained criticism was the most effective spur towards efficiency."[20] Insull probably would not have disagreed. "If necessary," he recalled, "I would ride roughshod over opposition to accomplish what my chief desired should be done."[21]

Intent on building central generating stations across the U.S., including in smaller towns, Edison had Insull travel the country, persuading local businessmen and officials of the merits of Edison's system, identifying the best location for plants, setting up local utilities, convincing city councils to grant franchises, and arranging financing and construction. Some councils were corrupt, had received kickbacks from gas companies, and expected similar under-the-table deals with Insull. He excelled at all aspects of the job.[22]

Zealous about enforcing financial discipline throughout the Edison companies, Insull also adeptly courted investors, primarily New York investment bankers, to meet the constant demand for more growth capital. Most sought quick profits from licensing Edison's inventions and were unenthusiastic about funding the time-consuming building of power plants or the manufacturing of dynamos, light bulbs, and other components of the system. They were stingy with loans for these endeavors and often called in such loans at awkward times, feeding Insull's lasting dislike of New York banks. The bankers, though, thought highly of Insull. When they masterminded the creation of GE, he was the only Edison Company employee to be offered a senior position, the number three job with a princely salary of $36,000 per year, equivalent to more than $900,000 today. Insull, though, never modest, wanted to be the top dog and began looking for a job elsewhere.[23]

When two directors of Chicago Edison, a licensee of the Edison Company, approached him for help in finding a new president, Insull remembered Edison had once said Chicago was "one of the best cities in the world for our line of business." Insull knew the company well—he had helped design its plant and underground grid—and offered himself for the position. The board was enthusiastic. Based on his hard-earned lessons trying to raise financing for Edison, Insull insisted as conditions of accepting the job that the directors and shareholders take responsibility for raising capital, they agree to build a new generating plant, they pay for it by issuing $250,000 in new stock, and they sell the stock only to him. The directors accepted, and Insull borrowed the money to buy the stock from department store magnate Marshall Field, who admired the young man's confidence.[24]

When Insull took over Chicago Edison, it faced fierce competition, including the larger Chicago Arc Light and Power Company and more than twenty smaller electric companies. Chicago Edison was also competing with itself. Despite the central station strategy, the company was selling dynamos to stores and factories so they could generate their own electricity. By 1893, those "isolated plants" were powering 50 percent more lights than the central station. What's more, none of the utilities had enough market share to reduce production costs and charge low enough prices to compete for the isolated plant market or put their competitors out of business.[25]

Insull came up with a brilliant solution for unleashing growth, later called his "grow-and-build strategy." The plan was to reduce rates in order to increase sales volume, which would allow the installation of newer, larger generators, creating greater economies of scale, which would in turn allow for yet further reduced costs—a virtuous cycle. The strategy required that the company rapidly build up its generating capacity, which Insull planned to do through acquisitions. His longer-term aim was to create a monopoly.

Samuel Insull in about 1894, two years after becoming president of Chicago Edison. (*Courtesy of Loyola University Chicago Archives & Special Collections.*)

In an ambitious move, he bought all the stock of his largest competitor, Chicago Arc Light, at a premium of about 15 percent above the market price. He never paid cash when he could avoid it, offering 6 percent debentures instead and making the sellers into financers of his company. More significant for the long run, he gave

Arc Light shareholders the right to buy future Chicago Edison stock offerings. He used this tactic throughout his career, creating pressure to ensure that his share prices were always rising. He succeeded for thirty-eight years.[26]

Within a few years, Insull had managed the purchase of all of the remaining electric utilities in Chicago and throughout Cook County. With no threat of competition, he continued his grow-and-build strategy and added a "gospel of consumption," increasing demand by reducing prices and by aggressively advertising and seeking new markets. One tactic was to tie low rates to a five-year contract. He was confident that improvements in technology and greater economies from progressively larger generators would bring his costs down over that time, eventually making the contracts profitable. He dubbed the strategy "massing of production," which his staff shortened to "mass production" and which would be popularized two decades later by a former chief engineer of Detroit Edison, Henry Ford.[27] In addition to cutting rates for existing residential customers, he offered incentive rates for new customers to wire their homes. One sales campaign offered the installation of six free outlets, and a deferred payment plan often convinced homeowners to incur the cost of wiring a whole house.[28] In his first three years in Chicago, his production quadrupled, and it doubled again in the next three. Electricity in the home had been a luxury of the wealthy. Now he was bringing it to the middle class.

As he solidified his leadership of Chicago's electrical world, Insull was introduced to the corrupt world of Chicago politics—a cesspool of bribery, government franchises, dummy corporations, and extortion. A quick learner, he outsmarted the boodlers and beat them at their own game. In 1897, the city's streetcar overlord had been unable to issue long-term bonds because several of his franchises were due to expire in a few years, and he persuaded the Illinois legislature to give cities the authority to provide fifty-year utility franchises. But in the wake of a public uproar about his bribery, the city council was unwilling to grant him one. Using the new law, though, a bi-partisan group of city councilmen suggested to Insull that it might be worth several hundred thousand dollars to keep them from creating a competing electric utility with a longer-term franchise. When Insull angrily refused to pay, they went ahead and established a new corporation, the Commonwealth Electric Company, and voted it a fifty-year franchise.[29]

They hadn't counted on Insull's preparation.

Commonwealth's managers soon discovered that he had locked up the Chicago and Cook County rights to sell the equipment of every major electrical manufacturer, and their utility was worthless. As a peacemaking gesture, Insull bought Commonwealth and its franchise for only $50,000. Two years later the legislature repealed the franchise law, leaving Insull with the only fifty-year deal in Illinois and the opportunity it provided for long-term financing. He started to fill in the shell that was Commonwealth by buying a few small companies he previously thought were too far from Chicago Edison's territory.[30]

Technical obstacles prevented him from immediately merging Chicago Edison and Commonwealth Electric. He decided to keep his original company, which still provided DC, operating downtown under its old franchise and to set up Commonwealth as an AC company serving the rest of the city and county. Their unified management and interconnections at several points made it a simple matter to merge the two companies a decade later as Commonwealth Edison. Politically, though, Insull took no chances. He cut his rates three times in two years before seeking approval to carry out the merger.[31]

His expansion plan also targeted industry, where isolated generators were still powering most factories. Aided by rapid improvements in motors, the electrification of most new factories, Chicago's explosive growth, and his acquisition of other utilities, his sales to industry grew by an astonishing 66 percent per year on average between 1896 and 1902. Before more factories became customers, most of his demand was for home lighting in the early morning and after sunset, and his generators were largely idle during working hours. Because he didn't need to add any generating capacity to meet factories' daytime demand, he could afford to sell them power more cheaply than they could provide it with their own generators.[32]

The largest potential for additional demand came from electric railways. By 1902, ten years after electric streetcars began to replace horse-drawn cars in Chicago, street and elevated railways generating their own power used more than three times as much electricity as all of Insull's customers combined. The railways had a huge peak demand in the morning and evening rush hours, exactly the times when Insull's residential and factory customers were using less electricity. Even more than factories, streetcar company generators were idle much of the time. Because the capital cost of generators was the same whether or not they were in steady use, the companies' power costs for electricity used were high, and Insull offered them a lower rate. Within five years he was supplying 30 percent of the transportation power in the city, accounting for more than all of his other sales, and the percentage continued to grow.[33]

At about the same time, Insull began to buy the coal that fueled almost all of his generators from Francis S. Peabody, a politically well-connected coal distributor. Peabody wanted to own mines rather than just distribution rights, but he lacked adequate credit. Insull had plenty of credit, and he foresaw a need for previously unthinkable amounts of coal. The two signed a contract for Peabody to supply Chicago Edison indefinitely with coal at cost plus a reasonable profit. Peabody was able to use the contract to borrow the money he needed to buy mines.[34]

Insull then made an equally prescient decision. He knew that transportation was a major part of his fuel costs over which he had no control. Accordingly he bought a small railroad that would haul nothing but his coal. In time the savings from the contract with Peabody would pay for the railroad and yield generous dividends for Insull's stockholders.[35]

Perhaps the most remarkable thing Insull did for the electricity business, however, was to propose that it be regulated by the state— an idea that shocked his colleagues when he floated it in 1898. From the beginning, utilities had to deal with unsympathetic, often venal, city governments. Bribery was often necessary to obtain or renew a franchise, to prevent a competing franchise from being granted, or to avoid the threat of a municipal takeover. Although he was adept at working with the politicians in Chicago, he reasoned that state regulation would reduce the opportunities for extortion. He also believed that state laws could enshrine the concept of natural monopoly, which held that it was wasteful for competing companies to build duplicate systems to serve one community.[36]

Around the turn of the century, the powerful movement that gave its name to the Progressive Era drew attention to urban social problems that had arisen with the rapid growth of cities in the 1890s. Part of its focus was on municipal corruption and the abuses of monopolies, and some Progressive reformers took up the cause of utility regulation. Wisconsin and New York led the way.

In Wisconsin in 1907, Republican Governor Robert M. La Follette pushed through a bill for state regulation of private utilities.[37] Following the recommendations of the Progressive movement's National Civic Federation, the law incorporated what became known as the "regulatory compact." Utilities would be granted a monopoly in their territories and a fair return on their investment for agreeing to serve all customers and accepting state regulation of rates.[38] By this time many utility executives supported the law—Insull had been proselytizing—but it was opposed by a few progressives who supported municipal ownership, some city politicians who wanted to retain their authority and source of revenue, and others who disliked the guarantee of monopoly status. Milwaukee Mayor Daniel Hoan fumed, "No shrewder piece of political humbuggery and downright fraud has ever been placed upon the statute books. It's supposed to be legislation for the people. In fact, it's legislation for the power oligarchy."[39]

During the Progressive Era, Republican governors Robert La Follette Sr. of Wisconsin (l) and Charles Evans Hughes of New York established the first state utility regulatory commissions in 1907. (*Library of Congress*).

In New York, Charles Evans Hughes won election as governor in 1906 on the basis of his exposure of utility abuses. As counsel to a state senate committee, he had demonstrated that New York Edison's cost of production was only 3.664 cents per kilowatt-hour, but the average price paid by consumers was 12.27 cents.[40] His report also highlighted the uneconomical purchase of weak competitors, citing "the investment of millions in securities earning no dividends and intrinsically worthless, solely for the purpose of securing monopoly of control."[41] His bill establishing a state regulatory commission, modeled on the Wisconsin draft bill but enacted first, passed overwhelmingly in 1907.

Although some reformers feared the regulatory commissions would be ineffective or corrupt, positive early reports from Wisconsin and New York helped persuade skeptics, and many utility leaders who had opposed state regulation soon came around. Early rate decisions by the states gave them confidence that their companies would receive enough revenue to remain solvent, if not thrive, and they also saw that they would normally be protected against competition. One of the first New York commission decisions provided a ringing defense of utility monopolies: "It can doubtless be demonstrated . . . that better service and fair prices . . . can, as a general rule, be given by one corporation than by several, and that this can be done with the use of less capital." But in another decision, the commission allowed a new company to compete against an existing monopoly that had failed to give adequate service.[42] Massachusetts also established a commission in 1907, and other states soon followed. Harvard law professor Felix Frankfurter, an expert on public utilities, noted that in their early years "these commissions constituted a new political invention responsive to the presence of new economic and social facts." But he and many others would soon become more critical.[43]

While Insull was expanding his monopoly in the 1890s but using its power to reduce prices, avaricious "robber barons" like John D. Rockefeller and Andrew Carnegie were riling the public by using their oil and steel monopolies to raise prices. The country was embroiled in a great battle over the concentration of power in such industries and the role of government in limiting it, a battle that was soon to ensnare the electric power industry.

Farmers and ranchers first led the charge against monopolies, protesting punishingly high railroad freight rates and the control over prices by businesses that sold them equipment and purchased their crops and livestock. Grievances against monopolies or cartels in petroleum, steel, sugar, mining, and meatpacking led to passage of the Sherman Antitrust Act in 1890. But railroads continued to combine, and the first attempt under the Sherman Act to prosecute a manufacturing trust—a holding company that controlled almost 98 percent of U.S. sugar refining—failed. The case went to the Supreme Court, which in 1895 ruled that because the parent company that controlled all the sugar refiners did not itself engage in interstate commerce, it was not in restraint of trade.[44] Corporate lawyers scrambled to set up more holding companies and trusts to exploit this loophole.

In another powerful blow to the populists and progressives, pro-business Republican William McKinley won the 1896 presidential election over William Jennings Bryan. And, as a strengthening economy banked the fiercest fires of populist revolt, his Justice Department used the Sherman Act to file suits only against labor unions. The progressives nevertheless kept up the fight. Governor La Follette of Wisconsin decried the "corporations and masters of manipulation in finance heaping up great fortunes by a system of legalized extortion."[45] Bryan urged greater regulation of trusts even more floridly in 1899: "When I lived upon a farm . . . we used to protect property from the hogs by putting rings in [their] noses. . . . The thought came to me that one of the great purposes of government was to put rings in the noses of hogs."[46] In 1900, he roused an audience of 15,000 in Madison Square Garden by chastising McKinley and his running mate, Theodore Roosevelt, for supporting "trusts, gold, and imperialist wars of aggression."[47]

President Theodore Roosevelt's Justice Department filed suit in 1902 against the Northern Securities Company, a railroad holding company financed in part by J. P. Morgan and John D. Rockefeller. (*Library of Congress.*)

Roosevelt, formerly McKinley's assistant secretary of the Navy, had risen to national fame during the Spanish-American War with his bold charge up San Juan Hill at the head of the Rough Riders. He rode that fame and his reputation as a reformer to election as governor of New York in 1898, and he set his sights on the White House in 1904. But when early talk of his presidential ambition irritated McKinley's friends, he suppressed his embryonic progressivism and effusively endorsed the President for re-election in 1900. McKinley's first-term vice president died in 1899, opening the way for Roosevelt. Though Roosevelt feared he'd been sidetracked into a notoriously insignificant office, McKinley was assassinated six months into his second term.

The wealthy eastern aristocracy thought of Roosevelt as one of their own, but many party stalwarts considered him an unpredictable upstart. They were right. Roosevelt recognized a golden opportunity in early 1902 to score a progressive victory by checking J.P. Morgan's power, bolstered by the knowledge that public sentiment was largely on his side.[48] Morgan had recently twisted the arms of competing railroad owners to create the Northern Securities Company, a gargantuan system that would dominate rail traffic from Chicago to the Northwest. In a biting commentary, muckraking journalist Ray Stannard Baker wrote, "You can ride from England to China on regular lines of steamships and railroads without once passing from the protecting hollow of Mr. Morgan's hand."[49]

Financial circles reeled when Roosevelt's attorney general announced that a suit would be filed against the rail behemoth. The stock market suffered its greatest drop since McKinley's death, and Morgan paid a call on the President. "If we have done anything wrong," he said, "send your man to my man and we can fix it up." But Roosevelt didn't want to "fix it up."[50] When the case worked its way to the Supreme Court, a 5-4 majority in 1904 ordered the dissolution of Northern Securities. The tide had turned in the fight over corporate power.

Roosevelt took a bold step in redefining the role of the government not only in regulating industry but also, with regard to electric power, in sharing in the business of production. Leading with an enormous dam-building project in Arizona, he championed an ambitious federal program to reclaim thousands of square miles of unproductive desert land by building a number of massive dams to irrigate it, creating vast fields of green to attract settlers and transform the West. He agreed with famed explorer John Wesley Powell, who argued that large dams provided the only way to reliably fight drought and irrigate the region.[51] Roosevelt also asserted that building those dams was "an undertaking too vast for private effort."[52] Power production was a side benefit that eventually became an integral part of the plan.

He pushed the Reclamation Act through Congress in 1902 despite a report from the House Irrigation Committee arguing that the proposed plan was "so vast and expensive that the ordinary mind is staggered at its mere contemplation."[53] Roosevelt astutely warned eastern congressmen and the Speaker of the House, Joseph Cannon, that he might not sign their Rivers and Harbors appropriations bill, with the projects it contained for their districts, unless they supported the western dams. The suggestion did the trick. The new law provided for the sale of public lands to finance government dams in sixteen arid western states, earning the hostility of private companies by ending the practice of giving them water rights.

Among the first reclamation projects authorized was a dam on the Salt River about sixty miles east of Phoenix, then a town of about 6,000 people and the capital of the Arizona Territory. The scale of the undertaking truly was unprecedented. Far from good roads or railroads, the workers, many of them members of the Apache tribes, dug a nineteen-mile-long canal as well as a 2,400-foot tunnel underneath a creek, in which were installed large, innovative hydraulic gates. Construction did not proceed smoothly. In a span of seventeen hours in 1905 nature made one last, furious bid to thwart the audacious humans who wanted to confine and harness the river. The river rose thirty feet, the largest flood since 1891, taking out a railroad bridge and the telegraph and telephone lines to the construction site, as well as washing away much of the partially completed construction and a good deal of machinery. Repeated flooding in the next few months delayed repairs and the renewal of construction.[54]

Also unprecedented was the government's foray into work that would normally have been bid out to private contractors. In addition to a sawmill, a cement plant was constructed. In an early example of the fight over the roles of government and private industry, leading representatives of the national cement trust argued strenuously to the secretary of interior that the government had no business making cement. The plant would destroy the industry, they warned, and would harm the Republican Party. Their plea was unsuccessful, and their dire predictions did not come true. [55]

In a development that would be auspicious for the electric power industry and especially for public power, a hydro turbine generator, installed to avoid the high cost of bringing fuel oil to the remote site, proved to be so productive that the government was able to sell excess power to neighboring ranches. The seed of a big idea was planted. Why shouldn't the federal government include power plants in its plans for irrigation dams and reservoirs, selling power to help pay for construction while speeding the electrification of the vast rural terrain that had been spurned as unprofitable by the industry? The idea was incorporated in a 1906 amendment to the Reclamation Act, making electricity sales a central component of federal dam projects.

Roosevelt Dam and Lake on the Salt River in Arizona was the first dam built under the Reclamation Act and the first major U.S. government hydropower plant. (*Library of Congress.*)

On February 5, 1911, the final stone of Salt River Project #1, dubbed Roosevelt Dam by locals, was laid. The jubilation in Arizona, which would become a state just nine days later, was raucous. A huge crowd greeted the former president when he arrived in Phoenix in mid-March for the dedication ceremony. Roosevelt declared "the utter impossibility of expecting the larger schemes to be developed by private enterprise unless we were content to have the larger schemes become private monopolies."[56] He had opened the door to a major government role in the business of electric power—a cause his younger cousin would soon champion.

CHAPTER 3

THE GOLDEN YEARS

While Theodore Roosevelt and his progressive allies were cracking down on the abuses of railroad, oil, tobacco, beef, and other trusts, leaders of the electricity industry were about to create the first of the holding companies that would collectively come to be called the "Power Trust." These increasingly far-reaching companies would provide a solution to the overwhelming financial demands of the growing industry and help bring electricity to most American homes over the next two decades. But at the same time they were the result of a deliberate plan by a few owners to capture control of many utilities with a relatively small share of their securities—a lucrative but risky strategy.

Holding companies were already attracting criticism. Ohio Attorney General Wade Ellis in 1905 called them "the most effective, and most invidious, and the cheapest of all combinations in restraint of trade.... the promoters have the use of the investment of all the minority holders in all the corporations brought under their control. ... Thus a vast industry is brought under the domination of manipulators."[1] In the utility industry, these leviathans would also prove adept at avoiding effective rate regulation, thwarting the growth of municipal utilities, and beating back support for a larger government role in power generation that gained momentum following the success of the Roosevelt Dam model.

While Samuel Insull became the master of utility growth, monopolization, and consolidation, General Electric made the first move into utility holding company terrain. In 1905, the year after the Supreme Court upheld Roosevelt's effort to breakup J. P. Morgan's Northern Securities Company, GE president Charles Coffin got the idea of bringing together a number of small utilities that were in deep financial trouble. GE still owned large quantities of their stocks and bonds that its predecessor companies had accepted as payment for generators and other equipment. Ten years earlier, as part of his strategy for saving GE from bankruptcy following the Panic of 1893, Coffin had brilliantly bundled the best of these securities and sold them for thirty-three cents on the dollar, agreeing to hold them in trust until the economy recovered and the investors could buy them outright. The remaining securities were of companies that had little prospect of growth or the kinds of earnings that would attract investors.[2]

GE itself was now thriving, thanks to the recovery of the economy and to patent sharing and price fixing agreements that limited its competition with Westinghouse and other equipment manufacturers. Coffin thought investors might now be convinced to invest in the low-value utility securities if they could do so by buying shares in a holding company created by GE that owned a controlling interest in the small firms. To make the weak securities more attractive, GE would provide centralized financial, engineering, and administrative services to the utilities, improving their earnings and chances for profitability.

GE incorporated the new company as Electric Bond and Share and sold it the unattractive stocks and bonds of thirty local utilities. Bond and Share in turn issued its own stock, and transferred all of it to GE as payment for the low-grade utility securities. Bond and Share would issue more shares to raise additional funds as opportunities developed for the newly strengthened utilities to expand or for Bond and Share to buy additional utilities. Just as Coffin had anticipated, investors leapt at the opportunity to participate in a venture led by a company associated with the blue-chip GE.[3]

Samuel Insull didn't form his first holding company, Middle West Utilities, until 1912. His initial purpose was to raise capital for some small southern Indiana utilities he had personally taken over several years earlier at the request of Chicago bankers. He had put his younger brother, Martin, in charge. But Martin's rapid acquisitions of neighboring electric, gas, and streetcar companies were stretching Samuel's credit to the limit. His broker suggested that he form a holding company for all of the Indiana properties.

A majority of the capitalization of holding companies typically took the form of bonds and non-voting preferred stock, leaving all the voting rights with the owners of the common stock. Because a minority of voting shares is usually enough to exert control, this arrangement would allow Insull to control all the operating utilities with a minority of just the common stock of Middle West, a very small percentage of the total worth of the utilities. This practice of issuing preferred stock without voting rights, which was becoming increasingly common, was described by Harvard political economist and corporate critic William Z. Ripley as "a bald and outrageous theft of the last tittle of responsibility for management of the actual owners by those who are setting up these latest financial erections."[4] His admonition did not deter Insull. He anticipated acquiring many more utilities throughout the Midwest, with the holding company mechanism providing needed funds.

According to Insull's generally sympathetic biographer, his transactions "were recorded on the company's books in a way that would forever leave accountants' heads swimming." The Indiana properties were worth about $1 million, and to achieve the expansion and acquisitions Martin had in his sights would require another $3.5 million. Middle West bought the Indiana properties from Insull for $330,000, then issued $4 million of preferred stock and $6 million of common and sold it all to Insull personally for $3.6 million. To raise the money, Insull sold all his preferred stock and $1 million of his common stock for $3.6 million to the public, with his reputation as a financial wizard attracting investors to the new and unproved company. By the time his hocus-pocus was finished, Middle West ended up with the Indiana utilities and $3.567 million in cash for expansion and acquisitions, while Insull walked away with the $5 million in Middle West's common stock, for which he had paid essentially nothing.[5]

Insull's biographer writes that these transactions "left the company showing what appeared to be essentially water of something over $6,000,000."[6] The concept of watered stock goes back to nineteenth-century cattle-drover-turned-financier Daniel Drew. He allegedly inflated the value of his livestock by depriving them of water on their way to market and then allowing them to drink their fill and gain weight the night before they were sold. When he later became a speculator in railroads and realized how much money could be made by issuing and selling extra shares, he boasted about "watering the stock."[7]

Insull rejected allegations of stock watering in the industry, telling a meeting of Iowa utility executives in 1916, "When any one attacks the business to which I devote my life, I believe in standing up and hitting back." He argued that U.S. Census figures showed "the great public-utility businesses of this country, as a whole, are not over-capitalized."[8] He failed to mention that the Census reports were based on data provided by the utilities.

With the proceeds from Insull's original sleight of hand, Middle West proceeded to expand over the next five years, buying or building utilities to provide service to four hundred towns in thirteen states. As a few other owners did in the 1910s and many more would do in the 1920s, Insull began to layer holding companies on top of holding companies. Soon after he created Middle West, he used it to acquire Central Illinois Public Service Company (CIPSCo), a small holding company based about two hundred miles south of Chicago. This was a small first step in building an elaborate pyramid of companies that would drive the explosive growth of his vast empire. Each layer in a pyramid reduced the amount of money the owners at the top had to invest to control the operating utilities at the bottom, increased the amount of dividends paid to the owners, and enhanced the owners' ability to engage in additional acquisitions, insider trading, and padded service contracts. (See Appendix A, "How to Build a Holding Company Pyramid," page 223.)

CIPSCo controlled a small streetcar system, a twelve-mile inter-urban rail line, and part-time power plants in three small towns. Insull purchased its securities at a steep discount and, with his financial connections and reputation, quickly sold most of them, making a nominal $4 million profit that became real over the next decade as CIPSCo bought the lighting plants in fifty-six central and southern Illinois villages and hamlets and extended transmission lines into fifty-five others that had never had service. These high-voltage or high-tension lines, popularly called "high lines," could provide an economic boost to a town in the early twentieth century similar to that provided by the arrival of a canal or railroad in the nineteenth century.

But Insull was thwarted in his more ambitious plans for growth in downstate Illinois. He wanted to purchase the utilities and transit companies in larger towns, but businessman and Congressman William B. McKinley, no relation to the former president, controlled all the larger streetcar and electricity franchises in the area and refused to sell to Insull. Even worse, he spoke disparagingly to potential investors about Insull's efforts to electrify small villages, creating hostility between the two that would fester until they crossed swords after McKinley became a senator in the 1920s.

At about the same time he was creating and expanding Middle West, Insull became Chicago's electric railway and gas magnate, increasing his clout in the city but setting himself up for future headaches. By early 1911, with the encouragement of the mayor, the city's traction companies had been prepared to merge, since their finances were in tatters, but their credit was limited and potential investors doubted their ability to obtain legislation for the merger. Because Commonwealth Edison's credit was strong and the elevated railroad companies were its biggest customers, Insull agreed to underwrite a $6 million loan to begin integrating the lines, with stock in the companies as collateral. But within three years a new mayor had taken office, and the merger never occurred. The companies could not repay the loan, and Insull ended up with four-fifths of their common stock.[9]

In addition, Insull was tricked into becoming chairman of People's Gas. The owners were facing political difficulties and wanted Insull's influence, which had been built by cash contributions to both parties. After he declined an offer of $50,000 a year to become non-executive chairman in 1913, the owners decided to bluff. They knew that Insull's streetcar customers were crucial to his success, and they constructed a model natural gas engine and released statistics suggesting it would be more economical than an electric streetcar motor. The statistics were phony, but Insull was always attuned to the threat of revolutionary technologies. He took the bait and accepted the company chairmanship before he learned that the engine was impractical. He initially limited his role to general policy and financing, but took control of active management after World War I forced a dramatic rise in the price of gas. He gradually made the company profitable in a familiar way. He built up gas demand by introducing lower rates for industrial customers.[10]

Control of the gas and traction companies was just one aspect of Insull's growing clout. The outbreak of World War I in 1914 provided him an opportunity to develop additional skills in public relations and bond sales that would enhance the growth of his empire after the war. With his strong family and business ties to his native England, he was an ardent war hawk.

When the U.S. entered the war in 1917 and President Woodrow Wilson asked the state governors to set up councils of defense, Governor Frank Lowden asked Insull to chair the Illinois council. Insull enlisted a group of the state's most prominent leaders and assigned them to committees staffed largely with his own employees. One of them, the Committee on Public Information, skillfully turned small town newspaper editors into active war supporters by providing ghost-written material most papers could not develop on their own. It also established a speakers bureau in every county, where neighbors talked to neighbors and brought in war heroes and other celebrities to promote "appreciation of the ideals of true patriotism and love of country." And the Illinois council sold Liberty Bonds at a rate 50 percent above the national per capita average, raising more than $1.3 billion and reinforcing Insull's image as a financial miracle worker.[11]

His greatest contribution to the war effort, though, may have been to crush profiteering in coal. Coal companies, mineworkers, and speculators took advantage of the situation, and coal prices tripled. High demand and transportation bottlenecks justified some price increases, but his cost-plus contracts with Peabody Coal convinced him that the tripling of prices was unwarranted. Using his publicity committee to denounce the profiteers, including mine owners and miners, he threatened to take over Illinois mines in the name of his council and run them himself.[12]

Manufacturing had gone into overdrive beginning in 1914 to meet increasing demand from Europe for military and other goods. U.S. exports to Europe almost tripled during the four years of the war, and federal spending for war mobilization increased to $8.450 billion in 1918 from only $477 million in 1916.[13] About a third of the revenue was raised by taxes, including income taxes made possible by the 16th Amendment to the Constitution in 1913, but the remainder was borrowed in five war bond campaigns that relied largely on men and women who had never before invested in securities.[14] The frenetic industrial activity led to a new surge in electricity use by factories. Industrial and commercial consumption grew by 67 percent between 1917 and 1922, and utilities struggled to keep up.[15]

The president's Council on National Defense created a War Industries Board, headed by wealthy Wall Street investor Bernard Baruch, that inserted the federal government heavily into the electricity business, setting production quotas, allocating raw material, and encouraging the use of mass production procedures. The Board also ordered the price of coal to be cut in half, relieving Insull of his threat to take over the Illinois mines. To reduce transportation costs and accelerate war production, Baruch initially tried to concentrate manufacturing on the Eastern seaboard, but coal shortages and railroad congestion thwarted this effort. A major coal shortage in the winter of 1917-18 threatened public health and welfare and jeopardized war production. Plenty of coal was being mined, but loaded coal cars were tied up in traffic jams in rail yards along the east coast. Baruch drew up plans to divert work to areas like Chicago with more accessible coal and adequate power reserves.[16]

On December 13, in the midst of a severe cold snap, mobs of people who could not heat their homes stormed coal yards in New York and Philadelphia. Hundreds swarmed two barges docked in the Wallabout Canal adjacent to the Brooklyn Navy Yard and took whatever coal they could carry while police looked on. The Health Commissioner wired Washington to ask Fuel Administrator Harry A. Garfield to rush coal supplies to New York because deaths from pneumonia in the previous twenty-four hours were the largest recorded in five years.[17] In January, Garfield issued an "idle Mondays" order, closing non-essential industries in the East for five days and then every Monday until March 25. Businessmen howled in protest, but he replied, "This is War."[18]

Looking for other ways to stretch coal supplies, Garfield gave the utility industry a decisive boost in its campaign to supplant factory-owned power plants, which were grossly inefficient. While economies of scale allowed Commonwealth Edison's large plants to produce a kilowatt-hour of electricity with only two-and-a-half pounds of coal, and other large utilities were not far behind, many of the much smaller factory plants used eight or nine pounds. Insull had long argued that utilities could provide power to factories more cheaply than they could produce it themselves, and he had been successful in winning the business of some. But where energy was a small part of manufacturers' costs and where in-house generators were already installed, there was not a large incentive to switch. Inertia had often prevailed. To encourage change, the War Industries Board gave priority to utilities in the allocation of coal, forcing many manufacturers to switch from their steam-driven machines or self-generated electricity to utility-provided power.[19]

The War Industries Board also encouraged, and in some cases ordered, interconnections between utilities to reduce the inefficiencies of the smaller ones. While Insull's and other large utilities had been rapidly consolidating, links between smaller, separately owned utilities were still uncommon in most of the country.[20] But the pressing need for increased production and efficiency led to new appreciation of the merits of coordination and consolidation. Interchanges among California utilities, with their extensive hydropower, avoided the unproductive spilling of water over some dams when other systems were burning scarce and expensive oil.[21] Exchanges among three small utilities in Massachusetts, with different peak demand periods and different reserve capacities, had demonstrated how efficiency could be improved without adding expensive new generation.[22] These steps opened the eyes of utility owners and regulators alike to the benefits of size and accelerated the rush to consolidation after the war.

When industry insiders warned the Wilson administration that a severe shortage of electricity would occur if the war continued into the winter of 1918-19, the War Industries Board ordered Army engineers to survey the country's capacity.[23] Their report, completed after the war, confirmed that larger producers were more efficient and proposed that still more utilities should be consolidated or interconnected.

Despite Insull's heightened stature, political problems awaited him when he turned his full attention back to business after the war. Progressive leaders like Senators William Borah of Idaho, Burton Wheeler of Montana, George Norris of Nebraska, and Robert La Follette Sr. of Wisconsin dropped their attacks on munitions makers and war profiteers and directed their ire against profiteering utility monopolies. Rising rates and poor service provided by the gas and streetcar companies sparked intense anger in Chicago.

Insull dealt skillfully with the resulting threat. Before the war, Mayor "Big Bill" Thompson had played to Chicago's large Irish and German population with anti-war rhetoric, threatening to "crack King George one in the snoot" if he ever came to Chicago.[24] Out on a limb after U.S. entry into the war shifted public opinion, he seized on a new cause—municipal ownership of utilities. His proposal to abolish the state utility commission and return to "home rule" won support from the two Chicago papers of national newspaper baron William Randolph Hearst, who a decade earlier had narrowly lost an election for Mayor of New York as a candidate of the Municipal Ownership League. Not wanting to publicly oppose a popular mayor with a popular cause but aware that creation of a municipal utility was a threat, Insull joined with a bipartisan group of political leaders not under Thompson's control and appeared to yield to the pressure. They arranged for the legislature to abolish the Illinois Utility Commission with widespread publicity in the spring of 1920. But later in the year, with Thompson having moved on to other issues, the legislature quietly established a new Illinois Commerce Commission with all the authority of the former Utility Commission.[25]

Insull's foresight also paid reputational dividends. Thanks largely to his strategy of increasing sales to keep rates down, Commonwealth Edison had been the only coal-fired utility to avoid rate increases during the war. His cost-plus contracts with Peabody Coal cushioned him from surging fuel prices, and his "grow-and-build" strategy of adding generating capacity in anticipation of demand increases meant that he had to borrow and build less than other utilities when war mobilization pushed up demand.

Costs continued to rise sharply after the war. An annual inflation rate of 15 percent in 1919 and 1920, boosted by higher labor costs resulting from the devastation of the Spanish flu, were down from the 18 percent suffered in 1918 but higher than anything the United States has seen since.[26] Insull was not immune. Coal prices shot up when the government removed price controls in 1919, and his protection against labor disturbances ended quickly in October of that year when Peabody's erstwhile collaborator in Illinois, John L. Lewis, became president of the United Mine Workers and called a national strike to demand six-hour days and a 60 percent wage increase. The ensuing coal rationing, factory shutdowns, and loss of 25,000 jobs turned public opinion in Illinois strongly against the strike, and the governor stepped in and settled for far less than the union demanded. But several months later, Frank Farrington, a new leader of the Illinois mineworkers, called a series of short strikes. Temporary deals kept the mines open for two years, but when several scab workers were lynched in Herrin, Illinois, during another national strike called by Lewis, the Peabody mines were closed for five months in the uproar that followed. Commonwealth Edison had to buy coal on the open market for the first time in years, paying an extra $1,600,000 during that time. But with Insull's concurrence, Peabody managed to bring Illinois miners back to work by providing a wage of $7.50 per day, half again the wage for miners elsewhere, and a secret $25,000 annual payment to Farrington.[27]

Despite substantial difficulties faced by electric utilities in the next few years, Insull continued to pursue growth aggressively. With most factory-based generators having been closed during the war, sales to industry provided a tremendous opportunity for utilities in the post-war years. The problem for many of them, though, was that capital became increasingly scarce and expensive. Electricity sales, primarily for industrial use, jumped by two-thirds between 1917 and 1922, but the cost of borrowing was an obstacle to adding capacity.[28] Interest rates soared to levels unseen in over twenty years, and many utilities had trouble selling their preferred stocks and bonds even with high rates.[29] By 1920, the speculation-driven boom had crested, and the country slid into a recession, with unemployment peaking at over 11 percent in 1921.[30]

Insull, like other holding company owners, was able to meet some of his credit needs during this period by shifting money among the utilities he controlled. Greater consumption remained his gospel, and aggressive marketers were his evangelists. Economies of scale seemed limitless, and with streetcars and industries now providing large day-time demand, he sought more evening household consumption to balance the load. Between 1915 and 1925 the per capita use of electricity by Commonwealth Edison customers doubled, with total residential use tripling, making Chicago the national and world leader. Because each utility had a monopoly in its own territory, Insull shared the formula for his success with his fellow executives, most of whom studied and followed his model.[31]

He also skillfully combatted criticism of utilities during this time by bringing his wartime propaganda machine inside Commonwealth Edison. He simply changed the name of the Illinois Committee on Public Information to the Illinois Committee on Public *Utility* Information.[32] Polishing the image of utilities by equating their mission with patriotism and economic progress, he became a leader in modern public relations. He blatantly capitalized on growing public fear of the "red menace," branding municipal utilities as socialist. The American Socialist Party was an appreciable force during these years. With the Bolsheviks gaining power in Russia in 1917 and the formation of the Communist Party of America in 1919, non-socialists' fear of socialism intensified. Anarchists further fueled the fire by mailing bombs to prominent U.S. government officials and businessmen in 1919. Attorney General A. Mitchell Palmer, twice a target of assassination attempts, hired a recent law school graduate, J. Edgar Hoover, to round up and deport radical leftists and anarchists. The resulting "Red Scare" and the "Palmer Raids" created fertile ground for Insull's public relations campaign.

He piously advised Illinois utility executives, "I believe it is our duty to the properties we manage, to the stockholders who own them, and to the communities they serve, that we should enlighten those communities on the situation." His committee provided speakers to organizations throughout the state, and newspapers received a weekly newsletter explaining the principles of ratemaking from a utility point of view. Elementary school teachers distributed pamphlets touting the advantages of electricity and portraying private power companies as a benefit to the community, and three quarters of the high schools in Illinois used industry-supported materials in their classrooms.[33]

Insull warned his committee not to "promote a one-sided viewpoint, to spread 'propaganda,' nor to 'mold public opinion.'" But that is exactly what he intended. Reflecting a business-knows-best attitude, he argued, "The public is in no position to judge service and rates when it knows nothing about the multitude of details involved in furnishing service."[34]

Insull's campaign benefitted from a growing mood in the postwar years that the public should be free to forget about public affairs and pursue their private affairs without government interference. In the 1920 Presidential election, Warren Harding, who promised a return to "normalcy," won in a landslide over James Cox and his running mate, young Franklin D. Roosevelt.

But the country was actually not turning back, it was lurching forward. Major changes in lifestyles appeared and accelerated. Radio burst on the scene when Westinghouse established the first commercial station, KDKA, in Pittsburgh, broadcasting the Presidential election returns in November 1920. Popular music, major league baseball games, the Jack Dempsey-Georges Carpentier heavyweight championship fight, and the humor of Will Rogers quickly made the station a huge success. In two years the first radio ad appeared, and in four years 600 commercial stations had sprung up around the country. From virtually zero in 1920, annual radio sales shot up to $60,000,000 in 1922. Electricity was the link to this popular culture boom, with families gathering in their living rooms to listen to broadcasts.[35]

The power industry took full advantage of radio and other media to further stoke public support. Utility executives took note of how effectively Insull had blanketed newspapers and civic groups with pro-utility messages and headed off home rule and a possible city takeover of Chicago utilities, and they began to replicate his efforts. In 1921, the National Electric Light Association (NELA) created a committee to coordinate efforts nationally. An industry publicist boasted that they used everything except skywriting to shape public opinion.[36] In addition to touting electricity's benefits and disparaging "socialistic" municipal utilities, the campaign argued against stronger regulation and characterized private utility executives as selfless public servants. NELA's managing director, M. H. Aylesworth, claimed, "The impelling and underlying motive for constant improvement in the electric light and power field is service."[37] Results were not long in coming. When *Collier's* editorialized in 1921 that modern progress depended on the ability of utilities to produce low-cost power, the utility-oriented *Electrical World* reprinted the entire page and congratulated the industry for successfully advancing its agenda.[38]

Paid advertising by utilities contributed to the willingness of editors to provide free media. An Illinois director said, "We are trying to promulgate the idea rapidly among the newspapers that utilities offer a very fertile field for . . . their advertising columns . . . . Unless human nature has changed, we will have less trouble with the newspapers than we had in the past."[39] In 1922, the director of the Ohio committee boasted that utilities had received $100,000 worth of free space in that state's newspapers, mainly for reports of speeches to groups that were not told the speaker was being paid by utilities.[40] Historians Charles and Mary Beard wrote that the industry "had secretly subsidized newspapers and slipped their doctrines quietly into editorial columns. They had surreptitiously hired leaders in women's clubs, college professors and publicity experts to promote their cause . . . . The 'red badge' of communism they had deliberately pinned upon their opponents to discredit men and women who refused to accept their program wholesale."[41]

The industry's PR task itself was made easier by the rapid advance of electrification. In 1910, only one home in ten had electricity. By the time America entered the war seven years later, one in four did. As electric lights extended the day, reading and leisure time increased. Once houses were wired for lights, residents often bought electric fans and irons. As sewing machines, vacuum cleaners, water heaters, and washing machines appeared on the market and started to come down in price, they too began to appear on customer wish lists.[42] Increased utility marketing campaigns and the extension of consumer credit had more than tripled sales of appliances from 1915 to 1920, from $23 million to $83 million. Residential electricity demand increased by 129 percent between 1917 and 1922.[43] The increased use, along with continuing improvements in technology, continued to hold rates down, reinforcing the PR campaign.[44]

The great irony of the campaign, historian Arthur Schlesinger Jr. noted, "lay in the fact that the expenses were borne by the people themselves when they paid their electric light bills."[45] NELA's Aylesworth concurred, telling an industry convention, "Don't be afraid of the expense; the public pays the bills."[46]

Initially because of its huge public relations potential, Insull began to rely on a new source of financing to meet growing demand—sales of stock to his customers.[47] When he was a director of Pacific Gas and Electric before the war, he had seen experiments in "customer ownership" and had tried it on a small scale with some of his own companies. People with even a small ownership stake would begin to identify with the company's interests, and politicians who denounced utilities would be attacking these voters. Massive purchases of Liberty Bonds during the war had created a habit of saving and investing by the middle class, and after the war Insull directed all of his companies to start selling as much preferred and non-voting common stock to customers and employees as possible.[48] All employees—linemen, customer service representatives, appliance salesmen—received commissions for selling shares to customers, friends, neighbors, and family members.

Small investors were not always sophisticated, and Insull's salesmen touted the security of utility investments with the illogical but apparently persuasive slogan, "If the light shines, you know your money is safe."[49] Commonwealth Edison's public relations manager, Bernard Mullaney, proudly claimed in 1921, "The number of utility security holders in [Illinois] has been increased from 50,000 to nearly 500,000 now—an impressive figure, the significance of which is being conveyed to the utility-baiting politician."[50]

A year later Insull reported that he expected to meet 40 to 50 percent of his need for new capital from customers and, as he told the New York Bond Club in November, "It gets everybody yelling for us." Other utilities and other industries joined the trend toward broader stock ownership.

A growing population of average Americans had been encouraged to participate in a speculative market boom that gained ever-increasing momentum in the 1920s.[51]

The consolidation of power in the industry did have its critics, who argued that public power and better regulation would have brought rates down considerably more. It was true that regulation had become generally lax. Within a few years of their creation, many of the state regulatory commissions began to fall short of the early standards set by Wisconsin and New York. Despite the initial goal of "professional" regulation, many governors chose commissioners for purely political reasons. A new governor in New York, wealthy businessman John Alden Dix, appointed political cronies in 1911 to replace the experts chosen four years earlier by Governor Hughes, and it soon became clear that a lucrative job with a utility might await a friendly commissioner at the end of his term. Campaign contributions to state political leaders could also prevent the appointment of commissioners deemed unfriendly to utilities.

But even qualified commissioners with the best of intentions faced a challenge. A utility with superior resources could often overwhelm the understaffed commissions. Utilities had better information than anyone challenging their rates, and their ability to pass their costs on to their customers gave them almost unlimited resources to hire the best attorneys and expert witnesses for hearings on rate increases. They regularly and successfully challenged unfavorable commission decisions in court. Federal appeals courts ruled in favor of the utilities in 28 of 34 cases in the early 1920s, and the Supreme Court reversed the appellate courts in three of the remaining six.[52]

One of the broadest attacks on private utility dominance was launched in the early 1920s in California. In 1922, overcoming a decade of resistance from Southern California Edison, the city of Los Angeles created a municipal utility and took over the private utility's local network. In the same year public power advocates secured a vote on a statewide referendum reflecting their belief that private monopolies were reaping excessive profits from their control of a technology that was fast becoming essential to American life. The referendum was on creating a state board with authority to condemn and purchase private hydropower facilities, to sign sales contracts with municipal utilities, and to provide funds for towns to buy private distribution systems. Congregationalist minister and mayor Dr. Horace Porter of Riverside, a leader of the movement, asserted that people "can get light and power at lower rates by public ownership than by any other system" and "those who own and control the . . . power will own and control the state. We believe that the people themselves should be the owners and controllers."[53]

The initiative needed a two-thirds vote to pass, and private utility efforts crushed it. The vice president of Pacific Gas & Electric credited customer stock ownership programs with inhibiting the spread of municipals and helping to "keep our state clean from those sorts of reptiles."[54] In response to criticism of massive utility expenditures to fight this "vicious legislation," *Electrical World* editorialized, "Self-preservation has ever been recognized as the first law of nature, and in all things that make for or against the continued prosperity and usefulness of the electrical industry there is no exception to this law." In just a few years, this attitude would lead the industry into a political buzz saw.[55]

As the economy began to recover from the recession of 1920-21, more utility owners began to create holding companies, and owners of existing holding companies began to add layers. The burgeoning empires swallowed more than 300 private utilities each year, with municipal utilities also an attractive target. Electric utilities needed about six times as much investment as manufacturing companies to generate a dollar of annual revenue.[56] With the industry growing by leaps and bounds, equity provided by local business leaders and loans provided by local banks could never have met the need. Historian Thomas P. Hughes considers the holding company as important to solving the adolescent industry's capital shortage as Edison's inventions were to eliminating the infant industry's technological bottlenecks.[57]

The advantages were undeniable. The holding companies could provide good management advice, acquire capital on favorable terms, build larger and more efficient plants, and obtain better prices by purchasing in larger quantities. They could also apply more effective pressure on government, through campaign contributions or expert testimony before regulatory commissions, to keep rates from being cut as fast as technological advances might warrant.

Another reason for the layered structures was to concentrate power in the hands of a small number of owners, who could regularly mark up the value of the securities of their subsidiaries, increases that were magnified as they moved up the pyramid. Not all holding company owners were driven by such motivations, but the reputations of all utility industry officials suffered from their actions.[58] According to Professor Ripley, whose course on corporate concentration Franklin Roosevelt had taken at Harvard,[59] a "serious defect of overdeveloped holding company organization is the temptation afforded to presti-digitation, double shuffling, honeyfugling, hornswoggling, and skullduggery. Sound and defensible management shades off almost imperceptibly under stress of self-interest, given such concentration of control . . . into all sorts of nefarious dealings."[60]

The spreading reach of holding companies also made regulation less effective. When utility transactions crossed state lines, no single state commission could examine all relevant records. To these practical limits the Supreme Court would soon add a legal barrier, ruling in 1928 that neither state commission could regulate the sale of electricity between a Rhode Island utility and a customer in nearby Attleboro, Massachusetts. This gaping void in authority became known as the "Attleboro gap."[61]

With no effective regulatory scrutiny, holding companies could also pad the management and engineering contracts with their utilities. According to the Twentieth Century Fund, such contracts "provided opportunities . . . to drain considerable sums from operating companies into the pockets of a few people who controlled the holding companies." Frederick Lewis Allen of *Harper's Weekly* wrote that holding companies could siphon revenues from customers "so adroitly that a regulating commission could not see it go." (See Appendix B, "How to Make Dividends Flow Uphill," page 225.) The management and engineering services company for Insull's Middle West Utilities, for example, made a hefty profit of $2.8 million, or 171 percent, in less than five years, drawing more of the ratepayers' dollars up the pyramid.[62]

The highly leveraged structure of the holding companies relied on ever-rising stock prices to maintain the owners' control, because losses as well as gains at each level would be magnified. This drove some of the chicanery that incensed critics. While the transactions undertaken to shore up the holding companies or to extend their reach were in progress, insiders had the opportunity to speculate in the stock of the companies involved, profiting personally even as the pyramids they were building became ever more debt-laden and vulnerable.

Among the many questionable practices pursued by some insiders, perhaps none was shadier than the artificial inflation of the value of properties, as Insull had done when he created Middle West. The Federal Trade Commission later reported that this was the single biggest cause of write-ups. In one instance, Howard Hopson, the head of Associated Gas and Electric, traded ownership of a block of stock among subsidiaries thirty-seven times in thirty days in order to drive up share prices. In another, Insull's Middle West Utilities and its subsidiary, National Electric Power, exchanged securities valued at three million dollars more than their purchase cost. Because Middle West was at the apex of the pyramid, it registered an increase in value of six million dollars. Defenders of such practices argued that such writing up of assets was a legitimate way to recognize that all values were increasing with the growing prosperity of the industry. Critics replied that this was a circular argument because much of the industry's growing wealth was due to just such revaluations.[63]

By 1924, seven groups of holding companies controlled almost 42 percent of the privately owned capacity in the country. Insull and the GE Group, including Bond and Share, controlled more than half of this. Because most combines crossed state lines and did not themselves sell electricity, state regulatory commissions were unable to examine their books, and overpriced service contracts and unduly high rates on intra-system loans escaped scrutiny. Congress, the states, and the courts were generally reluctant to intervene even as the practices became extreme. The industry's public relations machine thrummed along like a powerful turbine, and continuing rapid electrification in the cities and suburbs kept most of the public happy. A few well-placed officials, however, doggedly argued the case for a stronger government role.[64]

By 1924 Samuel Insull was the widely recognized leader of the utility industry. His holding companies and the GE group controlled 21 percent of U.S. privately owned electricity capacity.
(*Courtesy of Loyola University Chicago Archives & Special Collections.*)

* * *

Al Smith was a people's politician and Tammany Hall loyalist from Manhattan's Lower East Side, growing up not far from Edison's Pearl Street Station. He had been elected governor of New York as a Democrat in 1918, and in his first address to the legislature he proposed allowing the state to develop massive hydroelectric dams on the Niagara and St. Lawrence rivers. He considered himself to be following in the footsteps of two illustrious Republican predecessors. As governors, Theodore Roosevelt had warned against giving "waterpower barons" a monopoly on the state's natural resources and Charles Evans Hughes had declared that New York's water power "should be preserved and held for the benefit of the people and should not be surrendered to private interests."[65] By the time of Smith's election, however, the Republican party had swung solidly behind private power, and the Republican-controlled Assembly buried his bill in committee. He returned the favor by vetoing their bill to lease the sites to private utilities.[66]

Republican Nathan Miller defeated Smith in 1920 and won passage of a law intended to place the hydropower sites in the hands of private developers. But before he could implement it, Smith ousted him two years later in a rematch charged with rhetoric that would echo down the years. Miller claimed that public power would be "wasteful and socialistic" and Smith argued that the rivers of the state should not be handed over to the "power barons."[67]

Back in the Executive Mansion in 1923, Smith fired his next salvo. He proposed the creation of a New York State Power Authority to develop dams and related transmission lines. Modeled on the Port Authority of New York, it would be able to issue bonds serviced by revenue from power sales, avoiding the need for legislative appropriations.[68] But the bill also stood no chance in the Republican legislature. *Electrical World* made the case for the utilities: "State development is not only uncalled for," but hydropower is "too important and too complex to permit it to be shoved off the well-built road of experience and sanity into the unpaved byways of adventure and socialism."[69]

As Smith was battling in New York, progressive Pennsylvania

Governor Gifford Pinchot took up the cause of government-driven rural electrification. He believed that the failure of utilities to serve rural areas was inexcusable, especially when large percentages of farmers in Germany, France, and the Netherlands enjoyed service at reasonable rates. He decided that he would change the practice in his state. The Republican governor was an appointee of two Presidents and adviser to three more. An early leader of the push for conservation, he was the first Director of the Forest Service under Theodore Roosevelt and a supporter of Roosevelt's Bull Moose candidacy in 1912. Despite a tenuous hold on his own party's loyalty, he claimed a mandate to regulate the coal and electricity industries more strictly. He proposed to build large power plants near coal mines to save the cost of shipping coal, and long-distance transmission lines to bring affordable power to people in all areas. The legislature provided funds for what he called his Giant Power Survey. "We can expect," he predicted, "the most substantial aid in raising the standard of living, in eliminating the physical drudgery of life, and in winning the age-long struggle against poverty."[70]

In 1923, Pennsylvania Governor Gifford Pinchot proposed a state government role in building power plants and promoting rural electrification.
(*Library of Congress.*)

To carry out the study he hired a fellow blue-blooded, progressive Republican, Morris Llewellyn Cooke, an engineer who had personally filed a successful rate case against the private Philadelphia Electric Company a decade earlier. In a speech written by Cooke, Pinchot warned the Conference of Governors that the consolidation of the electricity industry in the twentieth century was comparable to the development of railroad cartels in the nineteenth and that this transformational change could similarly alter society with head-spinning speed. But Pinchot ran into a legislative blockade, just as Smith had done. The Republican legislature refused to allow any of his proposals out of committee. Activists in other states picked up some of the ideas, but the fight for public power would also move forward on another front.[71]

While Governors Smith and Pinchot struggled to promote public power at the state level, a push to follow Theodore Roosevelt's lead and build more massive federal dams and power plants gained momentum. A progressive and fiercely independent Republican Senator from Nebraska, George W. Norris, decided to throw the weight of his flinty integrity into the fight. In 1910, as a young Congressman, he had won a reputation for independence and a place later in John F. Kennedy's *Profiles in Courage* by leading a successful fight to strip the Republican Speaker, "Czar" Joseph Cannon, of some of his untrammeled power. Born in poverty, he had traveled to the Northwest in 1912 and marveled at the untapped energy of a Columbia River tributary, knowing that the nearby farmers still pumped water by hand and lit their homes with kerosene or coal oil. Little had changed in the subsequent decade for those farmers, and millions of others all around the country.[72]

Norris's longest battle, and the most widely publicized public-private utility fight of the 1920s, grew out of a World War I defensive measure. Fearing the interruption of international supplies of nitrates, a key ingredient of ammunition and fertilizer, Congress authorized President Wilson to choose a site with abundant waterpower for a domestic nitrate plant. Wilson chose Muscle Shoals on the Tennessee River in northern Alabama—a thirty-seven-mile stretch of rapids and pools with a fall of 130 feet.[73] By the time of the Armistice in 1918, the plant had been completed but the dam to provide it with electricity had not.

With peace at hand, the War Department sought to sell the plant, but when scarce credit and the possibility that a new chemical process would make it obsolete kept bidders away, the Department pushed for a bill to create a government-owned corporation to finish the dam and run the plant.[74] With the defense rationale gone, the Red Scare at its peak, and the 1920 presidential election looming, Republicans attacked the plan as a socialist scheme and a dangerous precedent for public ownership of hydropower. It didn't stand a chance.

After President Harding's inauguration in 1921, the consulting engineer for the dam argued for completing it based on the need for additional power in the South. He recommended public operation because higher borrowing costs would make a private company unlikely to build it. But he opposed government distribution of the power, recommending that it be sold to private utilities at market rates. Opponents criticized the proposal from two directions. Some argued that there was no demand for additional power, and others pointed out that a lack of competition would require selling all the power to the private Alabama Power Company, which had the only transmission lines in the area. Congress rejected the proposal. The administration then asked for private proposals to operate the facilities. With credit more readily available and a Republican administration and Congress in control, two bidders submitted offers—Alabama Power and Henry Ford.[75]

Norris had become chairman of the Senate Agriculture Committee and took up the Muscle Shoals cause. Extensive hearings in 1922 convinced him that the two private proposals would be unconscionable giveaways. He introduced his own proposal for flood control and navigation improvements on the Tennessee River, government operation of the power and fertilizer plants, and sale of surplus power to area buyers, with municipal utilities receiving priority as purchasers.

None of the proposals won a majority in committee, but Norris and a growing conservation movement were beginning to make headway with their criticism of the exceptionally generous one hundred-year leases of dam sites previously granted to private interests with no payment required for the use of the water. The 1922 Teapot Dome scandal, in which oil companies had bribed officials to lease naval oil reserves, helped discredit private leases of natural resources. Underestimating the potency of the issue, the Republican leadership allowed the most junior Democratic senator on the Senate Public Lands Committee, Thomas Walsh of Montana, to chair the investigation. He won a reputation as a tenacious investigator and made Teapot Dome a watchword for Harding Administration scandals by regularly repeating the question, "How did Interior Secretary Albert Fall get rich so quickly?"[76]

In pre-historic times, the Gulf of California extended 150 miles north of its current tip south of the U.S.-Mexico border. Over time, silt from the Colorado River formed a natural dam and turned the northern part of the gulf into a huge, shallow, saltwater lake. The lake evaporated, leaving the region that became known as the California Desert dry but rich with alluvial soil. In the late nineteenth century an attempt to irrigate the area with water diverted from the Colorado near Yuma, Arizona, was temporarily successful. In the promoter's literature, the California Desert became the Imperial Valley and its farmland the richest in the United States. By 1904, with land available at $1.25 an acre under the Desert Land Act, seven thousand settlers were raising cattle, hogs, dairy products, fruits, and vegetables.[77]

It was too good to last. The initial irrigation canal began to silt up, and a replacement canal through Mexico was destroyed when a flood wiped out the intake from the Colorado, sending the river surging unimpeded toward the Imperial Valley and creating the Salton Sea, a sixty-foot deep lake with no outlet, covering 150 square miles. After almost two years the Colorado was wrangled back into its former channel, and the Imperial Valley farmers proposed an "All-American Canal" to provide irrigation. No more relying on Mexico.[78]

Imperial Valley Congressman Phil Swing introduced a bill in 1919 for a massive dam to tame the Colorado and redirect a portion of the flow to California. But opposition arose from an unexpected source, Arthur Powell Davis. The nephew of Grand Canyon explorer John

Wesley Powell and director of the Bureau of Reclamation that had enthusiastically built federal dams throughout the arid West, he opposed dealing with the river on a piecemeal basis. Congress agreed and ordered the Bureau to study the river basin as a whole. In 1922 Davis proposed a massive dam, the world's largest at the time, a sixty-story arch "at or near" Boulder Canyon on the Arizona-Nevada border. Swing and California Senator Hiram Johnson, joined by Norris, introduced a bill to authorize construction. In response to objections to the enormous $165 million price tag, they argued the sale of power would handily recover the costs, an argument that would become increasingly accepted as more dams were completed and began to generate revenue.[79]

The utility industry, led by Southern California Edison, which had earlier sought a permit to dam the Colorado, led the opposition. They were joined by most Republicans, who opposed a greater federal role in producing electricity, and by Arizona's senators, who claimed the dam would allow California to steal Arizona's water and stifle its growth. Secretary of Commerce Herbert Hoover negotiated a water sharing agreement that brought the six river basin states except Arizona on board, but the anti-government sentiment was too strong. Three times between 1923 and 1926 the Boulder Dam bill was considered, but industry leaders had built their influence in the halls of power shrewdly. Each time it was squashed without even getting out of committee. In recent years, along with extending the benefits of electricity to millions of people, the utility companies had dramatically increased their number of shareholders, conducted highly successful ratepayer-financed publicity campaigns, and started to dominate many state regulatory commissions. But their political machinations were about to catch up with them.

CHAPTER 4

THE TIDE TURNS

By the second half of the 1920s the stresses of the immediate post-war years were largely a memory. To be sure, farmers still struggled, but wages were rising, unemployment was falling, and business was riding high. The presidential election of 1924 had been a yawner, with the unexciting Democratic candidate John W. Davis losing in a landslide to the even less exciting Calvin Coolidge, who seemed to personify the nation's prosperity if not its exuberance.

The stock market continued its dizzying climb, with more and more Americans participating. The Dow Jones Industrial Average climbed from 955 to 2,215 between the end of the recession in 1921 and the beginning of 1926.[1] If the electrification of homes and the purchase of an automobile made people's lives more comfortable, ownership of a small piece of U.S. Steel, or of Middle West Utilities, offered the possibility of having more. Continued growth in the stock market and in electricity shares in particular came to be regarded as normal in many circles. Utilities were considered an investment in which it was not only "impossible to lose one's money, but one in which an increase in security values was to be regarded as the normal and natural course of affairs." It was easy to dismiss market pessimists or critics of business who would deny the dream.[2]

But the stock exchange was defined as much by rampant speculation and inflated values as it was by hope and dreams of prosperity. Electricity holding companies, with their incessant need for more capital, not only issued new shares frequently but regularly sold bonds for expansion. Because they routinely rolled the bonds over at maturity rather than redeeming them, investment banks prized them, each transaction incurring lucrative fees. The banks also earned double fees on mergers and takeovers, once when existing securities were recalled and again when new ones were issued. Wall Street firms soon began to form holding companies of their own to capture more of this utility business.[3] In their eagerness to enter the game, they bid against each other and the earlier holding companies to buy utilities, raising share prices to even higher levels.

In 1925, Insull chastised those who paid bloated prices for utilities, but he too was guilty. When a journalist asked the head of a large utility why he had sold out to Insull, the executive responded, "What in hell would you do if someone came along and offered you three times as much as your company was ever worth?"[4]

Other sectors of the economy were seeing consolidation as well, among them the newspaper world, typified by the success of the Hearst and Scripps-Howard chains. By mid-decade syndicated features and news provided by press associations began to dominate.[5] RCA, GE, and Westinghouse in 1926 established NBC, which operated two networks and gave radio news a national focus. As in other media, the public craved sensation, and stories about violent crimes, sordid scandals, and tragic accidents captured national attention. In that year, Insull and the utility industry became one of the stories, and the tide of public opinion began to turn against them. Campaign spending scandals provided the gravitational pull. Operating in a corrupt system, Insull had long tolerated and abetted political venality in Illinois and, although a Republican, he regularly contributed to both parties. But his serious political troubles started indirectly in 1926 with a corrupt election in Pennsylvania.

For weeks before the May election, stories had circulated about the unprecedented amounts being spent in the Republican primary for a U.S. Senate seat. Just four years earlier the Senate had "severely condemned" the campaign expenditure of $195,000 by a senator from

Michigan as "dangerous to the perpetuity of a free government."[6] A few days before the Pennsylvania primary, the *Washington Daily News* reported, "The campaign in Michigan, which shocked the country a few years ago, was pikers' play compared to the [Pennsylvania] fight .... Some think the expenditures may reach $5,000,000."[7]

The lavishly funded Philadelphia Republican boss, William S. Vare, defeated the favored incumbent, Senator George Pepper, and progressive Governor Gifford Pinchot, who charged that much of Vare's campaign money had come from utilities.[8] The day after the election the Senate created a committee to investigate, and in early June what was already being called the "Slush Fund Committee" elected as its chairman James Reed of Missouri, a Democrat with a prosecutorial bent and presidential ambitions.

A series of hearings in Philadelphia attracted national media attention. Pinchot reported hearing about large expenditures by the other candidates as well as seven thousand false registrations and other signs of election fraud. His manager for western Pennsylvania alleged that twenty thousand votes cast for Pinchot had been counted for another candidate and that nearly fifty thousand "poll watchers" were paid $10 each by the Pepper or Vare forces in Pittsburgh and Allegheny County, calling it a "pure purchase of votes."[9] By early July, the committee had received reports of spending approaching $3 million, the Senate Rules Committee had passed a non-binding resolution to bar seating anyone whose campaign spent $25,000, and Senator Thaddeus Caraway, an Arkansas Democrat with a biting wit, had created a sensation when he insinuated that the amount spent in the April Republican primary in Illinois had equaled or exceeded that spent in Pennsylvania. Even more explosively, he reported that the winner, Frank Smith, was chairman of the Illinois utility regulatory commission and had received massive utility contributions, including $500,000 from Insull. "The opportunity for corruption can not be denied," he concluded.[10]

Reed, alert to the publicity potential, lost no time in announcing hearings in Chicago. In the opening session, Smith estimated that his campaign had received about $100,000 from Insull. Later in the day an unapologetic Insull testified that he had given Smith $125,000, worth over $1.6 million today.[11] By early August the committee had received evidence of total contributions of over $1 million and numerous allegations of voter fraud. Insull refused to identify the local and state candidates to whom he had contributed, even though they ran on slates with the Senate candidates. This lack of cooperation elicited a threat from Reed to hold him in contempt. Smith tried to disprove any conflict of interest by pointing out cases in which his commission had reduced rates charged by Insull utilities. In fact, Insull's chief motivation for supporting Smith was his intense dislike of Smith's opponent, incumbent Senator William McKinley, who a decade earlier had refused to sell him some downstate streetcar companies and disparaged him to investors.[12] But motivation didn't matter. News services sent daily reports around the country, tarnishing the image of utilities in general and Insull in particular.

Congress did not reconvene until after the November elections, when both Vare and Smith were victorious. Attention then turned to whether the new Congress would seat them, with Senator Norris saying that it would mean "the domination of the Senate and the entire country by political machines, corrupt and immoral."[13]

Then fate intervened. On December 7, McKinley died, and Illinois Governor Len Small appointed Smith to fill his seat during the lame-duck session that would run until March 4. Republican leaders urged Smith not to accept, fearing more negative publicity. But Smith thought he could be seated because his credentials as an appointee were not based on the election that Insull helped fund. Will Rogers, a humorous commentator on the national drama during the 1920s and early 1930s, observed in his syndicated column, "He was not supposed to be thrown out of there till next session."[14]

In February, the Senate proved Smith wrong. After a month of national publicity and two days of debate, they refused to seat him until the Committee on Privileges and Elections had investigated.[15] Before the committee could complete its hearings, however, Smith's doctor ordered him to return to Illinois to recuperate from a painful abscess in the ear. The incomplete investigation meant that the decision on seating him, like Vare's, would be considered by the new Congress to which he had been elected.

The Congressional session was scheduled to end on March 4, when the new Congress would be sworn in. During the waning days of the current Congress, a cluster of electricity issues, including Boulder Dam, Muscle Shoals, campaign contributions, and the Power Trust roiled the Senate and captured national attention. In mid-February California Senator Hiram Johnson called up the Swing-Johnson bill on Boulder Dam, excoriating opponents "who believe that there is a God-given right in a Power Trust to make profit . . . out of the property that belongs to our people." The *New York Times* predicted a filibuster, and opponents of the bill obliged three days later.[16] Arizona Senator Henry Ashurst argued that the diversion of water to California would be unfair to his state, but Johnson claimed this argument was a smoke screen and it was the private utilities that stood "like a lion in the path" of the dam.[17]

On the same day the biggest lion in the pride appeared before the Reed Committee. Insull acknowledged contributions to local candidates that brought his total to $237,000, but he again refused to identify the recipients without their permission. He also denied that the money came from his utilities, admitting that he had borrowed it from Commonwealth Edison but claiming he had paid it back after the primary. Reed ordered him to return in five days with the cancelled check used to repay the money and encouraged him to seek permission from the recipients to identify them.[18]

The Boulder Dam filibuster continued for several days, interrupted only by short recesses for sleep and for routine business, with the Senate at one point in continuous session for over 29 hours, the longest in over a decade.[19] Advocates on the outside also weighed in. Pinchot urged passage of the bill, saying Boulder "will be incomparably the greatest of all dams . . . will be twice as high as any dam yet built and . . . will develop more water power than is now produced at Niagara."[20] The president of Brooklyn Edison, Matthew Sloan, summarized the utility position on public power in the *New York Times*: "What evidence can be produced that Government [can] do a better job, or cheaper job, or a more beneficial job for the public than the light and power industry has done?"[21]

In the middle of the filibuster the Federal Trade Commission submitted a report on GE and the Power Trust that absolved GE of monopoly control. But it declared that the problem of holding company pyramids "calls for a legislative consideration by Congress" because a small "investment in voting stock of the apex holding company" can control scores of underlying companies.[22] Also during the filibuster, Insull returned with the check he had used to repay Commonwealth Edison, but he said he had not attempted to seek permission from the candidates to disclose their names. Reed's committee reported to the Senate on his "further and continued obduracy" and recommended contempt proceedings.[23]

On the fourth day of the Boulder Dam filibuster, Johnson filed a cloture petition that would end the filibuster after up to another one hundred hours of debate, which would push other important bills off the calendar. As a result, Johnson doubted he could win the supermajority necessary to cut off debate, but he thought the favorable publicity about the dam had ensured that the Swing-Johnson bill would pass in the next Congress.

The major public-private power debate in the 1920s was over control of Wilson Dam at Muscle Shoals on the Tennessee River. (*Library of Congress.*)

Before the cloture vote, the Senate briefly debated a bill to allow private industry to control Muscle Shoals. Norris prevailed, and the Senate sent the bill back to committee, killing it for the outgoing Congress. When Boulder again became the order of business, rhetoric soared. Johnson asserted that the Imperial Valley was in "ever-present peril" of flooding by the mercurial Colorado River and that Arizona was fighting not for water but for a royalty on every kilowatt-hour of electricity generated at the dam.[24] Senator Cameron of Arizona denied that, declaring, "I am pleading for the future life of my state." He felt cutting off the filibuster would make Arizona "walk the plank without even a fighting chance for her life."[25] Despite majority support for the Boulder Dam, Johnson's fears were realized: Too many Senators wanted to avoid additional lengthy debate in order to preserve time for legislation they considered more urgent. The cloture petition, needing two thirds to pass, received barely half that.[26]

Following the vote, Montana Senator Thomas Walsh seized the moment to call for a comprehensive Senate investigation of holding companies. Quoting Professor William Z. Ripley's recently published bestseller, *Main Street and Wall Street,* he argued that antitrust law was never "more boldly defied or more generally and more notoriously violated than in the past five years." In the wake of the exculpatory report on GE, he claimed the Federal Trade Commission had become "either neutral or subservient to" the violators.[27]

Throughout the hectic final days of the session, Senator Reed of Missouri continually tried to extend the life of his investigative committee through the coming nine-month recess. Many Republicans opposed him, thinking he would use it only to investigate Republicans. The leader of this filibuster was David A. Reed, the junior senator from Pennsylvania, who was incensed that the committee had investigated Republican primaries while ignoring the nearly total absence of black voters in Democratic primaries in the South. The two Reeds held the Senate hostage, with Reed of Missouri refusing to allow major bills to be considered before his resolution and Reed of Pennsylvania refusing to allow the resolution to come to a vote. They controlled the floor for thirty-seven hours during the last week and for the entire three-and-a-half-hour morning session before the mandated adjournment at noon on March 4.

As a result, major bills for appropriations, public buildings, and veterans' benefits died along with the Boulder Dam and Muscle Shoals bills and the Reed and Walsh resolutions.[28] Will Rogers wrote about the ugly end of the session, "Don't ever tell us Friday is unlucky. Didn't congress adjourn today? The Republicans died fighting to keep from being investigated. The voters would like to investigate both parties as to their sanity the last few weeks."[29]

Congress did not reconvene until December 1927, at which time it extended the life of the Reed Committee and refused to seat Smith and Vare. Norris proclaimed that the issue regarding Smith "is not a question of Illinois being deprived of her two votes in the Senate." Rather, "it is a question of Mr. Insull being deprived of his votes in the Senate."[30]

The Reed Committee's contempt recommendation for Insull was still pending, but by this time the Chicago municipal elections had been held and the candidates could no longer be damaged by disclosure of Insull's contributions. When the committee summoned Insull again, he avoided prosecution by providing their names, which proved to be uncontroversial.[31]

Swing and Johnson reintroduced their Boulder Dam bill in the new Congress, and this time the devastation wrought earlier in the year by the Great Mississippi River Flood brought many Midwestern and Southern senators on board, helping the bill survive another filibuster. President Coolidge reluctantly signed it into law at the end of his term, knowing it would be passed again and signed by President-elect Hoover if he did not.[32] Norris also introduced his version of Muscle Shoals legislation on a rising tide of support. Both houses of Congress passed the bill shortly before adjournment in May 1928, but Coolidge killed it with a pocket veto. Norris nevertheless claimed a victory, believing that leasing the facility to a private interest would no longer be possible.[33]

Thomas Walsh also reintroduced his resolution for a Senate investigation of the Power Trust and its holding companies, intending it to be tougher than the Federal Trade Commission investigation. His opponents feared the same. One senator said of Walsh, referring to his Teapot Dome investigation, "He is like a tiger who tastes human blood and then becomes a maneater for the rest of his life." After a bitter debate, supporters of utilities succeeded in amending the resolution to assign the investigation to the Federal Trade Commission. But theirs was a Pyrrhic victory. A new solicitor general of the commission was appointed who had a Walsh-like sense of justice and public interest but had a conservative temperament and appeared less partisan. The consequences would be far-reaching. Still, the most consequential development of 1928 would occur not in Congress, but in the public arena, when a fighter with a more powerful punch joined the battle.[34]

The United States was changing rapidly in 1882 when Franklin Roosevelt was born. In the midst of the swiftest economic growth in previous U.S. history and the accompanying Gilded Age, immigration reached its highest annual level, urban population exceeded 50 percent of the total in the Northeast, the rollback of Reconstruction in the South was six years underway, and Thomas Edison was about to open the first central station electric utility. But little of the turmoil of the times intruded on Roosevelt's privileged and comfortable childhood. His mother Sara supervised his upbringing with an intense love that could have been smothering but in fact contributed to his lifelong sense of confidence.[35] His father imparted to him a sense of responsibility to others, and his favorite tutor, Mlle. Jeanne Rosat-Sandoz, instilled in him a concern for social welfare and sympathy for the disadvantaged that distinguished him from many others of his class.

At fourteen he entered Groton, where the headmaster, Endicott Peabody, sought to cultivate in upper-class American boys "manly, Christian character, having regard to moral and physical as well as intellectual development."[36] He threw himself enthusiastically into sports despite being, according to Peabody, "too slight for success." He excelled only at "high kick," a game that entailed crashing to the floor after trying to kick a can hung from the ceiling. It required little athletic ability but a great deal of courage and tolerance for pain, traits that would come to serve Franklin well.[37]

Peabody's advocacy of public service helped prepare the ground for Franklin's interest in politics. A more important role model, though, was Theodore Roosevelt, his fifth cousin but not at all distant in the close Roosevelt family. Franklin followed "Cousin Teddy" to Harvard, where he was among the privileged elite in a socially stratified institution but distinguished himself from many of his wealthy classmates with hours spent volunteering at a boys' club in Boston and active membership in Harvard's social service group. The school newspaper, though, the *Harvard Crimson,* was his principal activity and the one that most developed his leadership ability and self-confidence.[38]

After her husband's death in Franklin's freshman year, Sara lived primarily through her son, moving to Cambridge each winter and expressing her love in a direct, often imperious, manner. Franklin struggled to assert his independence in the face of her forceful personality and her control of the family fortune. Because he sought to avoid conflict and wanted not to hurt her, he often defended his autonomy by appearing to yield while in fact maintaining his position. On issues that were important to him, when his tact or deception failed and a conflict became overt, he usually stuck to his position and prevailed.[39] The tactic of vaguely agreeing with others and then going his own way would become a central part of his political modus operandi.

Following Harvard, he enrolled in law school at Columbia and married another distant cousin, Theodore's niece Eleanor. At age 25, he started his first job at a Wall Street firm, defending corporations against suits in small claims court, learning about people in circumstances very different from those he knew even while arguing against them. Eleanor's volunteer work teaching at a settlement house on the Lower East Side, where she was exposed to misery beyond any she had imagined, also affected Franklin's worldview. He once accompanied her to a run-down, overcrowded, multi-family tenement house with shared outhouses. "My God," he said, "I didn't know anyone lived like this."[40]

Sometime during his three years at the law firm he told friends that he intended to run for office at the earliest opportunity, and "thought he had a very good chance to be President." His plans tracked Theodore's experiences, a fellow junior attorney later recalled, "first, a seat in the State Assembly, then an appointment as assistant secretary of the Navy . . . and finally the governorship of New York."[41]

The first opportunity was not long in coming. In 1910 he eagerly accepted the Democratic nomination offered by party officials for a difficult state senate race in the Republican Hudson Valley district that included his Hyde Park home. He won with a vigorous and effective campaign, aided by the Roosevelt name. The first important task for the legislature was the selection of a new U.S. Senator—the direct election of senators was still three years away—and he seized the opportunity to demonstrate leadership and solidify his reputation as a reformer by opposing the Tammany Hall machine. He was "outwitted and outgeneralled," according to the *New York Post*. But the publicity he won as a reformer boosted his political prospects.[42]

He supported fellow reformer Woodrow Wilson's Presidential nomination in 1912 despite Tammany's opposition. When Cousin Teddy's third-party candidacy opened a fissure in Republican ranks and led to an easy Wilson victory, Franklin won appointment as assistant secretary of the Navy, "the one place, above all others, I would love to hold."[43] During the next seven years in Washington, he learned to be an effective administrator, and he solidified his relationships with labor through his management of shipyards. A rapprochement began with Tammany, whose support he would need to achieve his larger political goals; in turn the organization sought the shade of his good-government umbrella in order to reduce its reputation for corruption.

When the United States declared war in April 1917, the hawkish and politically ambitious Roosevelt wanted to serve in the military, as his cousin had done to his great political benefit during the Spanish-American War. In the summer of 1918, Secretary of the Navy Josephus Daniels finally allowed him to go to Europe, where he visited field hospitals and managed to get near enough to the front lines to pull the lanyard on a French artillery piece. At the time he wrote in his diary of "my partially successful efforts to see the real thing," but by 1936 he would embellish the story on the stump, "I have seen war on land and sea. I have seen blood running from the wounded. I have seen men coughing out their gassed lungs."[44]

Democratic losses in the 1918 Congressional elections and the approaching end of Wilson's second term foretold a lean period for Democrats, and Roosevelt made plans to set up a law practice with two friends after he left the Navy.[45] At the same time his famous name, his national visibility, and the importance of New York's electoral votes gave him some credibility as a candidate for vice president in 1920. He worked hard to win Tammany's support at the convention in San

Francisco, asking to second the presidential nomination of Governor
Al Smith, who was running as New York's favorite son to hold the
state's delegates for later bargaining. He also burnished his credentials
as a progressive when he seized the New York banner from a Tammany
stalwart to join in a demonstration in favor of the League of Nations.
Future Secretary of Labor Frances Perkins, whom he had not impressed
during his days in Albany, considered him "one of the stars of the show.
I recall how he displayed his athletic ability by vaulting over a row of
chairs to get to the platform in a hurry."[46] When the deadlocked convention turned to Ohio Governor James Cox on the forty-fourth
ballot, Cox recommended the young and attractive Roosevelt, whom
he had never met, as his running mate.

Democratic presidential candidate James M. Cox and VP candidate Franklin
Roosevelt campaigning in Dayton in August 1920.
(*Courtesy Franklin D. Roosevelt Library.*)

Few observers expected a Democratic victory in 1920, and Roosevelt was no exception. He nevertheless resigned from his Navy job
and threw himself into the effort, traveling extensively, enjoying himself immensely, delivering hundreds of speeches, reaping copious local
press attention but little national coverage, and receiving a first-rate
education in how to run a national campaign. Although Warren G.
Harding won the Presidency with 61 percent of the vote, no one
faulted Roosevelt, and he built a massive list of contacts among

Democratic activists while establishing himself as a future Presidential prospect.

Roosevelt still needed to make a living, and in January 1921 he unenthusiastically assumed his duties in his law firm. As he later wrote to one of his partners, routine matters "bore me to death."[47] A deep-pocketed Democratic businessman soon came to the rescue, offering him a position as vice president of the New York office of his Maryland surety bond business. The generous salary came with the understanding that the type of civic and political activities that would add to his reputation would also be valuable to the firm.

In early August 1921, Roosevelt arrived at his family's summer home on Campobello Island in the Bay of Fundy for a vacation. At the end of a strenuous day, he felt a chill and dragged himself to bed, assuming he was coming down with a cold. By morning he was unable to move his legs. After several painful and terrifying days and misdiagnoses by two doctors, a specialist determined that he was suffering from polio.[48]

Two cover-ups started almost immediately. His close political aide, Louis Howe, hid from the press Roosevelt's need to be carried on a stretcher when he was taken off the island, and Dr. George Draper, his physician, deceived his patient as well as the public, telling reporters, "You can say definitely that he will not be crippled." Early in his treatment Draper wrote of his approach, "He has such courage, such ambition, and yet at the same time such an extraordinarily sensitive emotional mechanism, that it will also take all the skill which we can muster to lead him successfully to a recognition of what he really faces without utterly crushing him."[49]

Roosevelt's condition was irreversible, but he seems never to have accepted this fact, nor did Draper push him to do so. Over the next seven years, he struggled mightily to regain some use of his legs by swimming and exercising in warm water while Eleanor and Howe worked to keep him in the public eye. His most visible role was as titular chairman of Governor Al Smith's campaign for the Democratic presidential nomination in 1924.

Smith threw his hat in the ring with William Gibbs McAdoo, President Wilson's treasury secretary and son-in-law, as his principal primary opponent. The fight was personal for Smith. Not only did McAdoo refuse to disown the support of the anti-Catholic and anti-immigrant Ku Klux Klan[50]—a force at the convention, as illustrated by a proposed platform plank condemning the Klan losing by only a single vote, 543 to 542—but also his chief supporter was William Randolph Hearst. In 1918, at a time when babies were dying in New York City due to scarce and expensive milk, Hearst's New York papers had attacked Smith as a baby-killer and a pawn of the of the Milk Trust. An enraged Smith won the ensuing public fight with Hearst, but it was the beginning of a lifelong feud that would have lasting consequences for the election of a president.[51]

Franklin Roosevelt nominates New York Governor Al Smith for President at 1924 Democratic Convention. (*Courtesy of Franklin D. Roosevelt Library.*)

Although Smith considered Roosevelt a lightweight, his close adviser, Joseph Proskauer, persuaded him to choose Roosevelt as his campaign chairman and to ask him to give the nominating speech

"because you're a Bowery mick, and he's a Protestant patrician."[52]
Roosevelt knew that Smith was not favored to win the nomination
and that Democratic chances in 1924 were slim, but he happily
accepted the marriage of convenience. He was able to keep his name
in the news and his career hopes alive without extensive travel, and
he relished the opportunity to issue statements on the candidate's
behalf, to renew his 1920 connections by writing regularly to Democratic leaders around the country, and to give the national
convention in August its most memorable moment with his electrifying nominating speech.

There would be no vaulting over chairs this time. Determined not
to be wheeled into Madison Square Garden, he "walked" to his seat
every day with most of his weight on a crutch under his right arm
while he gripped his son James's arm with his left. When he struggled
down the aisle and appeared at the stage for his speech, the delegates
greeted him with thunderous applause, in relief and in appreciation of
his obvious courage. Then James handed him his second crutch, and
twelve thousand people seemed to hold their breath as he slowly and
painfully struggled for the last fifteen feet alone, sweating heavily and
twisting his shoulders back and forth to swing one braced leg forward
and then the other—exactly as he had practiced it many times at home.
When he reached the lectern and grasped it with both hands, unable
to wave but with his head thrown back in what would become a signature gesture, the relieved crowd stood and roared for three minutes.
He smiled and nodded, "seem[ing] to be sharing his personal victory,"
according to Frances Perkins.[53]

The thirty-four-minute speech itself was equally successful.[54] With
his rich tenor voice amplified by electricity and broadcast to the
nation—this was the first convention covered live by radio—Roosevelt
pleaded for unity in a divided party and, in a line written by Smith's
staff, gave the candidate his lasting nickname, "The Happy Warrior."
Although neither of the frontrunners could achieve the two-thirds
vote required for the nomination and the weary delegates turned to
the charisma-challenged Wall Street lawyer John W. Davis on the
103rd ballot, Roosevelt had "bridged a chasm between the party's elite
progressives and its working-class liberals," helping to create the

modern Democratic Party. He had also restored his place on almost everyone's list of possible future Presidential candidates.[55]

While Coolidge defeated Davis in November 1924 by a wide margin, Smith won re-election as Governor by defeating Theodore Roosevelt Jr. with Eleanor's enthusiastic help. She delighted in following her cousin to his appearances throughout upstate New York with a papier-mâché teapot on her car continually spouting steam, a not-too-subtle reference to his indirect connection with the Teapot Dome scandal and a satisfying settling of scores for his campaigning against the Cox-Roosevelt ticket in 1920.[56]

Back in Albany, a key part of Smith's program was to consolidate state government, which included abolition of the pro-utility Water Power Commission, but Republican control of the legislature ensured that his proposed New York Power Authority and public development of hydroelectric sites could not go forward. As with Muscle Shoals and Boulder Dam at the national level, resolution of the dispute would require the voters to speak with a more certain voice. Smith won again in 1926 in a landslide, with electricity again a major issue thanks in part to national publicity about Insull and utility campaign contributions. Smith's opponent, Congressman Ogden Mills, had charged that the incumbent governor intended to put the state into the power business, which he would turn over to Tammany to be milked. Smith noted that many Republicans supported Boulder Dam and pointed out that Mills had a conflict of interest because his relatives owned stock in companies seeking power licenses.[57]

In the summer of 1927, President Coolidge announced he would not run for re-election in 1928. Roosevelt wrote to his contacts developed in the 1920 campaign to say that only Smith had a chance of being elected as a Democrat, despite his Catholicism and his opposition to Prohibition. "The South will hold its nose and vote for him."[58]

Smith swept the early Democratic primaries and went to the convention as the clear favorite. Roosevelt served as his titular floor manager, looking stronger than in 1924, foregoing his crutch in favor of "walking" with a cane and a hand on his son's arm. He again nominated Smith in a strong speech prepared, he said, "wholly for the benefit of the radio audience" of fifteen million.[59] Smith easily won the nomination on the first ballot. The party that could not even truly condemn the Ku Klux Klan four years earlier had nominated a Catholic, although the convention broke with tradition and failed to make the nomination unanimous.

During the campaign Smith supported public control of hydropower and criticized the holding companies and their lobbying activities, leading Will Rogers to remark, "He told the truth about the power trusts. When you hop on the power trusts, you are standing on the very arches of the Republican party. I had a joke about the power lobby in the papers and I got so many letters from power magnets (*sic*) saying 'there was no power lobby' that it almost made me lose faith in rich men. So sic 'em, Al. Yours for everybody owning their own river."[60]

Although never completely out of touch, Roosevelt had been away from New York over half of the time from 1924 to 1928, largely at Warm Springs, a once run-down spa in Georgia where he believed swimming in the buoyant, mineral-laden waters improved his mobility and where he loved helping other polio patients attracted by his presence. Although it is doubtful that the therapy significantly improved his physical condition, it provided psychic rewards and made him more comfortable with his limitations. In an automobile fitted with hand controls, he also became familiar with the hardship of people in the impoverished countryside surrounding Warm Springs, and he bought a farm on Pine Mountain. Both provided him with an understanding and a trove of anecdotes that he used effectively for the remainder of his life.[61]

Smith faced an uphill campaign in the '28 general election. Prosperity was continuing, except for farmers, and he failed to achieve much traction outside East Coast cities. Catholic, anti-Prohibition, and urban, he faced stiff resistance from fundamentalist, dry, rural and small-town America. His inner circle, seeking someone to run for governor who could help him win New York's electoral votes, focused on Roosevelt. But they worried that he could be a future political threat to Smith. When they expressed these concerns to Smith, who thought the job required exceptional stamina, he replied, "He won't live a year."[62]

Roosevelt resisted pressure to run. Although it was the logical next step on his long-planned political path, he and Louis Howe believed

1928 would be a Republican year and preferred to seek the statehouse in 1930 or 1932 and perhaps the Presidency in 1936. He also hoped to regain more strength in his legs. He skipped the state convention for Warm Springs, but when Smith called and asked what he would do if he were nominated in spite of his reluctance, he refused to answer, perhaps because he didn't want to be seen as rejecting the party when it needed him. "Thanks, Frank," said Smith, "I won't ask you any more questions." The next day the convention nominated Roosevelt by acclamation.[63]

Albert Ottinger, New York's activist attorney general, was a formidable opponent. The first Jewish nominee of either party for governor, he was expected to cut into the Democratic margin in New York City. He was solidly for private development of the state's hydroelectric resources, while Roosevelt pledged to continue Smith's policy of public control of the Niagara and St. Lawrence dam sites. At Syracuse, Roosevelt gave what one historian called "the most effective single speech" of his campaign, likening GOP efforts to privatize the state's water resources to theft from the people. He also strongly supported federal operation of the dams at Muscle Shoals and Boulder Canyon.[64]

It was clear by 9:00 p.m. on Election Day that Smith would be swamped in the presidential race, and Roosevelt went to bed after midnight when the early editions of the morning papers proclaimed a Republican sweep in New York. Shortly after 1:00 a.m. Ed Flynn, the Bronx Democratic boss, thought he detected a hint of a positive trend in the upstate returns and called him. Roosevelt didn't believe it and said that Flynn was crazy to wake him. By morning the hint proved solid, and Roosevelt won by about 26,000 out of more than four million votes.[65]

By the mid-1920s, Samuel Insull personally controlled 9 percent of the nation's private electricity capacity and was the face of the industry.[66] Raising capital became easier as his reputation soared, and Chicago bankers virtually thrust money at him. But over the course of the next few years he put the stability of his empire in jeopardy by overpaying for badly run utilities.[67] Newly created holding companies were competing to buy utilities, and Insull was nothing if not a competitor. As a consequence, he began to take on additional debt to expand, leveraging his companies more extensively.

From the beginning, Middle West had indulged in questionable accounting practices. In the frothy markets of early 1928, Insull increased its estimated market value by about 70 percent with the purchase of two highly leveraged, pyramided holding companies that had engaged in similar practices and controlled forty-nine other companies. His younger brother Martin had arranged the deal, but Sam had the final word. His attorney described the meeting at which he made the decision: "Insull studied the figures, agreed that the underlying properties were excellent, and said, 'It will take us ten years to tear down this pyramid and make this a reasonable investment.' But then he shrugged his shoulders, and signed the documents."[68] The purchase compounded his risk by venturing into the Northeast, where J. P. Morgan and its allies were beginning to exert greater control of the industry. According to his biographer, Forrest McDonald, "In the end, this invasion of the East proved to be as successful as Napoleon's invasion of Russia."[69] Insull's harsh winter was about to arrive.

He felt the first chill a few months later when he noticed that Cyrus Eaton, a Cleveland financier, was buying large blocks of stock in his companies and trying to cover his tracks. Other interests that might have been surrogates for Eaton were also buying significant shares. Insull knew that several owners had lost control of their utilities, but he had never before had to worry, because ownership of his companies was widely distributed among banks, friends, employees, and customers in Chicago. Eaton made no attempt to take control, then or later. He was engaging in greenmail—acquiring enough shares to be a threat and intending to sell them back at a premium. But Insull was convinced he was planning a takeover.[70]

By mid-1928, Insull learned that Eaton's holdings were greater than his own, and late that summer he became certain that his empire was threatened. He and Eaton happened to be crossing the Atlantic on the same ship, and they shared several friendly conversations. But during the crossing, Eaton's agents bought a substantial additional quantity of Commonwealth Edison shares. Insull knew it, yet Eaton didn't know he knew and said nothing about it. Insull assumed the worst. At about the same time, in the speculative bull market, the skyrocketing price of Middle West shares was jeopardizing the popular ownership that he counted on. The company also had substantial high-interest debt. In a major refinancing operation, he split its stock ten for one, retired its debt and, to preserve funds for expansion by its operating utilities, began to issue dividends in stock rather than cash. The maneuvers seemed to work, as Middle West ended up with no debt and almost eliminated its fixed cash charges. A few years later, though, Federal Trade Commission investigators had a less benign interpretation. They accused Insull and his investment adviser of manipulating the price of the thinly traded stock.[71]

Insull took another defensive step in January 1929. He created Insull Utility Investments (known as IUI), an investment trust that would sit above and control his principal companies—just the kind of structure he had long criticized. He, his family, and his close allies exchanged their shares in the underlying companies for shares in IUI, including all of its common stock. He set a low price per share to deflect any criticism of overvaluing the stock, and the family was allowed to buy a large additional block of shares at a small premium above the original price. The purpose, as his press release openly stated, was "to perpetuate the existing management of the Insull group of public utilities."[72]

But there was a chink in his armor. Existing shareholders in the subordinate companies had the right to buy additional shares of IUI common stock before they could be offered for public sale. An outsider with more shares than Insull, like Eaton, could theoretically accumulate enough IUI common stock to take control. And no one had counted on the manic stock market of 1929. Commonwealth Edison shares went from $202 to $450 and Middle West rose from $169 to $529 between January and August. The boom had made it unreasonably expensive for IUI to purchase enough stock in the underlying companies to ensure continued control.[73] To solve the problem, in October 1929 Insull created yet another investment trust, Corporation Securities Company of Chicago, commonly known as "Corp," with inflated share values and without advance purchase rights for existing shareholders.[74]

But Corp was more than another layer on top of the pyramid. IUI and Corp were completely interconnected—IUI owned 28.8 percent of Corp, while Corp held 19.7 percent of IUI—and together they controlled Commonwealth Edison and Middle West. The interlocking companies had assets of nearly $3 billion and were highly leveraged. A potential raider would have to target both in order to dislodge Insull from any part of his empire, and their extensive debt made them both unattractive. But the high ratio of debt to equity that helped deter raiders in a rising market would make the companies highly vulnerable if share prices dropped. Insull had very little equity for such a substantial empire, and the entangled finances of the companies meant that a weakness anywhere would threaten the entire edifice.[75] According to John Rowe, a recent CEO of Commonwealth Edison and its successor, Exelon Corporation, "To the extent that his failure was overestimating future cash flows, that is a very common sin. I have no doubt that he was swept away by hubris in his later years. That too is a very common sin."[76]

Insull's risky actions were just one part of the massive consolidation in the utility industry. "The year 1929," *Time* reported, "may well be famed as the year in which the House of Morgan became also a Power House." The private investment bank gathered several existing holding companies into United Corporation, a new super-holding company. A history of the firm called it "a sure sign of impending disaster when the House of Morgan cast aside its traditional aversion and joined the flurry of stock promotion," but the large returns of utility holding companies were too tempting for even these conservative bankers to resist. With twenty times the capitalization of U.S. Steel, United gained control of one fifth of all electricity production in the country, roughly equal to GE's Bond and Share and Insull's companies combined. Through a complex system of cross ownership, interlocking directorates, and old-school ties, almost all the major utility holding companies, except Insull's, were now in J. P. Morgan's orbit.[77]

In late October the stock market crashed, ending the brittle prosperity of the preceding years and the speculative boom that accompanied it. Investors who had gambled on stocks during the euphoria of the nine-year bull market now faced margin calls and financial ruin. "As prosperity had never been so ostentatious," wrote historian Henry Steele Commager, "collapse was never so spectacular nor ruin so widespread."[78] Inopportunely, *Time* magazine celebrated Insull with a cover story a week after the Crash, unaware of the thin ice on which he skated. Insull, however, believed the economy was structurally strong. After all, weren't electricity sales increasing? On the day after Black Tuesday, he offered collateral from his own accounts to employees owning stock in his companies and facing margin calls. His actions appeared generous, but they could also be seen as self-serving. If his employees had sought to cut their losses or meet their margin calls by selling stock, they would have driven the share prices down even further.[79*]

Still optimistic, Insull borrowed more money to peg the falling Middle West stock at $220 so shareholders would exercise their options to buy additional shares at $200, providing the financing he needed. When President Hoover invited business leaders to the White House to declare that conditions were "fundamentally sound" and to urge them to keep investing, Insull committed to $200 million in new expenditures in 1930, an increase over 1929. This also required more borrowing. As the market partly recovered in November and December, his confidence seemed justified. An *Electrical World* headline in December trumpeted, "Samuel Insull Asserts 'Business As Usual.'"[80]

Following the precipitous drop in stock prices, bond markets revived and financing switched even more heavily to debt. Both IUI and Corp borrowed to complete the stock purchases that were the purpose of their creation, and the interest payments burdened the entire empire. Despite Insull's dangerously insufficient equity, his self-confidence was reassuring to the market, his credit was good, and buyers snapped up each of his bond offerings. As a result of his bitterness toward New York banks dating to his years with Edison, he still excluded them from the profitable business, and at the 1930 dinner of the Chicago Stock Exchange, he brashly poked the tiger, blasting the concentration of financial power in New York.[81]

Eaton doubted that banks would indefinitely loan money to Insull, and in April he offered through an intermediary to sell him a combined

---

* This is one of several parallels between Insull's collapse and that of Enron and its CEO, Kenneth Lay, seventy years later.

158,000 shares of common stock in Insull's companies at $400 per share, saying he would sell the shares to a banking syndicate if Insull declined. Their market value at the time ranged from $318 to $329. Insull made a counter offer at $350, with 85 percent payable in cash over four months, and Eaton accepted. But Insull made the agreement without first making arrangements to finance the purchase.[82] Pledging IUI and Corp shares as collateral, he again borrowed heavily. Many of the loans were from his own companies, leaving them even more burdened with debt. But Chicago banks could not make up the difference, and he had to borrow about $20 million from New York. With minor exceptions, he later recalled, "This was the first borrowing made from a New York bank."[83]

McDonald, Insull's forgiving biographer, speculates that the banks set out to drive down the price of his securities, forcing him to put up more shares as collateral. If so, the forces of the bear market were doing much of the work for them, but Insull put up a good fight. In early 1931, the strong performance of his underlying utilities and continued aggressive stock sales to small buyers kept their share values higher than they had been in early 1929. But the stock market overall had resumed its decline in mid-April 1930 and continued downward. IUI and Corp were forced to put up more and more shares as collateral. By December 1931, they were out of unpledged securities.[84]

In March 1932, a committee representing the bankers, led by GE Chairman Owen D. Young, met with Insull. Young informed him that a newly formed accounting firm, Arthur Andersen, would oversee all the companies' transactions. Andersen concluded that the unique method of depreciation devised by Insull and used by most utilities was too generous, and he replaced it with the straight-line depreciation system used in other industries. This made Middle West retroactively insolvent. It had only appeared solvent due to bookkeeping methods that disguised a steady depreciation of assets.[85]*

Insull knew that IUI and Corp would have to go into receivership,

---

* Seventy years later Arthur Anderson, by then one of the world's largest multinational accounting firms, forgot its roots and brought about its own demise by assisting Enron Corporation in another improper scheme to survive by keeping its share value high.

but he hoped to salvage Middle West by raising $10 million to refinance notes coming due on June 1. Then the auditors began to uncover his many questionable intercorporate loans. The final blow was a disclosure that his brother had issued $268,000 in unsecured company loans to help cover margin calls on his individual brokerage account, and that Insull had perhaps unknowingly signed the checks. When he heard this, Insull wept. In a meeting in Young's office in April to discuss the refinancing, he learned that there would be no more help for Middle West. "Does this mean a receivership?" he asked. "It looks that way," said Young. "I'm sorry, Mr. Insull."[86]

Parts of the empire were still healthy—Commonwealth Edison, for example, would go through the Depression without missing a dividend—but Insull knew his days were numbered. In late May, the bankers and outside directors of his companies decided to oust him. When he left his office on June 6, he told a waiting swarm of reporters, "Well, gentlemen, here I am, after forty years a man without a job."[87] His fall was widely publicized, and he soon left for Paris—in flight from the law, his critics claimed, or to relax in the wake of a stressful situation, his biographer averred.

In September a Republican prosecutor in Chicago, an Insull friend facing a tough re-election race, initiated a very public investigation of the causes of Insull's financial collapse. Eight days later, Franklin Roosevelt gave his campaign speech railing against "the Ishmael or Insull whose hand is against every man's." In early October, a grand jury indicted Insull on charges of embezzlement and larceny, and he left Paris for Greece, which had no extradition treaty with the United States.[88]

Early in his first two-year term as New York governor, Roosevelt had begun to implement his campaign pledges on electricity and became identified nationally as a public power advocate. He railed against court decisions that based utility rates on replacement cost, and he proposed state hydroelectric facilities on the St. Lawrence as a yardstick against which to measure private rates. Private companies would transmit and distribute the power from the dams "if possible," but only at rates based on their actual investment. "If not," he warned, sending shudders down the spines of utility executives, "then the State may have to go into the transmission business itself." He called for a new commission to take bids, negotiate a contract for the dams, and report back to the legislature by January 15, 1930.[89]

To no one's surprise, the legislature killed his proposal in committee, with no hearings. The Republican majority instead authorized a nine-member commission to investigate the Public Service Commission, but this was a hollow gesture. The governor was allowed to appoint only three members, while the legislative leaders appointed six, who Roosevelt claimed were "not merely conservative but definitely reactionary." Knowing that his appointees could do little more than "see to it that the progressive side of the case obtains adequate publicity," he nominated utility experts James Bonbright of Columbia University, recommended by Harvard law professor Felix Frankfurter, and Frank P. Walsh, a prominent progressive lawyer and close associate of Senator Norris.[90]

The consolidation of upstate New York's three largest utility systems into the Niagara Hudson Power Corporation in July 1929 drew Roosevelt's ire. The new holding company would have a monopoly on transmission in the state, which would eliminate any possibility of competitive bidding to transmit power from the St. Lawrence.[91] He studied power issues intensely in the summer and fall, tutored by Bonbright and Walsh, and he asked Howe to collect data on rates within the state and to compare them with those in Ontario. Howe found that rates for a typical household's monthly consumption in New York ranged from a high of $19.50 in Albany to a low of $5.53 near Niagara Falls. The bill for the same monthly use in Ontario was $2.79.[92]* On the Fourth of July, Roosevelt gave a speech on electric power at Tammany Hall in which he warned of a "new kind of economic feudalism." Will Rogers observed that the speech "just about threw him in the ring as the next Democratic candidate" for president.[93]

The stock market crash and growing unemployment strengthened the electoral prospects of Democrats everywhere. Blame fell on

---

* Private utilities claimed that Ontario had more access to hydropower and forced industrial and commercial consumers to subsidize household rates. FTC, 71-A, 363. Emmons argues that although Howe's comparisons were crude, more sophisticated analyses also supported Roosevelt's conclusion. "FDR, Utilities, and Competition," 884.

business leadership in general, with owners of electric utilities attacked with special bitterness,[94] and Roosevelt concluded that power issues could help fuel a presidential campaign. He used radio to speak to upstate New York voters about the economy in general and about rural access to electricity. Crystal sets or early radios known as TRF (tuned radio frequency) receivers allowed some farmers without electricity to hear his message.[95]

In late 1929 and early 1930, he attacked utility holding companies in national magazine articles. Ironically, in one speech he criticized a utility for proposing to reduce rates to increase consumption, the Insull strategy that would become a centerpiece of his public power policies.[96] He also talked of adding a Rural Power Authority to the Power Authority previously proposed by Al Smith and won passage of legislation establishing his St. Lawrence Power Development Commission.[97]

Governor Roosevelt built on the work of former Governor Al Smith in expanding the New York Power Authority and developing hydropower on the St. Lawrence River. (*Library of Congress.*)

In an election eve speech in Brooklyn in 1930, he said that citizens suffered "when you pay six dollars a month for electricity instead of two," and he won a second two-year term with a margin twice as large as the previous record. The struggling economy was the main cause, but electricity issues helped him carry upstate counties and precincts that had not voted for a Democrat in decades.[98]

In early 1931, Roosevelt appointed Walsh and Bonbright to his St. Lawrence Commission. On the recommendation of Gifford Pinchot, recently returned to the Pennsylvania governorship on the power issue, he also named Morris Cooke, who was to play a key role in his future rural electrification efforts. As expected, the Commission proposed a New York Power Authority, and Roosevelt orchestrated a "spontaneous" public outpouring of support to ensure approval by the newly Democratic legislature. The Authority would develop hydropower and sell it to Niagara Hudson, but only if the holding company agreed to deliver it at actual cost plus a profit not to exceed eight percent. Otherwise, the Authority would build its own transmission lines. In April, Roosevelt signed the bill and appointed Walsh to chair the Authority's board.[99]

The fruits of victory were exceedingly slow to ripen. Power projects on the St. Lawrence were linked to proposals for the St. Lawrence Seaway, a series of locks and canals to allow ocean-going shipping to reach the Great Lakes. Both required the agreement of the Canadian government. Roosevelt believed that Hoover was delaying the treaty to keep one of his popular issues out of the news during the coming election and cabled him to urge prompt "initiation of this vast project—one which means . . . cheap electricity . . . for the primary interest of homes, farms and industries." He declared his readiness "to go to Washington on forty-eight hours' notice at your convenience." One cheap shot deserved another, and Hoover responded to the vacationing Roosevelt: "It will not be necessary to interrupt your cruise."[100*]

As 1932 approached, Democrats anticipated recapturing the White House. Four million more Americans lost their jobs in 1931, and millions more were working part-time or for lower wages.

---

* A St. Lawrence Seaway treaty was in fact signed late in 1932, but railroad interests and lobbyists for ports in the United States blocked ratification until after World War II. The first hydroelectric plant, the St. Lawrence–Franklin D. Roosevelt Project, on Barnhart Island in Massena, NY, went into operation in 1958.

Unemployment increased still more in 1932, and over 2,200 small-town banks failed when beleaguered farmers could not repay their loans.[101] Hoover's frequently stated belief that free markets would lead to recovery was widely derided, and the shantytowns that cropped up in and around many cities were dubbed "Hoovervilles."[102]

In contrast to Hoover's optimism—"The fundamental business of the country . . . is on a sound and prosperous basis"—and his opposition to government programs to provide jobs or relief—"federal aid would be a disservice to the unemployed"—Roosevelt was a leader in proposing public works and relief programs, "not as a matter of charity, but as a matter of social duty." Taking a lesson from the Progressives at the turn of the century, he urged his colleagues at the National Governors Conference to see the states as "48 laboratories" to test "programs to protect [their] citizens from disaster."[103]

His activism fueled the perception that he was the frontrunner for the presidential nomination, but he faced obstacles within his own party. Some thought his lack of mobility was disqualifying, especially at a time of crisis. Others considered him all surface charm and no intellectual depth. The nation's most prominent journalist, Walter Lippmann, considered him an equivocator "skilled at carrying water on both shoulders" and famously called him "a pleasant man who, without any important qualifications for the office, would very much like to be President."[104] The most important hurdle, though, was the requirement of a two-thirds vote to win the nomination. This rule, as Roosevelt well remembered, had caused the exhausted convention delegates to bypass the frontrunners and nominate a weak compromise candidate in 1924.

Roosevelt announced his candidacy in January. His strongest potential opponent, Al Smith, declared in February that he would not campaign for the nomination but would accept if the convention chose him. He encouraged states to nominate favorite-son candidates to prevent Roosevelt from winning on the first ballot. Both camps wanted an ally in the potentially decisive position of convention chair in case of a brokered convention. After a weeks-long standoff, they came up with a compromise, Smith's choice as chair and a Roosevelt supporter as keynote speaker. Smith's team sent an emissary to get Roosevelt's personal commitment to the deal. "Here," in the words of author Jonathan Alter, "Roosevelt double-crossed his rival in a way that would sound familiar to his New Deal critics of later years. His move was cunning, shameless, and effective." Roosevelt "commended" the compromise, but when the convention convened, he said that "commend" was not the same as "endorse," and his campaign won a vote to make his choice the convention chair.[105] Even some of his supporters criticized his flip-flopping and hairsplitting, but winning was his goal. As he wrote to a friend, "There is a difference between ideals and the methods of obtaining them."[106]

On the first ballot in Chicago, Roosevelt won 666 votes, short of the 770 needed. Smith had 201, House Speaker John Nance Garner of Texas had 90, and the remaining 196 were spread among seven others. After two more ballots, Roosevelt had crept up to 682 and Garner had 101 votes, most from Texas and California. His support could put Roosevelt over the top. Negotiations began between New York Democratic chairman James Farley and Texas Congressman Sam Rayburn, the campaign managers for Roosevelt and Garner. Roosevelt needed votes soon, before he lost momentum, and Rayburn wanted the vice presidential nomination for his fellow Texan. With the encouragement of Garner's principal supporter and Al Smith's long-time enemy, William Randolph Hearst, the deal was done.[107]

The candidate broke with tradition and flew to Chicago to deliver his acceptance speech in person. He began his speech by acknowledging that his appearance was "unprecedented and unusual, but these are unprecedented and unusual times." He continued, as he would throughout the campaign, by recognizing the severity of the nation's economic problems, expressing them in human terms, criticizing the failed Republican leadership, promising action, and offering few specifics about his proposals. Hoover called him "a chameleon on plaid" for saying different things to different groups, but Roosevelt understood that voters cared less about what he said than how he said it. "If Roosevelt's program lacked substance," according to biographer William Leuchtenburg, "his blithe spirit—his infectious smile, his warm mellow voice, his obvious ease with crowds—contrasted sharply with Hoover's glumness."[108]

As the campaign approached its end and the economic decline persisted, Roosevelt continued to promise progress and offer hope to a desperate nation. Despite efforts by the utility industry to portray him as an untrustworthy eccentric, he became more confident of victory.[109] He campaigned vigorously to the end, partly to rebut any lingering doubts about his physical capability but primarily in hopes of winning a landslide that would give him a strong mandate for action.

CHAPTER 5

CREATING TVA

By eleven o'clock on election night, it was all over. Roosevelt won 57.4 percent of the popular vote, the highest total for a Democrat up to that time. With unemployment at 25 percent, he had offered hope to the devastated country, promising to wage war against "the 'Four Horsemen' of the present Republican leadership—the Horsemen of Destruction, Delay, Deceit, Despair."[1] President Hoover had merely offered more of the same to voters seeking dramatic change. Nonetheless, Roosevelt's margin surprised many, as did the strength of his coattails, as Democrats transformed razor-thin minorities in both houses of Congress into huge majorities.

The economic challenge increased, but Roosevelt's hand was strengthened by continued financial panic in the weeks following the election. A late 1932 epidemic of bank failures triggered a national series of bank runs. In February, Detroit's banks collapsed, and Michigan's governor declared an eight-day bank holiday. Several days later, a run on Baltimore's banks broke out, and Maryland's governor instituted a three-day holiday. The panic was contagious, and all around the country customers stood in lines to withdraw their money from the banks that were still open.

Inauguration seemed a long slog away, not to be held until March 4.* Throughout the interregnum Roosevelt evaded attempts by Hoover to enlist him in a joint statement about the soundness of the economy, seeing them as an attempt to tie him to the lame duck president's unpopular policies.

Instead Roosevelt began laying the groundwork for swift action on his own agenda. The federal dam projects he outlined in his Portland campaign speech, with their promise of jobs, were among his priorities, and he invited Senator Norris to join him on a January 21 visit to Muscle Shoals. In brief remarks nearby, he repeated his promise to develop the power of the river to assist the poorest region in the nation.[2] At the dam site, watching most of the Tennessee River's water rushing unused down the Wilson Dam spillways, Roosevelt called Norris over to his car and said, "This ought to be a happy day for you, George." According to *New York Times* reporter James Hagerty, Norris replied with tears in his eyes, "It is, Mr. President. I see my dreams come true."[3]

Roosevelt (l) thrilled Senator George Norris (in bow tie) with his speech in support of government development of water power at Muscle Shoals in January 1933. (*Courtesy of The Landrum Collection.*)

---

* The Twentieth Amendment, which moved the inauguration to January 20, had been passed early in 1932, but the necessary three-fourths of the states wouldn't ratify it until January 23, 1933.

Later that day, in remarks to about twenty thousand people at the Birmingham railroad station, Roosevelt referred to his visit to "a great plant built by the United States Government and now lying idle. I want to make that great plant work once more for the people." That evening, speaking extemporaneously at the state capitol in Montgomery, he made it clear that his vision was national. "Muscle Shoals gives us the opportunity to accomplish a great purpose for . . . the whole Union. Because there we have an opportunity of . . . tying in industry and agriculture and forestry and flood prevention . . . into a unified whole."[4]

While people in the region responded favorably to his message, critics were unmoved. The *Washington Post* contended there was no justification "in this period of hard times" to "waste still more of the taxpayers' money on this futile project," and Republican Congressman Joseph Martin of Massachusetts said, "Painting rainbows is always a delightful and inspirational pastime."[5] But Roosevelt understood that many in the South associated economic growth with cheap energy and believed investment decisions by Northern banks and holding companies had retarded their progress.[6] In fact, support for big dams extended well beyond the Tennessee Valley, particularly in the South and West, and Roosevelt's confidence in this support steeled his determination.

His mandate was further bolstered in the prelude to his inauguration by another outbreak of bank closings. On Friday, March 3, banks withdrew $109 million from the Treasury, and their frightened customers immediately withdrew and hoarded most of it. By that evening twenty-seven states had restricted bank withdrawals. By Saturday, March 4, Inauguration Day, thirty-eight states had closed their banks, and that morning the governors of New York and Illinois, home of the two most important financial centers, followed suit.[7]

The country expected immediate and strong action from Roosevelt. Some business supporters were so frustrated by indecision in the economic crisis that they proposed giving the president dictatorial powers. *Barron's* wrote, "A genial and lighthearted dictator might be a relief from the pompous futility of such a Congress as we have recently had."[8] Columnist Walter Lippmann suggested, "A mild species of dictatorship will help us over the roughest spots in the road ahead."[9]

The *Wall Street Journal* acknowledged on the morning of Inauguration Day, "All of us the country over are now ready to make sacrifices to a common necessity and to accept realities as we would not have done three months ago."[10]

At one o'clock in the afternoon Roosevelt "walked" down a specially constructed ramp on the East Front of the Capitol, and Chief Justice Charles Evans Hughes administered the oath of office. In his inaugural address, Roosevelt offered hope but few specifics. Pledging not to "shrink from honestly facing conditions in our country today," he asserted, "This great nation will endure as it has endured, will revive and will prosper." The most famous phrases, "new deal" and "the only thing we have to fear is fear itself," attracted little attention in the moment. More resonant with the temper of his audience were his attacks on financiers, "The money changers have fled from their high seats in the temple of our civilization." The audience welcomed his bold assertion of presidential authority. If Congress failed to act energetically on his plans, he warned, he would seek "broad executive power to wage war against the emergency."[11]

Throughout the weekend his advisers met with bankers, businessmen, and outgoing Hoover Treasury officials to work out an immediate response to the crisis. On Monday morning, he declared a three-day national bank holiday, after which he would call Congress back for a special session to pass emergency legislation. That morning Will Rogers had reflected the public's support for dramatic action: "The whole country is with him . . . . If he burned down the Capitol we would cheer and say, 'Well, we at least got a fire started, anyhow.'"[12]

On Thursday, the House passed an Emergency Banking Act by voice vote, before it had even been printed and distributed. The Senate passed it by a vote of 73-7. Just seven hours after it was introduced Roosevelt signed the bill, which gave him near total authority over the banking system. He extended the bank holiday through Sunday, March 12, and gave his first "fireside chat" that evening to explain what he had done and how he would quickly re-open sound banks. He explained in simple language how the system worked—"a comparatively small part of the money you put into the bank is kept in currency . . . which in normal times is wholly sufficient to cover the cash needs of the average citizen." But, "because of undermined confidence on the part of the public, there was a general rush by a large portion of our population to turn bank deposits into currency or gold."[13]

Roosevelt's "fireside chats" took him into people's living rooms and allowed him to speak to the public directly and in simple terms.
(*Courtesy of Franklin D. Roosevelt Library.*)

He reassured the millions who had tuned in that their money was safe—"No sound bank is a dollar worse off than it was when it closed its doors last Monday"—and he subtly discouraged immediate withdrawals when banks reopened: "It is my belief that hoarding during the past week has become an exceedingly unfashionable pastime."[14] On Monday morning, people around the country heeded his call, pulling cash out from under their mattresses and re-depositing it in banks. In just ten days, he had started to restore public confidence.[15]

Roosevelt's dramatic response impressed even many of his critics, but some progressives still worried that his prominent business supporters would thwart more bold legislative initiatives. When it came to electric power, though, hopes were high for swift and dramatic changes because the new president had gone toe to toe with utilities and supported government dams in New York and had raised hope for rural electrification. Meanwhile, the collapse of several holding companies after the stock market crash and a steady drumbeat of disclosures of stock watering, insider trading, and other financial shenanigans from the Federal Trade Commission investigation continued to discredit the industry.

His first move was to initiate federal dam projects, starting on the Tennessee and Columbia rivers. Although public opinion was divided on spending taxpayer money to build hydroelectric dams, and on government ownership of the power generated, Roosevelt was determined to follow through on his efforts as governor and the promises of his Portland speech. He shrewdly justified his actions in terms of the construction jobs they would create and the regional economic development they would catalyze.

A week after his inauguration, Roosevelt asked Norris to introduce a bill to create the Tennessee Valley Authority (TVA).[16] He agreed with Norris that TVA should have the authority to construct additional dams and reservoirs on the Tennessee and its tributaries, adding to the power generated at Muscle Shoals, as well as government transmission lines to allow the sale of power directly to municipal utilities and other large consumers. He wanted a public power "yardstick" that would allow people to measure the expected lower rates for power against private rates, as he had promised in his Portland speech. During a working dinner at the White House, Norris asked him, "What are you going to say when they ask you the political philosophy behind the TVA?" Roosevelt replied, "I'll tell them it's neither fish nor fowl, but whatever it is, it will taste awfully good to the people of the Tennessee Valley."[17]

In a soaring message to Congress on April 10, he asked for "legislation to create . . . a corporation clothed with the power of Government but possessed of the flexibility and initiative of a private enterprise." Describing the dam at Muscle Shoals as "but a small part of the potential usefulness of the entire Tennessee River," he emphasized that "Such use . . . transcends mere power development; it enters the wide fields of flood control, soil erosion, afforestation, elimination from agricultural use of marginal lands, and distribution and diversification of industry."[18] While national planning would have been a bridge too far, regional planning to alleviate poverty and unemployment was not. A proposal to build government power plants for the sole purpose of replacing private power might not win Congressional approval or pass muster with the Supreme Court, but power production in conjunction with flood control and navigation would probably be acceptable.[19]

Reflecting the sense of urgency, Majority Leader Joseph Byrns said the House would proceed at top speed "to complete the enactment of the Roosevelt national rehabilitation program." The bill would be taken up right after a farm-mortgage bill the following day.[20] Norris predicted that "an army of men" could be put to work almost immediately after enactment of what was still informally called the Muscle Shoals bill.[21]

The next day Norris introduced the bill in the Senate and Mississippi Congressman John Rankin introduced it in the House, the opening salvos in what historian Thomas McCraw called "one of the most intense struggles between government and business in American history."[22] For the rest of the decade, this dramatic contest played out in public opinion, Congress, and the courts. Faced with such a skilled advocate as Roosevelt, the power industry needed a persuasive and tough fighter to lead its cause. It found just the man in a young Hoosier named Wendell Willkie.

At the time the Muscle Shoals bill was introduced, Wendell Willkie was president of Commonwealth & Southern (C&S), one of the largest holding companies and the principal owner of the major utilities TVA would threaten in the Tennessee Valley. He was particularly well suited to lead the opposition, as he was not the expected Wall Street blueblood or stiff corporate suit.

He was born in 1892 in the frontier-like town of Elwood, Indiana, which was just beginning to boom due to the discovery of a large natural gas field. The fourth of six children of educated and ambitious parents, he took pride in his immigrant grandparents, who had come from Germany in the early and mid-nineteenth century. He internalized the family story that a chance for freedom and opportunity had called them to America. His maternal grandmother Trisch crisscrossed Indiana by horseback to conduct revival meetings, emblematic of the radical preachers spawned by the Second Great Awakening, a religious movement that related moralism to social justice. This concern for justice and a gift for oratory were among her bequests to Wendell, while he inherited restless energy and a strong work ethic from his father and paternal grandfather. His mother read law after the fifth of her children was born and, her children claimed, was the first woman to be admitted to the Indiana bar, as well as the first woman in Elwood to smoke cigarettes. Her independence, non-conformity, and ambition both for herself and her children helped shape Wendell's individualism. Books, liberal politics, and constant discussion filled the Willkie home, and active dinner table conversations honed his political interests and debating skill.[23]

Waging battle seemed to come naturally to him. As an undergraduate at Indiana University, he was a member of the debate team and active in campus politics, becoming known as a radical for his opposition to fraternities and his support for socialism, although his girlfriend persuaded him to join a fraternity in his senior year and his interest in socialism may have been primarily intellectual. After a year off to earn money for law school, he returned to Indiana, where he was elected as class orator for his graduation. He gave what the embarrassed university president called "the most radical speech you ever heard," criticizing the law school faculty and the state supreme court justices sitting behind him for being too conservative.[24]

After graduation he returned to Elwood, became president of the Young Democratic Club, and joined his parents' law practice. In one of his first trials, before he had built up a clientele of his own, he substituted for the deputy county prosecutor and eloquently argued the case despite insufficient evidence. His presentation to the jury prompted his father, the defense attorney, to tell the jurors, "I believe my son will be a great lawyer, he can make so much out of so little."[25]

When the United States declared war in April 1917, Willkie signed up for Officers' Training Camp and received his commission as a first lieutenant in August. Then he marked time in various training assignments for over a year, with the boredom relieved only by his wedding in January. His regiment finally sailed for Europe in

September 1918 and arrived in France with the war almost over, leaving him as disappointed as Roosevelt at not seeing combat. After he was mustered out, local Democratic leaders encouraged him to run for Congress. Unlike Roosevelt ten years earlier, though, he was unwilling to run in a Republican district that he could not expect to hold for more than one term.

A political contact arranged a job for him with Firestone Tire and Rubber in Akron, Ohio. Firestone offered its employees generous fringe benefits, including free legal advice, which Willkie was hired to provide. Like Roosevelt, he soon tired of the routine legal work, and he found other outlets for his energy. He began giving political speeches, at first about his war experiences and later in opposition to the re-emerging Ku Klux Klan. He was something of a showman, often jumping down from the stage and pacing the aisle waving his arms. His ability to appear earnest without ever talking down to his audience or taking himself too seriously gave him strong public appeal, again much like Roosevelt.[26]

He became a leader in the Akron Democratic Club and commander of the local American Legion Post, and a prominent law firm offered to hire him at a substantial increase in salary.[27] When he accepted, Harvey Firestone told him, "Young man, I like you, but I don't think you will ever amount to a great deal." "Why not?" Willkie asked. "You're a Democrat," Firestone replied. "No Democrat can ever amount to much."[28]

Though Willkie was not radical, he did champion social justice. Elected as a delegate to the 1924 Democratic national convention, he won the notice of the Klan, a serious force in Ohio and at the convention, by supporting the unsuccessful resolution to censure them. He subsequently led a successful effort to defeat the Klan majority on the Akron school board.[29]

While making a name for himself, he learned a new type of debating in Ohio courtrooms, a quick-on-your-feet, forceful, sensitive-to-the-jury style that would later make him stand out as a witness before Congressional committees. He also became versed in utility law, representing Northern Ohio Power and Light before the Ohio Public Utilities Commission, a body not in the forefront of protecting customers' rights.[30] "He seems to have taken the system much as he found it," according to his friend and biographer Joseph Barnes, "trying to improve it where he could but basically interested in making it work, in serving his clients, and in making money."[31]

When B. C. Cobb, the founder of Commonwealth & Southern, wanted to hire a lawyer to ensure that legal policies were consistent among all the companies under the C&S umbrella, he settled on Willkie. Willkie had not thought of leaving Akron, he recalled. "I thought I was fixed for life. I wanted to stay right there." But he accepted Cobb's lucrative offer and moved to New York in October 1929, settling into a seven-room apartment on Fifth Avenue overlooking Central Park just weeks before the bottom dropped out of the stock market.[32]

Soon after his arrival he had his first and only brush with Samuel Insull. In a speech to a group of utility executives, Insull denounced critics of big business as dangerous and said they should be silenced. In the question period, the large, tousle-haired, and rumpled Willkie argued that everyone had a right to be heard. The small, meticulously groomed and attired Insull dismissed him with the comment, "Mr. Willkie, when you are older, you will know more."[33]

In truth, Willkie was no neophyte. He teamed with Cobb to make changes at C&S that put the holding company in a much more secure position than many following the financial crisis. In the three years following the stock market crash, the gross earnings of C&S dropped nearly $40 million and its dividends fell from 70 cents to 1 cent per share. But Willkie and Cobb hired hundreds of salesmen to attract new customers, increased efforts to sell appliances, and offered discounted rates to customers who used more electricity. They also eliminated one layer in the pyramid, dissolving the three sub-holding companies that Cobb had combined to create C&S, and consolidated 165 utilities into eleven operating companies, one in each of eleven states in the Midwest and Southeast.[34]

They merged the three separate engineering and financial services companies into one and claimed that the new company only charged the operating utilities the actual cost of its services. It is unclear whether these steps were part of the original plan behind Cobb's creation of C&S or were a response to the Federal Trade Commission investigation of the power trust. Although C&S had been formed with watered stock, much of the water was squeezed out in write-downs following the market crash, and the company emerged looking more like a traditional holding company and less like an investment trust designed to milk its subsidiaries. Indeed, in a book criticizing utility holding companies, Roosevelt adviser James Bonbright held up C&S as an exception to the rule.[35]

In January 1933, three days after Roosevelt's visit to Muscle Shoals, the C&S board accepted Cobb's request to make the forty-year-old Willkie president. A nervous breakdown the following year forced Cobb's resignation in June, and Willkie became, in name as well as in fact, chief executive of the company. He proved he was his own man by promptly replacing four directors from Wall Street with officers from operating power companies, and he abolished the title of chairman as "too damn stuffy. I would have to be dignified."[36]

Willkie presented a striking appearance as he approached middle age. Large and attractive, if not conventionally handsome, he exuded energy and interest in his audience, whether a full auditorium, a Congressional committee, or an individual. His dark mane was noticeable for an unruly forelock, which he periodically threw back in place with a toss of his head. By the time of the Muscle Shoals hearings, he had become an old hand at winning over a room. A Midwestern drawl and a sense of humor gave him an air of informality, which he cultivated. He regularly put his feet on a table or threw his leg over the arm of a chair, and *Time* quipped that he could make an expensive suit look like it came from Macy's bargain basement.[37] Hoosier author Booth Tarkington called him "a man wholly natural in manner, a man with no pose . . . American as the courthouse yard in the square of an Indiana county seat." No pose? Far from it. As Roosevelt biographer James MacGregor Burns observed, "Inside this rustic form was an urbane New York cosmopolitan."[38]

With the president and Congress eager to show progress, the TVA bill was on a fast track. On April 12 the Senate Agriculture Committee, chaired by Senator Norris, unanimously reported out the bill in twelve minutes, without hearings or amendments. A day later Norris steered the bill, substantially as written, to a 63 to 20 victory in the full Senate.[39] Chairman John McSwain of the House Military Affairs Committee held hearings and invited witnesses from both sides. Willkie, the leadoff witness for the utilities, sought common ground with the committee. He acknowledged that the public did not think highly of the utility industry and added, grinning, "I know you gentlemen will not take this amiss; but, frankly, I think Congress is in the same boat with us. It is not very popular."[40]

He praised "the magnificent development plan for the Tennessee Valley" and said the industry had "heard with gratification that President Roosevelt has no desire to impair the investments already in the valley, and we don't believe the protection of our investments would impair that development."[41] The bill would establish a planning authority with broad powers, as well as funding the addition of powerhouses to dams planned for flood control and navigation, and Willkie did not object to either of those provisions. But he and officers of C&S-controlled Georgia Power and Tennessee Electric Power testified that the generating capacity in the Tennessee Valley was already 66 percent in excess of demand, so the plan for new power development wasn't needed.[42]

He quickly zeroed in on the major threat—government-owned transmission lines that would allow TVA to sell power directly to current C&S customers. To "take our markets is to take our property," he argued. Instead, government-generated power should be sold to private utilities for delivery.[43] The threat was real. C&S would not only lose its exclusive right to buy all the power generated at Muscle Shoals and future TVA dams but also its monopoly on selling electricity in the region. In addition the bill called for TVA to give preference in the sale of its power to municipal utilities and cooperatives. This "preference clause" put a heavy thumb on the scale in the battle between private and public power. Up until now, small municipal utilities had suffered from being unable to achieve economies of scale.[44]

The charge of socialism was a convenient criticism at the time of any new government action, and Congressman Martin of Massachusetts shouted that TVA was "patterned closely after one of the Soviet dreams." Representative Everett Dirksen of Illinois warned in his deep, honeyed tones: "Some of you gentlemen who are giving birth to this beautiful child, I am afraid, will not be as proud of it after it grows up." The *New York Times* editorialized that the bill was an attack on private power: "The power plants are to be made a weapon in the war on the 'Power Trust,' with Government-built transmission lines spreading their tentacles in every direction."[45]

Despite Willkie's skilled protestations and so much heated political opposition, Congress acted quickly. Democrats commanded large majorities in both chambers, public works jobs could alleviate economic hardship, people distrusted the power industry, and Roosevelt was the man of the hour. While the House heeded Willkie's warning and seriously weakened the bill's provision for construction of transmission lines, it passed the bill by a vote of 306 to 91. Roosevelt successfully pressured the conference committee to accept the Senate version, with his original transmission provision intact, and he signed it into law on May 18, presenting the pen to Norris.[46]

The extent of the territory to which TVA would deliver power, and at what rates, now had to be hashed out with the utilities in the region, led by Willkie. Roosevelt selected a three-man board of directors to run TVA. For chairman, he picked Arthur E. Morgan, the president of Antioch College. He was not an expert on electricity, but he had been trained as a civil engineer and had been in charge of planning and dam construction for the Miami Conservancy District in Ohio, created in the wake of the 1913 Great Miami River flood. He was a Republican who had voted for Hoover, but his imagination was fired when Roosevelt questioned him about whether the economically and socially underdeveloped Tennessee Valley could be transformed by regional planning. He was an enthusiastic supporter of social reform, coming from a long line of reform ministers, whose religious zeal he had translated "into a secular passion to make the world over." Yet as much as he desired reform, he was disdainful of the political process required to achieve it, as well as of politicians who cared only for short-term benefits.[47]

His bullishness about the potential for planning convinced

Roosevelt to appoint him, and the president asked him to find the other two directors. The only conditions were that one be a Southern agriculture expert and the other an electricity expert. Morgan recommended President Harcourt A. Morgan of the University of Tennessee, a popular former dean of its college of agriculture who knew county agents and farmers all over the state. The third directorship was offered to a rising star of utility regulation, David Lilienthal, who, according to his biographer, "may have been the best-schooled utility lawyer in the country, young or old."[48]

Lilienthal was also a passionate advocate of social reform, but with a substantially more aggressive view than Arthur Morgan's of making electricity more accessible to rural communities. Morgan, like Roosevelt, considered TVA a "designed and planned social and economic order," weaving together economic and social concerns—conservation, flood control, agricultural improvement, small scale industry, and education as well as access to electricity. He was not, though, a supporter of public power. At each of the five dams he had erected on the Great Miami River, he had installed a granite block inscribed, "The dams of the Miami Conservancy District are for flood prevention purposes. Their use for power development or for storage would be a menace to the cities below."[49]

He supported the creation of a small but effective power distribution component to TVA, using only a small portion of the power output of the dams, with the rest distributed by private utilities. The scope he envisioned was extremely limited. A single demonstration farm, one farmer cooperative, and one municipal power company would be enough to cause private power companies to copy their success. There was no need for extensive territory or multiple examples to create a public power yardstick against which to measure private companies' rates.

Lilienthal, on the other hand, saw TVA's goal as Norris did, becoming a major provider of lower cost power to rural communities in the region broadly. He envisioned providing TVA power to municipal utilities and to farmer-owned cooperatives modeled on a few that already existed elsewhere, believing that people would not give credit to TVA for the cheaper power if it were distributed by the private utilities. TVA could prove that lower cost electricity would be an economic boon, creating greater demand. He wanted TVA by its example to create political pressure for better regulation of private utility rates. What's more, based on his experience in Wisconsin regulating private utilities, with what he considered their inflated valuations, he doubted that Willkie would sell C&S assets to TVA at a fair price. And, in stark contrast to Chairman Morgan, he thrived on political agitation. Arthur Morgan had made no effort to determine whether Harcourt Morgan's and Lilienthal's views about TVA were compatible with his own. He was soon to discover what a tough adversary Lilienthal was.[50]

Like Willkie, Lilienthal was reared in small-town Indiana. The two shared the formative experience of growing up in a family with a strong mother, a father they admired, a love of books, and politics in the atmosphere. At DePauw, a liberal arts college in Greencastle, Indiana, he won election as student body president, boxed as a light heavyweight, and earned a Phi Beta Kappa key, demonstrating early the political skill, combativeness, and intellect that would mark his career. More importantly, he developed a close friendship with Helen Lamb, a woman two years ahead of him and his future wife. After their friendship had turned into love, he wrote to her, "Platonic friendship is the gun you didn't know was loaded."[51]

His interest in regulation was sparked at Harvard Law School in the public utilities class taught by future Supreme Court justice Felix Frankfurter, and his passion for social reform was matched by great ambition. He wrote to Helen while there, "I am ambitious . . . . I don't often admit it, even to myself—this inordinate desire for leadership, but that I have it, I never can honestly deny." His models, he told her, included Frankfurter, Justice Louis Brandeis, renowned attorney Clarence Darrow, and Frank Walsh, co-chair of President Wilson's War Labor Conference Board and later one of Roosevelt's electricity tutors and chair of his New York Power Authority.[52]

When Lilienthal wrote to Walsh asking for assistance in finding a job, Walsh recommended him to Donald Richberg, an Insull adversary, who hired him in his Chicago firm. There he received a practical introduction to utility law, representing the city of Chicago in several cases against Insull. He also made an initial foray into party politics by helping Richberg qualify Senator Robert La Follette Sr. for the ballot as the Progressive candidate for president in 1924.[53]

After three years with Richberg, Lilienthal set up his own practice concentrating on utility issues, and he began teaching utility law at Northwestern University. His 1929 *Columbia Law Review* article was the first to examine the difficulties state commissions had in regulating out-of-state utility owners. Recommended by Richberg, he earned his spurs battling the power industry in the administration of Wisconsin governor Philip La Follette, a progressive Republican who had won the 1930 election after calling for utility regulation "that will make it possible for Wisconsin to develop unhampered by restrictions of monopoly, and unretarded by exorbitant power and light rates."[54]

By the time Lilienthal took office as a member of the Wisconsin regulatory commission in March 1931, he had drafted a utility reform bill, which the legislature passed within weeks. The *New York Times* called it "the most far-reaching regulatory measure ever put into force in the country." He then used the new powers the law gave him at breakneck speed. Within a week, the commission ordered a comprehensive investigation of Wisconsin Power & Light, shunning the traditional one-by-one examination of complaints. Four days later, every public utility in the state was ordered to disclose all relationships with holding companies. Less than two months after he took office, *Public Utilities Fortnightly* identified Lilienthal as a face of the growing national reform movement."[55]

In January 1932, as Middle West Utilities was teetering on the financial brink, a shaken Insull lieutenant asked permission for their Wisconsin subsidiary to sell more bonds to reinforce the parent company. The commissioners refused to put local consumers and investors at risk and even suggested that the local utility cease paying dividends, a large portion of which were going to Middle West. An avid journal keeper, Lilienthal recorded the dilemma: "If the company should 'blow,' the question could fairly be raised whether we had met our obligations to senior investors in permitting dividends to continue to be paid . . . . [But] if we issued a public order . . . terminating payment of dividends to the holding company, it would probably precipitate receiverships." After conferring with La Follette, the commission refused the request to issue more bonds but did not block dividend payments.[56] Lilienthal humblebragged to his journal, "Here was the ruthless businessman brought to bay, asking for mercy from [the Chairman] . . . and a kid. But the consequences—a general collapse and panic! What a situation for man of 32 to be in!"[57]

With the Depression serving as a drag on most incumbents, La Follette lost his re-election bid in 1932, and Lilienthal worked all of his contacts in hopes of obtaining an appointment in the Roosevelt administration. Nothing materialized, and by mid-May he was discouraged. Then Arthur Morgan came calling.[58]

The three TVA directors met for the first time on June 16, 1933, at the venerable Willard Hotel in Washington. Arthur Morgan mentioned a letter he'd received from Willkie asking for a meeting and reported that he had assured Willkie of TVA cooperation. Lilienthal was appalled. He believed the role of TVA was to compete with private power, not to cooperate. Lilienthal and Harcourt Morgan agreed that it was fine for the chairman to meet with Willkie, but they cautioned him against any premature commitments.

Arthur Morgan also took Lilienthal aback in the meeting by proposing that TVA negotiate on a friendly basis for the transfer of a small number of representative urban and rural areas from C&S to TVA. He thought an impartial panel of economists should devise accounting methods to compare the operations of these TVA yardstick areas with areas served by private companies, and that their conclusions would guide policy. Most of the power TVA would generate should be sold to private utilities—most owned by C&S—for distribution to customers. He did not want a public-private power fight to jeopardize TVA's broader agricultural, industrial, and educational mission. Lilienthal, who had been in the regulatory trenches and distrusted the utilities, considered Morgan's approach naïve. He was circumspect but prescient in writing about the meeting in his journal. "There was some difference of opinion as to tactics and strategy expressed as between myself and Chairman Morgan, with Harcourt Morgan acting as a mediator. This will require a good deal of working out."[59]

Lilienthal and Harcourt Morgan also discovered in that meeting that Arthur Morgan was an abysmal administrator. Lilienthal recollected, "Dr. Arthur Morgan had on his lap a great stack of letters .... Most of these letters inquired about employment opportunities, or key specific matters, one completely unrelated to the other .... Harcourt Morgan was completely caught off base with this way of beginning a big enterprise, without ... any proposals for organization, without any ideas about staffing or where we go from here .... (and) said in effect, 'What do you make of this fellow? We can't go on like this.'"[60]

On June 28, Chairman Morgan met Willkie at the University Club in New York to discuss the range of territory to which TVA could deliver power. The law said only vaguely that the agency's authority extended beyond the Tennessee Valley to its "adjoining territory," and that TVA could send power to customers "within transmission distance," a similarly ambiguous phrase. At the extreme, this would allow the authority to reach all of the southern territory of C&S as well as cities such as Pittsburgh, St. Louis, and Atlanta. The two therefore had much to wrangle over, and they reached no agreement.[61]

At an August 5 meeting in Knoxville, where the directors had decided to establish TVA headquarters, Lilienthal and Harcourt Morgan responded to the continuing disorganization by forcing through a three-way division of responsibilities among the directors. Arthur Morgan would be responsible for TVA's engineering business, Harcourt Morgan for agriculture and forestry, and Lilienthal for power operations and the legal department. Chairman Morgan said later that accepting the arrangement was a horrible mistake. Lilienthal recollected that he and Harcourt Morgan knew the lack of unified leadership was unsound, but they saw the arrangement as their best option given an untenable situation.[62]

The new division of labor did not resolve the tensions between Lilienthal and the chairman, and later that month their disagreement about how widely TVA should distribute its power reached the boiling point. They took it to Roosevelt, who liked his subordinates to bring conflicting views to him for resolution, but in this case he just suggested a few possibilities for compromise and told them to work it out. The directors reconvened at the nearby Cosmos Club and agreed on a way forward, which they captured in a surprisingly comprehensive press statement. Lilienthal had won the day. No details of the discussion survive, but Roosevelt's suggestions may have tilted the field in Lilienthal's direction. Their statement put Willkie and the private utilities on notice: "The interest of the public in the widest possible use of power is superior to any private interest. Where the private interest and this public interest conflict, the public interest must prevail." The statement also affirmed the "undeniable" right of communities to own and operate their own electrical facilities. While it acknowledged that the adverse economic effects on private power companies should be "a matter for the serious consideration of the board," these effects should not be "the determining factor" of the extent of TVA's territory.[63]

The press release described that territory, which included Northern Alabama, Northeastern Mississippi, and a wide swath of Tennessee. Looking ahead, the statement also projected substantial growth, potentially incorporating the drainage area of the Tennessee River in Tennessee, Kentucky, Alabama, Georgia, and North Carolina. It would include several substantial cities, such as Chattanooga and Knoxville, and "ultimately, at least one city of more than a quarter million, within transmission distance, such as Birmingham, Memphis, Atlanta, or Louisville." In a nod to the power companies, the directors said they would make "every effort" to purchase existing distribution lines "on an equitable basis" rather than constructing duplicate systems.[64] The concession failed to reassure Lilienthal's potential targets. According to a corporate history of Southern Company, a direct descendent of C&S, the press release "essentially served notice to C&S and other utilities in the region that TVA intended to run them all out of the valley."[65]

Lilienthal quickly pushed ahead. The next challenge was to establish a rate structure for the municipal utilities that were clamoring to switch to TVA power. Based on his belief that lower rates would increase consumption, Lilienthal decided to base TVA's rates on the assumption that the average household would use 1200 kilowatt-hours a year—twice the national average at the time. He announced the proposed rates in another dramatic press release in mid-September. A typical customer would pay 2 cents to 2.7 cents per kilowatt-hour, a huge cut. Alabama Power's customers were paying 4.6 cents at the time and Tennessee Electric Power's 5.8 cents. The next day, Lilienthal added that TVA's rates had assumed costs not actually incurred by TVA— such as taxes and interest—which did have to be paid by private companies, making clear that he was asserting C&S and other power companies should be able to offer comparable rates.[66]

The statement caused a drop in private utility stock prices, but utilities knew the risk he was taking. Only three percent of the farms in the Tennessee Valley had electricity, and average farm income before the Depression was only $1,000 a year. Without the huge increase in consumption Lilienthal was counting on, TVA could bankrupt itself. But Roosevelt had promised bold action in the face of the economic crisis, and only the federal government could undertake such an experiment.[67]

Lilienthal explained to Roosevelt's staff the need to increase demand. "The private utilities had substantially all the market in our area, and have installed capacity approximately 30% in excess of the present requirements . . . . The only way we could get the 'yardstick' operating was to take away their market. This would greatly increase their unused facilities . . . . [W]e sought to devise some means of increasing the demand for electricity so as to make room for the existing systems as well as the system which we are creating. We concluded that this can only be done by large-scale distribution of appliances, and the lowering of rates."[68]

To achieve the former goal, he created a consumer credit affiliate, the Electric Home and Farm Authority, to provide low-interest installment loans to farmers. Increased employment by appliance manufacturers during the Depression was a corollary benefit. TVA supplemented the program with research on new farm uses of electricity, such as blower drying of hay in barn lofts, and with publicity and demonstration programs to work with customers and appliance dealers.[69] In an adroit move, he announced that customers of private utilities would also be eligible for the TVA affiliate's loans, which gained Willkie's support for the program. So eager was Willkie to

make the program a success that he offered to help persuade manufacturers to develop simpler, cheaper, standardized appliances "shorn
of some . . . gadgets." He also designed a system for consumers to repay
their loans on their monthly electric bills, whether they were served
by a private or municipal utility, or eventually a cooperative.[70] This
cooperation was a major exception to the adversarial relationship
between Willkie and Lilienthal over the next five years.

The next salvo in the TVA battle had them at loggerheads again.
The War Department's original agreement to provide power from
Wilson Dam to Alabama Power, a subsidiary of C&S, was due to
expire on January 1, 1934. TVA would lose most of its anticipated
revenue unless it either renewed the contract or found another large
customer or group of customers. Willkie and Lilienthal met in Washington on October 4, 1933, to negotiate terms for the contract renewal.
Willkie went on the offensive with a proposal that the C&S companies
buy all of TVA's power, suggesting that this would relieve it of the need
to look for other customers and would provide greater independence
from Congressional appropriations. He also patronizingly suggested
that the young lawyer with a family might damage his career by taking
too tough a position against C&S. Lilienthal recalled of the meeting,
"We were two exceedingly cagey fellows who met at lunch that
noon."[71] He didn't agree to Willkie's proposal, but he felt the heat,
writing in his journal that he was "somewhat overwhelmed by his
cocksureness" and "pretty badly scared."[72]

Five days later Lilienthal suffered a setback when Birmingham, a
city of over 250,000, voted against a proposal for municipal operation
of its electric utility. *Electrical World* crowed, "Birmingham was a fair
test sample." But ten small towns had already stated their intention to
terminate their arrangements with C&S affiliates and buy their power
from TVA, and the people of Knoxville voted two-to-one to buy its
distribution system from another holding company and join the TVA
network.[73]

Before his next meeting with Willkie, Lilienthal strengthened his
hand even further. In November he completed an agreement for TVA
to sell power to the municipal utility in Tupelo, Mississippi, the
hometown of Congressman Rankin, the House sponsor of TVA. At

a "New Power Era Celebration" on Armistice Day, November 11, Rankin told his cheering constituents that the agreement "means an armistice—an end—in the war of the people against private power interests." Frankie Kirkpatrick, a thirteen-year-old farm boy, later remembered, "Everybody was talking about getting electricity; only people downtown had lights."[74]

Now the question was whether Willkie would refuse to sell his company's distribution systems in these towns at a reasonable price. If he refused, TVA had a way to bypass him. The Public Works Administration (PWA), an early New Deal job-creation program headed by Secretary of Interior Harold Ickes, could grant funds to towns to build their own distribution lines. Ickes, a progressive Republican utility lawyer who had tangled with Insull in Chicago, encouraged towns and cities nationally that were unhappy with the rates charged by private utilities to apply for these grants and loans—a policy called "extortionary" by private utilities.[75]

For weeks Willkie and Lilienthal sparred over the terms by which C&S would sell their local systems to the communities that had voted to buy TVA power. Willkie especially wanted to prevent TVA from building a transmission line right through the heart of Tennessee Electric Power Company (TEPCO) territory, from Norris Dam, then under construction near Knoxville, to Wilson Dam. At one point he offered to sell all of TEPCO to TVA for $100 million, but Lilienthal thought the price was inflated and was reluctant to take such a big step so soon, one which would require additional legislation.[76]

Holding several high cards, Lilienthal eventually issued an ultimatum: cede to TVA certain counties in northwest Alabama, northeast Mississippi, and eastern Tennessee and the transmission lines to serve them at reasonable prices, or TVA would build duplicate lines there. Willkie blinked, and they worked out the details in a few short weeks.[77]

When they signed the contract renewal for Wilson Dam power on January 4, 1934, Willkie told reporters, "It's tough to negotiate with a pistol at your head." But it was not a one-sided deal. The small systems sold to TVA were responsible for only about two percent of the $50 million earnings of C&S's southern holdings. In return TVA agreed to continue selling C&S the surplus power from Wilson Dam, and Lilienthal agreed not to compete for further markets in the territory for five years or until the Norris Dam was complete, whichever came first. The January 4 contract was the apogee of cooperation between Willkie and Lilienthal.[78]

While Mississippi Power sold its properties to Tupelo and smaller towns as agreed, Alabama Power stymied the intended sales in its territory, insisting on receiving cash payment for the full book value of its properties, an impossible challenge for small towns during the Depression. When Lilienthal threatened to seek PWA funding for the towns to build duplicate facilities, Willkie proposed that instead TVA purchase the properties and resell them to the towns. But a New York bank refused to relinquish its lien on the Alabama properties, and TEPCO refused to transfer the Tennessee properties until the Alabama problem was resolved. The private utilities also won preliminary injunctions from courts to prevent construction of duplicate distribution systems by municipalities. Friendly courts often issued such orders at hearings without formal testimony and sometimes after another court had already denied the request.[79] Ultimately only two of the fourteen towns covered in the January 4 agreement were able to purchase their distribution facilities.

But Lilienthal was not to be discouraged. In January 1934, he and other TVA officials met with several farmers and businessmen in the rear of Will McPeters's furniture store in Corinth, the seat of Alcorn County, in the hill country of Northeast Mississippi. Mississippi Power operated a small, inefficient power plant there that served fewer than a hundred households and under one percent of the county's farms. The agriculture-based economy of the county had been devastated by low cotton prices, its banks had closed, and most farmers cashed their checks and received limited credit at department stores.

The community leaders who met with Lilienthal that morning organized the first electric cooperative in TVA territory. The member-owned Alcorn County Electric Power Cooperative received a charter from the state on January 17 and then, with one of the first such loans from the PWA, bought the Corinth power plant that TVA had purchased from Mississippi Power. On June 1, the co-op signed a contract to buy wholesale power from TVA. Rates were immediately reduced to half of what Mississippi Power had been charging, and within a year the co-op had repaid half of its debt. TVA also began construction of rural distribution lines, mostly short extensions from the town at first, which the co-op agreed to buy over time.[80]

Workmen erect poles for the electricity cooperative in Alcorn County, Mississippi. The first co-op in TVA territory, it became a model for the Rural Electrification Administration as well as TVA.
(*Courtesy of Alcorn County Electric Power Association.*)

Hookups to the lines began slowly. D.F. Wright, whose job was to sign up new members, recalled, "People were very skeptical at first, having never heard of an electrical co-op. They didn't believe we could keep the rates low for very long." Some were also "really scared of electricity; they thought lightning would strike if their house was wired." These fears soon faded, however, and another early employee of the co-op, Joe Brawner, said, "It was the greatest thing in the whole business, bringing electricity to those people. We wired the houses, brought out the appliances, put in the meter, with the families crowded around waiting. When the first switch was turned on, they literally cried and shouted with joy."[81] Alcorn County would become a model for a national rural electrification program.

CHAPTER 6

ENLARGING THE BATTLEFIELD

While the creation of TVA took center stage in 1933, two other electricity initiatives also began to take shape—plans for federal dams in the Northwest and a national rural electrification program. Roosevelt had declared in his 1932 Portland speech, "The next great hydroelectric development . . . must be on the Columbia River," which drained an area six times as large as the Tennessee and carried 40 percent of North America's potential hydroelectric power. In 1931, during the Hoover administration, the Army Corps of Engineers had proposed a series of ten dams—from Grand Coulee, seventy-five miles northwest of Spokane, downstream to where the river cuts through the Cascade Mountains, near North Bonneville, forty miles east of Portland. Bonneville would be a "run-of-the-river" dam, with no reservoir to regulate the river's flow. The dam and reservoir upstream at Grand Coulee, and eventually those at sites between, would be "adjustable flow," allowing the dam's power production to more closely match demand. Although the plan included extensive hydropower development, the Corps had recommended government funding only to make navigation of the river possible, not for the construction of any power plants. Hoover was still president, and power plants were supposed to be developed by private companies.[1]

Under Roosevelt, that policy changed. The economy of the

Northwest, dependent primarily on agriculture and forest products, was hard hit by the Depression, and employment in the region in 1933 was only about half what it had been in 1926.[2] Early in 1933 Roosevelt proposed the National Industrial Recovery Act to bring industry, labor, and government together to create codes of fair practices, set prices, and regulate wages in order to stimulate economic recovery. The bill the president signed in June authorized both the Grand Coulee and Bonneville dams, but it was uncertain whether sufficient funding would be available in the early 1930s to start construction on both projects.[3]

As in the Tennessee Valley, opponents of public power in the Northwest were skeptical that a market existed for the massive amounts of electricity the government intended to generate. Republican Congressman Francis Culkin claimed, "Up in the Grand Coulee area there is no one to sell the power to except the jack rabbits and the rattlesnakes." Private utilities disparaged Bonneville and Grand Coulee as "white elephants in the wilderness." But Roosevelt was confident, as were Norris and Lilienthal, that cheap power would stimulate demand.[4]

Bonneville, with a greater focus on navigation, was logically a Corps of Engineers construction project, and Grand Coulee, with its emphasis on irrigation, was within the purview of the Bureau of Reclamation. Before 1931, the Bureau had supported a "gravity plan" for Grand Coulee, which would use a low dam with canals and tunnels to bring water from the Columbia's tributaries to the dry areas of south central Washington. The 1931 Corps report, though, had made a convincing case for the economics of a more expensive high dam and reservoir with greater hydroelectric potential. In a quick about face, the Bureau supported the high dam and made a case to build it.[5]

The fear that appropriations would not be adequate to start both dams caused a conflict between Oregon and Washington over which should be built first. Oregon promoted Bonneville, where the river formed the border between the two states, while Washington pushed for Grand Coulee. Both focused their pressure on Roosevelt rather than Congress because Congress had already appropriated large amounts of money, primarily to the Public Works Administration

(PWA), for economic recovery. During the campaign Roosevelt had promised Democratic Senator Clarence Dill of Washington that he would build Grand Coulee. But after the election Dill mentioned a $450 million price tag, which was for the high dam. Roosevelt, who had campaigned on cutting government spending, balked, pointing out that even the Panama Canal had not cost that much. As a compromise he suggested settling for a low dam, which would provide irrigation but little power. Dill accepted as long as the design could accommodate a future high dam, for which he would fight. [6]

The PWA announced a grant to start construction of the low dam at Grand Coulee first, distressing Senator Charles McNary of Oregon, the new Senate Republican Leader and a Roosevelt friend. He pressed the president to reconsider, showing him a favorable report on Bonneville that the Corps had submitted to PWA Administrator Ickes in mid-August, and the president agreed to provide funds for it as well. As he signed the papers for the PWA grant in October, he commented, "I've got to give 'Charlie Mac' his dam." With an alacrity dictated by the state of the economy, the Corps began to build a construction camp within three weeks and issued an excavation contract three months later. [7]

The rural electrification program had less planning to build on. The TVA Act called for preference in the sale of power to, among others, "cooperative organizations of citizens or farmers" to "promote and encourage the fullest possible" rural electrification. But it was limited to one region, and its first cooperative, in Alcorn County, did not start up until 1934.

In June 1933, Morris Cooke, author of Pennsylvania's electricity plan in 1923 and a member of Roosevelt's St. Lawrence Commission in 1931 and 1932, wrote a memorandum to the president recommending that he create a commission to study the issue. In the blizzard of proposals in the early months of the administration, it was shunted aside by staff in the White House. Receiving no response, Cooke vented his frustration to an aide to Harold Ickes, who, like Cooke, was a long-time progressive Republican. Shortly thereafter Roosevelt summoned Cooke and asked him to head a committee to propose ways of developing the Mississippi Valley, where rural electrification was rare, low agricultural prices were forcing people into the cities, and memories of the Great Mississippi Flood were still raw.[8]

Cooke's eventual recommendations included flood control, soil conservation, and other subjects, but he gave priority to rural electrification. He suggested to Ickes the creation of a joint government-utility commission to consider how to achieve the rural electrification goals, but Ickes, with his deep distrust of utilities, replied, "I'll have nothing to do with the sons of bitches!" Cooke seized the moment and asked, "Then will you consider a plan wholly under control of public authority?" Ickes encouraged him to develop one.[9]

Ickes' skepticism about utility cooperation was matched by the industry's wariness of government intrusion into their business, heightened by Roosevelt's support for public power and his attacks on holding companies and utility ratemaking. An official of Philadelphia Electric, which had a contentious relationship with Cooke going back to before World War I, said an "impetuous plunge" into rural electrification would be "the greatest error we could make." *Electrical World*, disparaging TVA's early rural electrification efforts, editorialized that the government should give whatever funds might be available to private utilities and let them run their own programs. Cooke consulted with industry representatives as he developed his recommendations, but they did not sway him.[10]

Determined that his proposals not be buried again, Cooke invited several of the nation's top newspaper, magazine, and book editors to a lunch in New York to discuss how to present them. They recommended keeping things short. Cooke did more than that; he hired an artist and draftsman to "take a rather ordinary document and doll it up so that it stood out." He heard that Ickes liked red barns, so every barn in the illustrated report was red.[11]

When he delivered two copies to Ickes in February 1934, Cooke's cover letter cited the famous words attributed to urban planner Daniel Burnham, "Make no little plans. They have no magic to stir men's souls."[12] The letter also stated that the report could be read in twelve minutes, with details in the appendices. One copy was given to Roosevelt the next day and was later read by key administration officials.

"Perhaps its bizarre black-and-white-striped cover," Cooke wrote, "kept it circulating among those in high place and so out of the waste-basket." He believed that its positive reception ensured a vigorous commitment to rural electrification.[13]

Cooke's plans were indeed not little. He proposed a new agency, the expenditure of half a billion dollars in twenty years on power generation, and a hundred million dollars for a revolving fund for loans to farmers and cooperatives for appliances and line extensions. Antic-ipating challenges to the legality of the program, he included a lawyer's opinion that the Constitution's grant of spending power to Congress to "provide for the ... general welfare" provided the authority required. Knowing that Ickes was an ally, he also shrewdly proposed that the program report directly to the interior secretary.[14]

Cooke also sought allies for the program by tying it to other New Deal initiatives, recommending that it play an active role in planning the rural use of power from Boulder, Bonneville, and other federal dams and that it cooperate with TVA's Electric Home and Farm Authority in promoting the use of appliances. Finally, expecting resis-tance from both private utilities and perhaps from some state and local governments, he proposed that applications for projects should be welcomed from both private and municipal utilities as well as from rural cooperatives.[15]

Roosevelt's long-standing interest in rural electrification would have made him receptive to Cooke's proposal in any case, but according to Harry Hopkins, head of the Federal Emergency Relief Administra-tion, its greatest appeal was the possibility that it could help reduce rural unemployment and the resulting migration to cities. Cooke received a green light, and during the remainder of 1934 and early 1935 he consulted widely and fleshed out his plans.[16]

The administration's hand continued to be strengthened in all of its electric power initiatives as more abuses by private utilities were reported during 1934, keeping the industry on the defensive. The stories included Alabama Power reselling Wilson Dam power it had purchased from TVA at thirty times its cost of production, a New York Senate investigation of lobbying activities by Associated Gas and

Electric, and the Federal Trade Commission's investigation of holding companies.[17]

The biggest story in 1934, though, was the extradition and prosecution of Samuel Insull. The Cook County state's attorney had indicted him in February 1933 on a new charge of using the mails to defraud investors. That was about the only way to prosecute securities fraud before New Deal legislation required investors be provided with financial information about securities and set standards for marketing them. In June the prosecutor further accused Insull of fraudulent conveyances of property to avoid bankruptcy claims.

Yielding to pressure from the U.S. State Department to extradite Insull, the Greek premier decreed in early March 1934 that his residency permit would not be renewed and he must leave the country. Claiming ill health, Insull received a brief delay and then evaded his government-assigned guards and left secretly on a small, chartered steamship. The *New York Times* reported that he "resented the American activity for his apprehension" and regarded it "as evidence of an intention to railroad him to jail." He cruised the Mediterranean for two weeks, with daily speculation in U.S. newspapers about his destination, disguises he was wearing, and his health. An Associated Press report even alleged he had "attempted suicide by trying to jump into the Bosporus." When he alighted in Istanbul, the Turkish government ordered his extradition after a sham hearing in which he had no interpreter.[18]

Transported back to the United States under guard, Insull had several lengthy conversations with his State Department escort. At one point he claimed, "What I did, when I did it, was honest; now, through changed conditions, what I did may or may not be called honest. Politics demand, therefore, that I be brought to trial; but what is really being brought to trial is the system I represented."[19] When his ship reached New York, his son gave him a statement prepared by a publicist. In part it summarized the defense he would use in his coming trials: "My greatest error was in underestimating the effects of the financial panic on American securities and particularly on the companies I was working so hard to build . . . . I made mistakes, but they were honest mistakes."[20]

In Chicago, he spent three nights in jail before being released on bail. His lawyers had been advised that his bail would be set at $100,000, but at his booking it was set at $200,000. One of the lawyers offered to raise the additional sum immediately, but Insull declined. He knew he would be judged by the public as well as by the courts, and a stay in jail represented an opportunity to transform his image from that of a rapacious swindler to a frail former public benefactor who was being vilified for the failings of an entire system.[21]

When his trial for mail fraud began in October 1934 the prosecutor presented two hundred witnesses, who gave four weeks of testimony. Finally, Insull took the stand in his own defense. "On the verge of tears," the *New York Times* reported, he told the story of his life, from his poverty as a boy in London, through anecdotes from his days with Edison and his daring gambles building giant steam turbines in Chicago, to the wealth created by his companies throughout the Midwest. His testimony "caused many in the packed chamber to weep," and the jury was mesmerized. The state's attorney tried to object at several points that none of this was relevant, but he relented when the jurors gave him dirty looks for interrupting.[22]

The prosecutor sought to undo the damage by introducing income tax returns showing that Insull had received huge salaries and dividends from thirteen companies from 1929 to 1931. But the tactic backfired when Insull's attorney established that he had donated more to charity than he had earned. When this came out, the prosecutor turned to the FBI agent who had collected Insull's income information and whispered loudly enough to be heard by the jury, "You son of a bitch. Why didn't you tell me that was in there, too?" In his emotional summation to the jury, Insull's attorney concluded, "I beg you by your verdict to remove the stain . . . . Send this old man back to his home." The jury took only five minutes to conclude that the seventy-five-year-old Insull was innocent but, fearing they would be suspected of accepting bribes if they returned too quickly, took two hours to celebrate a juror's birthday before announcing their verdict. The headline in the pro-New Deal *Chicago Times* concluded, "Insull and his fellow defendants—not guilty; the old order—guilty."[23]

Insull was also tried, along with his brother, on one embezzlement charge, with the verdict again being acquittal. The state then dismissed the remaining charges against him. One more set of charges still loomed over him. Federal prosecutors had charged him, his son, and his investment adviser with bankruptcy crimes—the transfer of large sums out of Midwest Utilities in advance of its bankruptcy to deprive creditors of their money—and they went ahead with a trial. After the prosecution presented its case, the judge concluded that criminal intent had not been proved and instructed the jury to find the defendants not guilty. After the trial the judge asked Insull privately why he had fled to Europe after his bankruptcy and dismissal. Insull said that he wanted "to give people an opportunity to quiet down. They were fearful of the future, and thousands of them wanted to take it out on me."[24]

Though Insull had been exonerated legally, his wife refused to settle again in Chicago, and they moved to Paris. In 1938, Insull died there of a heart attack on a subway platform, and his body was not identified for several hours. His wallet was missing, and because he had only a few centimes in his pocket the newspapers concluded that he had died a penniless death. In the epitaph of his biography of Insull, Forrest McDonald asserted, "In his death, as in his life, Samuel Insull was robbed, and nobody got the story straight."[25] His dual legacy lived on, as the business genius who created the modern utility and as the most visible perpetrator of the financial excesses that brought the industry into the crosshairs of the New Deal.

The 1934 mid-term elections demonstrated resoundingly that Roosevelt had strong public support. The Democrats added to their Congressional majorities, the first time since the Civil War that a president's party had gained seats in a mid-term election. Roosevelt understood well how to build on the momentum to stoke support for TVA and other controversial initiatives. On his way to Warm Springs after the election he stopped in Tupelo, the first municipal buyer of TVA's power, to tout increasing electricity usage and the importance of TVA providing a standard for rates, telling a crowd, "What you are doing here is going to be copied in every state of the union." He told Lilienthal the comment was "for the benefit of the newspapers all over this country."[26] The widely syndicated Will Rogers took the cue. "The

President made one of his best speeches in Tupelo, Miss., Sunday," he wrote. "He told that the people could make their own electric energy cheaper than they were getting it. And, say, by Monday morning he had all the companies talking 'new rates.' They all say the government can't do anything toward running any business but they break their necks to see that it don't try."[27]

Willkie had stepped up the level and tone of his public opposition to TVA in the recent months. While his criticism had initially focused on excess generating capacity and duplicative transmission lines, which he argued would threaten his markets, by fall he was persuaded that TVA's low rates would also lead to heavy losses for utilities and their investors. In a series of speeches, he began echoing the charges of socialism common among other utility executives. In response to Roosevelt's Tupelo speech, he counterpunched, saying TVA's yardstick was "rubber to the last inch." He also asserted that "tax moneys that are being used to give Tupelo its well publicized 'yardstick' rate" mean "the Tennessee River waters four states and drains the nation." As he explained in his speeches, the argument that TVA rates should serve as a yardstick for all power providers had serious flaws. For one, TVA's electricity at the time was 100 percent hydropower, substantially cheaper than power from coal-fired plants. What's more, in calculating its rate structure, Lilienthal had logically allocated some of the cost of its dams to navigation and flood control, reducing the portion of the capital costs attributed to electricity. TVA's rates also reflected its access to low-cost government financing and its exemption from state and local taxes.[28]

Realizing the battle for public opinion was not going their way, the private utilities decided to take the fight to the courts. In the fall of 1934, a legal memo was prepared for the former National Electric Light Association, which after the scandals of the previous decade had rebranded itself as the Edison Electric Institute to take advantage of the still-revered inventor's name. It declared the TVA "palpably unconstitutional." Lilienthal responded, "The mask is off . . . . We now have, in the open, a clear issue between the people who use electricity and those who have controlled it." In the first major suit, *Ashwander v. TVA*, a small group of Alabama Power shareholders sought to block the sale of their company's transmission lines to TVA under the January 4 contract negotiated by Willkie and Lilienthal. They argued that government transmission was a marketing activity that, unlike generation at dams, was unrelated to navigation and flood control and was therefore unconstitutional.[29]

Willkie denied speculation that he was behind the suit. "An absolute and unqualified falsehood," he told Roosevelt's press secretary Steve Early, stressing that the suit was brought against Alabama Power, a C&S subsidiary, as well as against TVA. But Lilienthal had good reason for doubt. Willkie was a director of the Edison Electric Institute, which helped fund the suit, and Alabama Power launched the second major legal attack on TVA, challenging the authority of the PWA to offer grants for municipal electricity projects.[30]

Meanwhile, though, TVA was building momentum. By the end of 1934, the agency had received applications for service from over three hundred towns, and Lilienthal was intent on attracting the "cities of substantial size" he had projected in his 1933 press statement. Although he and his allies failed in their pursuit of the Birmingham market, they fought fiercely for a referendum in the spring of 1935 to establish a municipal utility to replace TEPCO service in Chattanooga, TEPCO's headquarters. A local newspaper editor, George Fort Milton, called it "the Hindenburg line of private power." The TEPCO newsletter groused that TVA promised the city "if it would go to the polls and vote for the good old TVA, the good old TVA would build nice little Chattanooga a $28 million dam." But TEPCO also played for keeps, establishing a "Citizens and Taxpayers" committee, staffed with TEPCO employees, to oppose the referendum. The company even purchased two empty lots to use as the bogus addresses for voter registrations of 120 non-resident employees. The referendum nonetheless passed by a crushing three-to-one margin.[31]

The prospects for TVA's expansion dimmed, however, in December 1934. A U.S. district court judge in Birmingham decided in the *Ashwander* case that the Constitution did not allow TVA to engage in the electricity business, except for the sale of "surplus" power. He annulled the January 4 contract between Alabama Power and TVA and blocked the transfer of transmission lines. He also enjoined the Alabama towns from accepting PWA grants while his decision was appealed. Although the judge did not rule on the constitutionality of TVA itself, Senator Norris declared, "The effect of the injunction is practically to nullify the whole TVA Act."[32]

Yet the legal fight wasn't over. In July 1935, the circuit court in New Orleans overturned the district court's injunction, and the private utilities promptly appealed the decision to the Supreme Court. TVA's prospects were also bolstered when the administration persuaded Congress to amend the TVA Act to allow TVA to issue up to $100 million in government-backed bonds. That extra financing would allow the authority to move forward despite its short-term inability to sign up many new customers. Willkie testified against the amendment in April, focusing particularly on how the low-interest loans would further prop up TVA's ability to compete unfairly with private utilities. Pointing out that the average interest on C&S's debt was five percent, he argued that with a government guarantee he could issue bonds at two percent or less.[33]

David Lilienthal testifies in favor of an administration proposal allowing TVA to issue up to $100 million in government-backed bonds. (*Library of Congress.*)

While Lilienthal was pressing to expand TVA's reach, President Roosevelt personally took the lead on another major legislative effort. After his stirring Tupelo speech in November 1934, he invited Lilienthal and several other advisers to join him at Warm Springs to plan a strategy for reining in holding companies. Over whiskey and soda after dinner, the president asserted that they could not be regulated effectively and therefore should be abolished. Lilienthal recorded in his journal that he agreed with the president's premise, but Frank McNinch, chairman of the Federal Power Commission, had reservations. McNinch believed that stronger regulation would be sufficient and knew that neither his commission nor Roosevelt's National Power Policy Committee, chaired by Ickes, was proposing total abolition. Roosevelt was not swayed by McNinch, and he asked for legislation to be drafted that would destroy the companies by taxing their intercorporate dividends as profits moved up the pyramid, the approach favored by his Hudson Valley friend and neighbor, Treasury Secretary Henry Morgenthau.[34]

When Roosevelt returned to Washington in early December, he pressed the case. Chairman Joseph P. Kennedy of the Securities and Exchange Commission (SEC), established in 1934 to carry out the regulation of securities transactions required by early New Deal legislation, had sent the president new evidence of holding company malfeasance. Roosevelt forwarded the information to McNinch and Morgenthau. The president also advocated his tax solution with the National Emergency Council, which had been established a year earlier to coordinate the activity of federal agencies. McNinch and others on the National Power Policy Committee still preferred strict regulation, and they requested a briefing with the president to make their case. McNinch suggested arguing against the tax in a meeting rather than in a written report, which might be leaked, embarrassing the president. Ickes agreed and urged that legislation be drafted promptly, in strict secrecy. Rumors that legislation was being written nonetheless spread.[35]

Roosevelt meanwhile scheduled a series of meetings with utility leaders, including Willkie, which he reported were amicable. Willkie, who had not previously met the president, diplomatically told reporters that he and Preston Arkwright, president of Georgia Power, "were very favorably impressed with President Roosevelt's attitude on the power question." But the telegram he sent his wife was more candid. "Charm exaggerated stop I didn't tell him what you think of him." None of the executives took much hope from the meetings, and their sense of the president's intentions was on target.[36]

On the morning of the State of the Union address, January 4, 1935, Willkie and three other utility executives met with McNinch at the Federal Power Commission (FPC) in an effort to head off the most draconian version of the legislation. McNinch made it clear that he was not speaking for the full FPC or the president as he outlined tough requirements he believed the industry would have to meet, including stricter regulation of its securities and prohibition of holding companies owning other holding companies. The executives strenuously objected, insisting that such radical steps would destroy the value of their securities.[37]

The president's speech that evening indicated there was scant probability that legislation could be thwarted. He called for the outright "abolition of the evil of holding companies." But he had mistakenly departed from his written text, which only advocated "abolition of the evil *features* of holding companies," and he subsequently corrected himself. But as historian Arthur Schlesinger Jr. later asserted, "there was great truth in the slip," as abolition was still Roosevelt's preferred course. At his behest, federal agencies stepped up their criticism of holding companies. The FTC also released additional parts of its report suggesting that various methods—compulsory federal licensing, direct elimination, or taxation—could be used to solve the problem.[38]

In late January any remaining hopes of cooperation were dashed. Three utility executives, Willkie, Clarence E. Groesbeck of Bond and Share, and Harvey C. Couch, president of a holding company in Arkansas, Louisiana, and Mississippi, sought a meeting with the president. They wanted to clarify his views on holding companies, rural electrification, and government dams. Lilienthal and Commissioners McNinch and Basil Manly of the Federal Power Commission also attended.

Roosevelt ran through a list of holding company abuses, and

Lilienthal wrote in his journal that he could see Willkie "getting hotter and hotter . . . . Finally, he took his glasses out of his breast coat pocket and using them as a pointer, he leaned over and pointing this object at the President as he spoke, said, 'If you will give us a Federal incorporation law, we can get rid of holding companies.' He didn't preface it by 'Mr. President,' and he didn't say it with the courtesy that you would accord if you were addressing the vice president of a bank, much less the President of the United States. And from the moment he did this pointing job, the conference was on a completely different basis."[39]

Although Roosevelt was sympathetic to a federal incorporation law, which would require corporations operating across state lines to be chartered by the federal government rather than by one of the states, Willkie's manner shocked Groesbeck and Couch "as if Willkie had suddenly produced a gun and started shooting." The previously reasonable discussion degenerated into a hostile argument, with the president demonstrating less and less tolerance as Willkie continued to argue and point his glasses. Lilienthal wrote that the exchange ended decisively. "Finally Willkie said, 'Do I understand then that any further efforts to avoid the breaking up of utility holding companies are futile?' . . . . The President gave him one look and said simply, 'It is futile.'"[40]

But while Roosevelt wanted to see the holding companies abolished, or at least considerably reined in, he did not want the fervent advocates of public power in Congress, particularly Norris and Rankin, to outflank him by proposing legislation to establish government ownership of utilities, as they desired. As he had noted in his Portland speech, he believed utilities, with limited exceptions, should remain private.

Eager, therefore, to send a holding company proposal to Congress as soon as possible, Roosevelt summoned his advisers on January 21 to make the critical decision about whether to regulate the structure of holding companies directly or to destroy them by taxation. He initially favored the tax proposal, but after an animated discussion he acquiesced to the regulatory approach. He made the proviso, though, that multistate holding companies must be eliminated because state commissions could not effectively regulate them. All holding companies would have to register with the SEC, which at first would work with them to flatten and geographically limit their structure on a voluntary basis. But after January 1, 1938, the SEC could eliminate any that still controlled more than one geographically integrated system. This soon became known as the "death sentence," a label for which Willkie claimed credit. It was the lightning rod for an all-out lobbying offensive by the industry to kill the proposal.[41]

On the same day Roosevelt decided on the regulatory approach, Willkie led the opponents' charge in a debate with Lilienthal in the overflowing grand ballroom of the Hotel Astor in New York. Willkie attacked government enterprises as inefficient and unfair, denied that utility stocks had been watered, and said the industry was a piker compared to the government when it came to propaganda. Lilienthal warned that it was not government but the holding companies that were endangering their own investments, suggesting not only that stock had been watered but also, less persuasively, that there was "serious doubt of the existence of any substantial equity for common stock" in many utilities.[42]

McNinch and the FPC quickly signaled their own dissatisfaction with the draft bill, but for jurisdictional and political reasons as well as substantive ones. They wanted jurisdiction over the regulation of utility holding company securities that the bill gave to the SEC. They also sought to attach to the bill separate legislation giving the federal government authority over interstate sales, which they feared might be neglected if submitted separately. The dispute was taken to Roosevelt, who condoned combining the two bills but left the regulatory authority with the SEC.

The administration quickly completed the bill and sent the final version to the chairmen of the Congressional commerce committees, Senator Burton K. Wheeler of Montana and Congressman Sam Rayburn of Texas. On February 6, 1935, they introduced what became known as the Wheeler-Rayburn bill in their respective chambers. Title I of the bill was the Public Utility Holding Company Act of 1935, which included the registration requirement and the "death sentence" authority for the SEC. Title II amended the Federal Water Power Act, renaming it the Federal Power Act and giving the Federal Power

Commission regulatory authority over interstate electricity sales, which by this time amounted to nearly one-fifth of all electricity sold. With that measure, the "Attleboro gap" left by the 1928 Supreme Court decision would finally be plugged.[43]

Press reaction was mixed. Some papers suggested that the bill went too far, proposing destruction of holding companies when only regulation was needed. But Arthur Krock of the *New York Times* wrote that taking on the unpopular holding companies was "essential politics" for Roosevelt as well as "personal conviction." Columnist Walter Lippmann, who had characterized the New Deal as a "dangerous centralization of power," initially cast favor on the bill for being a "revival of old-fashioned 100% American trust-busting." He later, however, turned against the death sentence provision.[44]

A five-week utility lobbying campaign led by Willkie followed, which Roosevelt biographer Kenneth Davis said "raised such a hue and cry as had not been raised against a single measure, perhaps, since Stephen Douglas's Kansas-Nebraska bill was before Congress in 1854." As part of this effort, utility executives launched a fierce letter-writing campaign to urge their shareholders to write their Congressmen, opposing the measure. The company heads had learned the political value of having many small shareholders from Insull. Georgia Power, a subsidiary of C&S, reported in its newsletter, "Quick death for the holding companies by execution is proposed. And slow death for the operating companies." Thomas N. McCarter of Public Service Corporation of New Jersey told shareholders the bill endangered their property, and Alex Dow of Detroit Edison said it "seriously affects the values of all utility securities, those of operating as well as holding companies."[45]

Supporters of the bill also went into high gear. Even Will Rogers got into the act: "A Holding Company is a thing where you hand an accomplice the goods while the policeman searches you." After this gibe generated an outpouring of criticism from industry supporters, he wrote in a subsequent column, "Well I dident (*sic*) figure that little half witted remark would upset the whole holding company business. But I forgot that a remark generally hurts in proportion to its truth."[46]

Rayburn moved with great haste to push the bill through, scheduling

House hearings for the week after he introduced it. Once again Willkie was the leadoff witness for the utilities. He paced up and down before the committee, raising his voice in anger and dropping it to little more than a whisper as he defended the industry. Yet he said he would support virtually all of the provisions of the bill, zeroing in on the death sentence for his attack. Reasonable regulation, he asserted, could prevent the notorious practices that had occurred in some companies. "There is no reason for the abolition of holding companies like Commonwealth & Southern, who have enlightened policies in reducing rates, promoting business, and fostering its subsidiaries throughout the Depression." Some of his colleagues strongly disagreed with his willingness to accept most of the bill. But with his persuasiveness as a reasonable witness and his rhetorical skill at inspiring his allies, he burnished his position as the industry's national leader. His wit and deft touch with the press also bolstered him. On his departure from New York for the hearing, he commented that he was going to Washington "to see that my contempt for the New Deal remains founded on familiarity."[47]

As letters and telegrams opposing the bill flooded Congressional offices, Roosevelt decided to weigh in. On March 12, 1935, he sent Congress the final report of his National Power Policy Committee. In an accompanying memorandum he wrote, "It is idle to talk of the continuation of holding companies on the assumption that regulation can protect the public against them . . . ."[48] Yet Willkie and his colleagues were anything but idle. In a May 1 article in *Forbes*, Willkie attacked the bill, "178 printed pages . . . more verbiage than is contained in the Magna Carta, Bill of Rights, Declaration of Independence, Constitution and the Emancipation Proclamation combined," and its authors, "junior members of the so-called Brain Trust who never had the remotest contact with the operation of a public utility." He asserted that the case against the industry was based on examples of mismanagement that were isolated and long since corrected.[49]

When the House committee met in private to discuss the bill, it became clear that Rayburn did not have the votes for the death sentence. But its prospects in the Senate looked better. On May 14 Wheeler's committee reported a bill with the death sentence intact.

However the Democratic majority in the full Senate was in fact divided.

While the lobbying and legislative maneuvering proceeded, several challenges to other New Deal legislation moved forward in the courts. In May alone, the Supreme Court ruled against the constitutionality of Title I of the National Industrial Recovery Act, the Farm Bankruptcy Act, and the Railroad Pension Act. A common criticism of the National Industrial Recovery Act was that it created or strengthened monopolies or cartels, but Chief Justice Hughes wrote for a unanimous Court in *Schechter Poultry Corp. v. The United States* that the overbroad delegation of legislative power to the president was what made it unconstitutional, a decision that gave hope to opponents of other expansive administration initiatives. The number of unfavorable opinions and their broad sweep made it appear likely that the Court would severely limit the use of government power to achieve the New Deal's goals. Roosevelt told reporters, "We have been relegated to the horse-and-buggy definition of interstate commerce."[50]

With the summer recess looming, Roosevelt pressed for rapid action on a number of bills. On June 4 he sent Congressional leaders a list of nine major bills he said must be passed before adjournment, which typically occurred early in the summer. It included the Social Security Act; the Wagner Act mandating collective bargaining; the Wealth Tax Act, which increased income and estate taxes and created a corporate income tax; and the Holding Company Act.[51]

During a heated two-week Senate debate—at one point Norris lectured his colleagues for five hours—William Dieterich, a Democrat from Illinois, announced that he would offer an amendment to strike the death sentence. When a rumor spread on the morning of the vote that Roosevelt was prepared to accept Dieterich's amendment, Wheeler rushed to the White House, where the president was still having breakfast in bed, to urge him to issue a statement dispelling the rumor. Rather than a press statement, the president scrawled out a short note, handing it to Wheeler and saying, "You can show this to the boys."[52]

When that afternoon Dieterich claimed that Roosevelt supported his amendment, Wheeler read from the president's note: ". . . any amendment which goes to the heart of the major objectives of [the death sentence] . . . is wholly contrary to the recommendations of myself." The amendment was defeated by a single vote, 45 to 44. But the strength of the utility lobby was demonstrated when twenty-eight Democrats voted in favor, including twenty previously loyal New Deal supporters—the first serious break in the president's bloc. The bill then passed with a comfortable majority, 56 to 32.[53]

In the House, the committee remained divided. On June 22, unable to obtain the votes for the death sentence, Rayburn reported the bill without it. But Roosevelt wasn't willing to concede defeat. Although a preliminary count indicated the administration might be forty votes short of a majority to restore the death sentence in the House, the perpetually optimistic Roosevelt thought he could hold most Democrats if they were forced to vote on the record, allowing loyalists to be rewarded and dissidents to be punished. Rayburn personally asked the Rules Committee to allow such a recorded vote, but Chairman John J. O'Connor, a conservative Tammany Democrat, would allow only a teller vote with no record of how each Congressman voted. On July 1 each Congressman walked between two tellers, who tallied only 146 votes for restoring the death sentence and 246 votes against, giving Roosevelt the first major House defeat of his Presidency. On the following day the House approved the weakened bill 323 to 81.[54]

Roosevelt wasn't to forget the slight. Although O'Connor's brother was the president's former law partner and the president of his Warm Springs Foundation, when the Congressman was favored to be elected House Majority Leader in 1936, Roosevelt signaled his support for Rayburn. The loyal New Dealer went on to win and became Speaker four years later, serving as Speaker or Minority Leader until his death in 1961.[55]

With the normal August recess a little more than a month away, Roosevelt still held out hope for a bill including the death sentence, even though Rayburn expected a House-Senate conference committee would eliminate it. He told the president that the utility lobby was the "richest and most ruthless lobby Congress has ever known."[56] But Roosevelt was a master of the system. He had Vice President Garner appoint supportive Senate conferees and instructed them to hold strong.

The pressure for and against the bill was already intense, but it reached a crescendo by July. A particularly heated row ensued over accusations made by a Republican Congressman from Maine, Owen Brewster. He charged White House lobbyist Thomas Corcoran with threatening to cut off funding for a Passamaquoddy Bay project to harness tidal power for electricity if he voted against the death sentence. The accusation was ultimately found to be false—the project, near Campobello Island and a Roosevelt favorite, was already funded—but it triggered investigations of lobbying in both houses. In the House, Chairman O'Connor had the investigation referred to his Rules Committee, where little came of it. In the Senate, though, a special investigating committee chaired by a crusading New Deal supporter from Alabama, Hugo Black, was especially vigorous. Black had called holding companies "a blood-sucking business, a vampire" and believed an exposure of utility lobbying practices would undercut the industry's credibility, and his tactics included broad subpoenas for messages between utility officials and their lobbyists. Civil libertarians objected vehemently, but he did not back down.[57]

Opening the hearings on July 12, Black said, "Tell the boys of the press to come in. The show is about to begin." The first witness was Philip H. Gadsden, chairman of the Committee of Public Utility Executives. Senate investigators had surprised him in his office that morning and rushed him to the hearing by taxi with no opportunity to prepare. He disclosed that the Edison Electric Institute had established and guided his organization in response to introduction of the Wheeler-Rayburn bill but had instructed him to keep no minutes of meetings and to keep the connection secret. Those revelations provided ample fuel for the continuing investigation. Black recessed the hearings to await information he had requested from holding companies.[58]

While waiting, Black heard from a Congressman who had received over eight hundred telegrams against the bill from a small town in his northwestern Pennsylvania district. Three out of four of the senders' names started with one of the first few letters of the alphabet, which suggested the names had been plucked out of a phone book or list of utility customers. When contacted, many of the supposed senders denied having sent them. Black's staff determined that the local office of Associated Gas & Electric (AG&E), a ten-layer holding company pyramid, had told one of its salesmen to generate the telegrams.[59]

The committee also discovered that AG&E had paid messenger boys three cents for each signature obtained. Black called one of them, nineteen-year-old Elmer Danielson, as a witness, asking the boy if the petitioners had known what they were signing. To much laughter, the unsophisticated teenager said he explained the complicated Wheeler-Rayburn bill to them. Corcoran later wrote that the exchange "really turned the tide of almost certain defeat for Roosevelt." Black told a friend, "Another revelation like that, and we will compel the House to approve the death sentence."[60]

But Black needed a better villain than a young messenger, and he found one. He had announced on July 14 that he intended to subpoena Howard C. Hopson, the founder and president of AG&E. Hopson was described by one writer as "the crown prince of corporate jazz" who surpassed Insull in "holding company legerdemain." In a farcical game of cat and mouse, Hopson evaded the committee investigators for two weeks. He changed hotels in Washington, and he drove around Virginia and West Virginia to avoid them. Eventually he agreed to appear instead before the friendlier House Rules committee investigation, chaired by O'Connor. As he left the House hearing after gentle questioning, a Senate process server confronted him, only to be shoved aside by Hopson's guards. After another chase, which a reporter compared to "Eliza crossing the ice, hotly pursued by bloodhounds," and another subpoena, which Hopson ignored, a unanimous Senate issued a warrant for his arrest for contempt of Congress.[61]

Hopson's testimony was worth the effort. Aided by his tax return, which Roosevelt ordered released, in violation of normal procedures, Black elicited a wealth of evidence against Hopson. Money that should have been paid as dividends had been diverted to Hopson as income. He'd also received millions in income from a personally owned utility service company. Prodigious revenues from ratepayers had been

devoted to lobbying, telegrams to Congress had been mass manufactured, and records had been destroyed. Hopson became the new face
of holding company abuses. But even these revelations didn't break
the logjam on the bill in Congress.[62]

Howard Hopson, the "crown prince of corporate jazz," explains the structure of
his holding company pyramid to Senators Hugo Black and Lewis Schwellenback.
(*Library of Congress.*)

With the House conferees buttressed by the strong vote against the
death sentence and their Senate counterparts reinforced by the publicity from the Black hearings and by administration pressure, the
debate in the conference committee was intense. A compromise on
the death sentence was the only way to advance. As the conferees met
into the second and third weeks of August, Rayburn suggested
allowing a holding company to hold two operating systems, rather
than only one, and of any size. This would mean Willkie's C&S and
other of the largest companies would survive.[63]

But Roosevelt championed a different proposal, based on a game
plan suggested by Felix Frankfurter. Procedurally, he persuaded the
Chairman of the House Ways and Means Committee to say that he

would hold a highly popular tax bill in committee to keep Congress in session until agreement on the Holding Company Act was reached. Tactically, he stated publicly that the House bill was unacceptable but hinted at compromise by acknowledging that no particular legislative wording was necessary to achieve his objectives. Substantively, he proposed a compromise suggested by Frankfurter: holding companies could control more than one system if the additional system could not economically stand alone. The additional company must also not be so large or so dispersed as to prevent efficient management and regulation. And no more than two holding companies would be allowed above an operating utility. The death sentence was out, but these conditions would spell the breakup of C&S, Bond and Share, and many other of the largest holding companies.[64]

A full-court press by Democratic leaders led to acceptance of the Frankfurter compromise in the conference committee, and the House passed the revised bill by a large margin—219 to 142. The bill gave Roosevelt most of what he wanted, complying with his 1935 State of the Union address as it was written, abolishing "the evil *features* of holding companies." He signed the final Public Utility Holding Company Act on August 26, 1935, saying that if Congress "had done nothing more than pass this Bill, the session would be regarded as historic for all time." When Congress adjourned the next day, concluding what became known as Roosevelt's "second hundred days," each of the nine significant bills the president had demanded had passed.[65]

Willkie, though, felt that holding companies had escaped from a certain death sentence only to be encumbered by excessive restrictions. "While a strait-jacket will keep a man out of trouble," he complained, "it is not a suitable garment in which to work." He was not ready to concede. He hoped that the narrow victory margin and the need to encourage investment and employment in a still-weak economy might allow a reconsideration in 1936 that would permit companies like his to avoid dismemberment. On November 23 he announced that C&S would not register with the SEC, as required, but would file suit to challenge the law's constitutionality.[66]

CHAPTER 7

PEAK POWER

TVA was only the first of President Roosevelt's initiatives to stimulate competition with private utilities and to reduce the growing gap between urban and rural America. On May 11, 1935, just days before the Commerce Committee voted to send the Holding Company Act to the full Senate, he established the Rural Electrification Administration (REA) by executive order. The organization and its mandate were based on the plan Morris Cooke had developed after nearly a year of extensive consultation, and the Senate confirmed Cooke as administrator of the REA a few days later.

Cooke wrote to private utility executives on May 20 inviting them to propose a program to work with the REA in providing rural service. He didn't completely share Ickes' hostility to private utilities, and he reasoned that they had the greatest experience in building transmission and distribution lines. But he specified two conditions: they must charge low rates and provide area coverage, meaning that all farms in an area must be provided with service.[1]

After World War I a debate had emerged between supporters of *line coverage* and those of *area coverage*. The cost per customer of serving sparsely populated areas was high, and farmers had low cash incomes. This led to the unfortunate but understandable practice of "cream-skimming."[2] Utilities seeking the highest return for investors occasionally built lines to selected groups of farms—line coverage—but only if farmers paid the cost of the lines and only if there were no more profitable opportunities to expand service in towns. "We called these 'snake lines,'" wrote Cooke, "as they went now in one direction and then in another in order to reach the cream of the business. Usually a territory, once covered in this haphazard way, is precluded from being economically developed on an area basis."[3]

Within several weeks the utilities responded to Cooke with a report that alleged government intrusion into the domain of private business yet failed to consider the social benefits of electrification along with the economic benefits to farmers. As an alternative they proposed a $238 million program, the equivalent of nearly $4.5 billion today, for private utilities to build 78,000 miles of lines to 351,000 new customers, two-thirds of them farmers. Of the total, the companies would provide only $13 million. The federal government would provide $100 million to the utilities for line construction and wiring houses, and farmers would be expected to pay the remainder, mostly for new appliances. Rates charged would be similar to those already charged in rural areas, which to date had achieved abysmally little electrification. Cooke rejected the plan as too small, too costly, too vague about rates, and unresponsive to his requirement that the utilities provide area service.[4]

As Cooke was reaching out to the utilities, he had to deal with a problem within the administration that could have smothered his plan in the cradle. Roosevelt had established the REA under the authority of the Emergency Relief Appropriation Act, and within weeks he issued an executive order applying to all relief agencies: each agency needed to spend at least 25 percent of its funds for labor and hire at least 90 percent of its employees from local relief rolls. Unemployment nationwide, although declining, was still above 20 percent in 1935.[5]

Cooke knew that the REA would not be able to comply because so much of the expense of extending electrical service was in materials and equipment. The labor required to string wires and hook up new customers also involved skills not often found on rural relief roles. Rather than directly creating jobs, the rationale of the rural electrification program was to improve lives. Its business model was to provide low-interest, long-term loans, a large portion of which would be used for appliances and farm equipment, providing the less direct benefit of creating jobs manufacturing appliances. With only 11 percent of American farms enjoying the benefits of electricity in 1935—less than one percent in Mississippi—Roosevelt understood the need to support the program even in the absence of large direct employment gains. In August he issued another executive order, allowing the REA to waive the labor requirement.[6]

Roosevelt's Columbia River initiative also moved forward in 1935. When the first of the government dams, Bonneville and Grand Coulee, had been authorized and initially funded in early 1933, the legislation was silent on how to market the power. Idaho Senator James Pope, a Democrat and strong Roosevelt supporter, introduced a bill in early 1935 to create a Columbia Valley Authority modeled after TVA, with broad regional planning responsibility and the authority to market all of the federally produced power in the Northwest, allowing it to prioritize bringing cheap electricity to both farms and towns.[7]

The Army Corps of Engineers was charged with planning and building Bonneville, and the Interior Department's Bureau of Reclamation had responsibility for Grand Coulee. Both considered power marketing to be part of their planning responsibility. Although Roosevelt had called for multiple regional planning authorities in his Portland speech, they wanted no part of an independent Columbia Valley Authority that would displace them—they had been given no role in planning or building TVA's dams—and they worked with Oregon's Republican Senators, "Charlie Mac" McNary and Frederick Stelwer, to develop an alternative to the Pope bill. Introduced in July, it called for Bonneville's power to be sold to private utilities, which without government intervention would resell it primarily to the tidewater region around Portland, the Northwest's most heavily industrialized area. This bill won the support of private utilities and of Portland-area businesses but was opposed by public power advocates. Congress adjourned after passage of the Holding Company Act in August without acting on either bill, and the knotty question of marketing the power in the Northwest would persist for most of the decade..[8]

The issue of whether Grand Coulee would be a low dam, primarily for irrigation, or a high dam with significant hydropower potential, was decided more quickly. Soon after excavation had started for the low dam in early 1934, calls for a high dam and greater power production intensified. By June 1935 Washington Senator Clarence Dill and his allies had won the day, and the Bureau of Reclamation agreed to redesign Grand Coulee as a high dam, not raise it later with a potentially unsafe seam between the lower and higher segments. In August Congress authorized funding for the new, more expensive design. Although Grand Coulee had been the first to receive funding, the delay caused by the change in plans meant that construction on Bonneville actually started first.[9]

On a western trip after Congress adjourned, Roosevelt dedicated Boulder Dam, which had been called Hoover Dam during the Hoover administration and would be again after the passage of a Congressional resolution in 1947. Along with Muscle Shoals, it was a symbol of government-produced power and a manifestation of the intense, fifteen-year struggle between public power advocates and the private utility industry. Roosevelt's speech on September 30, 1935, captured the national pride in "the greatest dam in the world," and linked that pride to TVA, the dams under construction on the Columbia, future power developments, and the economic recovery of private industry. "Expenditures on all of these works, great and small, flow out to many beneficiaries; they revive other and more remote industries and businesses." Supporters of large-scale public power took renewed encouragement from his reference to Boulder Dam as "the first of four great Government regional units," an echo of the call in his Portland campaign speech for "four great Government power developments ... in each of the four quarters of the United States."[10]

When the private utilities' proposal for cooperation with the REA proved to be unsatisfactory, Cooke sought the involvement of municipal utilities. He soon concluded, though, that legal obstacles to serving customers outside municipal boundaries and the political difficulties of asking town residents to subsidize the rates of their rural neighbors would prevent them from participating. As the private utilities realized that they were not going to receive REA funds on their own terms, and as their fight with the administration over the Holding Company Act heated up during the summer of 1935, most turned from tentative cooperation to outright opposition. Cooke's talks with them continued, but by the end of 1935 he concluded that the companies were using the delay to push construction of their own rural lines, many of which were snake lines designed to block area coverage by REA. He then turned his attention to cooperatives modeled on TVA's Alcorn County model, which proved the feasibility of publicly developed rural electrification in a depressed area with a high percentage of tenant farmers. The REA began to focus almost exclusively on building up the capacity of farmers to organize such cooperatives.[11]

Lilienthal was encouraged during the first week of October 1935 by his visit to small towns and rural areas in Tennessee and Alabama. "There is somehow a magic about TVA kilowatts," he recorded in his journal. "We have really stirred public imagination about electricity . . . while lower rates and the saving on electric bills means a good deal, to have electricity apparently open up a new world for people and to have the form of organization whereby electricity is brought to them through the beginning of cooperative activity in which they participate is really an accomplishment."[12]

REA architect and first administrator Morris Cooke signs off on seven early rural electrification projects in November 1935. (*Library of Congress.*)

Despite TVA's advances, Norris was disappointed with the REA's slow progress in achieving similar goals on a broader scale and was thinking about legislation to put it on a more permanent footing. He wrote to Cooke that it was "increasingly obvious that . . . we should adopt a more positive program for electrifying the largest possible number of farms."[13] In a favorable reply authorized by Roosevelt, Cooke threw the administration's weight behind a more aggressive national approach, claiming the private utilities' failure to electrify rural areas was due to "prohibitive costs of line construction, to excessive demands for cash contributions from farmers to pay for the lines which would serve them, to high rates which discourage the abundant use of current, and to the traditional policy of the private utilities of extending the monopolistic franchises as widely as possible, while extending their actual service only to those areas which are most profitable." He concluded by endorsing "a positive program of planning for construction on an area basis so as to effect the economies of mass construction . . . ." Publication of the exchange of letters initiated a national campaign for legislation, which was backed by the National Grange and the Farm Bureau.[14]

As this campaign got underway, the REA continued to struggle. Not all of the obstacles it faced were created by private utilities. TVA's Electric Home and Farm Authority, established in 1933 to serve only TVA customers, had been reorganized in 1935 as a public corporation separate from TVA that could make loans to customers of cooperating utilities throughout the country. The authority was expected to provide installment loans for appliances and wiring to farmers served by the REA, but under the tightfisted management of Jesse Jones, Chairman of the Reconstruction Finance Corporation (RFC), few of its loans went to cooperatives. A frustrated Cooke, the only authority board member not an employee of the RFC, complained to Jones in November 1935, ". . . this work has really never started . . . . I think we have lost some of the impetus which we inherited." He eventually quit the board in disgust.[15]

When Congress convened in January 1936, Benjamin Cohen and Thomas Corcoran, Felix Frankfurter's protégés and the New Deal's all-purpose legislative craftsmen, had drafted a bill to make the REA an independent agency. In addition to giving it a statutory basis separate from the emergency relief programs, the bill authorized funding to make loans that could be renewed or transferred to another cooperative when the first borrower repaid them, giving the agency some independence from the annual appropriations process. Norris introduced it in the Senate, and Agriculture Committee Chairman Marvin Jones expected to introduce it in the House and have it referred to his committee. But Commerce Committee Chairman Sam Rayburn, bruised and embittered by the fierce utility opposition to his Holding Company bill the year before, felt Jones was not tough enough. He charged into the House Parliamentarian's office and laid the bill on his desk, saying "Give it to me." He did.[16]

For several reasons the bill initially elicited little overt opposition. The REA was precluded from competing for customers of existing utilities, the private utilities could anticipate increased sales of wholesale power to the REA cooperatives for resale to new customers, the promise of so many new buyers for electric pumps, stoves and other appliances made it attractive to electrical manufacturers, and the utilities were gun-shy about heavy-handed lobbying after the previous summer's Black Committee hearings. The most compelling reason, though, may have been the utilities' belief that few poor and risk-averse farmers would ever be willing to go into debt for electricity.[17]

The Senate approved the bill with no formal hearings and with little debate. Some members of Rayburn's Commerce Committee, though, which was more supportive of corporations than the House as a whole, objected to a provision that made private utilities ineligible for REA loans. Rayburn wanted the bill more than he wanted purity, and he accepted an amendment broadening eligibility. He also yielded to pressure from public-power and farm lobbyists to set interest rates very low. The changes helped him pass the bill in committee, although with only a one-vote margin. The amendments also helped him win approval in the full House, as did his speech on the Texas experience: "When free enterprise had the opportunity to electrify farm homes—after fifty years, they had electrified three percent." But his two compromises led to a very contentious conference with the Senate. Norris strongly opposed any participation by the private utilities, and he argued that interest rates had to be higher in order to make the program self-liquidating.[18]

Norris recalled the negotiations, which he chaired, as "exceedingly bitter." After several weeks, Rayburn and his allies had failed to move the stubborn senator. Norris finally declared that compromise was impossible, that he would not call another meeting, and that he would take the issue to the voters in the next Congressional election, allowing farmers and other supporters to bring pressure to bear on opponents of the bill. Rayburn feared that the House would not be able to report the bill out again if it went back to committee, and he wanted electricity for his constituents, not a campaign issue. He followed Norris into the hall to plead for more time. Norris finally agreed, and Rayburn continued to work behind the scenes to find a way to break the deadlock.[19]

His work paid off. After a few more weeks, the conferees reconvened and accepted compromises on the two divisive issues. Private utilities would be eligible for loans, but the REA would be required to give preference to cooperatives and public entities. Cooke assured REA supporters among the conferees that private utilities would receive little of the funding because the emphasis on area coverage would discourage them from applying. The interest rate on loans would be based on the average for federal obligations having a maturity of ten years or more, or effectively about three percent.[20]

The final Norris-Rayburn bill gave the REA a ten-year life with an initial authorization of $50 million per year (worth about $950 million today) for the first two years and $40 million per year thereafter, when repayments from the cooperatives would presumably begin to arrive. The money was to be allocated among the states based on the number of unelectrified farms, thus favoring the South and Midwest.[21] The co-ops could use the money for building lines but also, unlike under the executive order, for 25-year loans to consumers for wiring homes and financing appliances. Within a few days both houses passed the bill by voice vote, and the president signed it on May 20, 1936.

Applications from co-ops began to arrive, more heavily at first from areas where TVA was active. All three of the co-ops that filed for incorporation in 1935 were in Mississippi, and six of twenty-two in 1936 were in Mississippi or Tennessee.[22] Cooke's prediction that private utilities wouldn't seek REA loans in large numbers was on target. They received only 3.5 percent of the first year's loans. They had access to credit with interest almost as low as the REA offered and without bothersome restrictions like area coverage. They weren't about to concede to Cooke's plans, however, and they worked in a number of ways to derail REA progress.

Cooperatives needed time to organize under state laws, and in the first several months after the bill was passed private utilities accelerated their previously anemic efforts and brought electricity to more farms than did REA-funded co-ops, in some places at a level and at rates they had previously said were impossible. Cooke and the REA claimed credit for spurring them to action, with some justification, because the utilities were going on the offense in an effort to preempt the REA. While this could be seen as healthy competition, the utilities concentrated their efforts on the most profitable customers, often running "spite lines"—another term for snake lines through areas seeking to form co-ops.[23]

In states where the utility regulatory commission had a reputation for being hostile to public power, including North Carolina, Virginia, Pennsylvania, and Massachusetts, utilities sought to bring the cooperatives under the jurisdiction of the commission and force them into expensive and lengthy rate cases. A single ruling by the Massachusetts Department of Public Utilities destroyed a cooperative with 700 farmers, the state's largest.[24]

Utilities also sought to undermine the business viability of the new cooperatives by charging them high wholesale rates for power while insisting on contracts that prohibited the retail sale of power at rates lower than the private utility charged its customers.[25] These practices were a direct threat to the REA business model, which relied on low rates to create greater demand. In a December 3, 1936, letter, Cooke called out Willkie of C&S and Groesbeck of Bond and Share for their behavior: "The cooperatives to be financed by this Administration are not receiving the service in the matter of wholesale rates to which they feel themselves entitled and which would accord with the industry's protestations of goodwill and cooperation." He was more critical in a note to his own staff. "Normally in negotiating a contract, a good buyer respects the interests of the man from whom he is buying, but this seems out of the question in dealing with an industry whose present day conduct is so largely influenced by its narrow past." He also began to add staff members with utility experience who could help cooperatives negotiate.[26]

Despite the utilities' tactics, new co-ops were formed at a rapid clip and loan applications to the REA accelerated. The $50 million provided for the first year proved to be well below the amount necessary to fund all applications that year, which came to $112 million. Cooke was creative in his response. He began to commit funds to applicants over a three-year period instead of all at once, allowing him to approve nearly $150 million in loans in the first year.[27] He also spurred participation by having his staff investigate in advance the best potential territories in terms of population density and the number of owner-operated farms. This legwork allowed his staff to evaluate more quickly the applications that came in from these areas.

Some private utilities cooperated with the REA. Georgia Power, a C&S subsidiary that was not directly threatened by TVA, lost rural customers during the Depression and generally found the cost of extending new lines to rural areas uneconomical. But it was able to contract with newly formed co-ops for services such as line maintenance and appliance repairs and as a result won virtually all of the REA's wholesale power purchases in the state.[28]

Mississippi, Alabama, and Tennessee, where TVA and the REA fought for customers in rural areas as well as towns, were different stories. In Alabama, TVA representatives attended community meetings to encourage people to form co-ops rather than sign up for Alabama Power service, sometimes implying that government employees would lose their jobs if they voted wrong. The company fought back, issuing a brochure with insinuating questions for potential co-op members to ask before signing up for TVA power: "If some of the members of the association fail to pay their bills . . . won't you have to help make up the amount they fail to pay? If there is an accident to someone, who will be liable?" Nonetheless, TVA was able to win the contracts for over half of the power sales to the co-ops in the state.[29]

As Cooke was fueling momentum for rural electrification, progress also seemed imminent in the Northwest. For one thing, the dispute over distribution of power from Bonneville appeared to be nearing resolution. The Oregon senators reintroduced their Columbia River bill when Congress convened in 1936, and Washington's senators introduced an alternative more favorable to public power and rural electrification. Roosevelt persuaded Senator Pope of Idaho to shelve his more ambitious proposal, saying there would be plenty of time later to consider a TVA-like arrangement. In a response to a Congressional request for their views on the bills, the Corps of Engineers and the Federal Power Commission proposed that the Corps generate power and build high-tension transmission lines for the Bonneville Dam and that the Commission market the electricity and set the rates. As a gesture to Washington's senators, they recommended a public-preference principle for sale of the power similar to the one in the TVA Act. All four senators co-sponsored the resulting compromise in May.[30]

Prior to hearings on the bill, Roosevelt's advisers sent him a report of the Pacific Northwest Regional Planning Commission. In addition to proposing a new agency with a TVA-style board to market Bonneville's power, it recommended high-tension lines to carry power to all parts of the region and uniform rates throughout the system to encourage power sales in remote areas. The dispute over these "postage-stamp" rates, as opposed to traditional rates based in part on transmission distance, became another bone of contention for the next few years.[31]

Bonneville Dam under construction in 1936.
(*Courtesy of the Franklin D. Roosevelt Library.*)

Bonneville was approaching completion with the prospect that there
would be no way to distribute its massive amounts of power. The marketing question had to be resolved. Roosevelt temporized, suggesting
that Congress establish an interim agency, buying time until Grand
Coulee was finished and a regional solution would be needed. In Senate
hearings other witnesses made the case for postage-stamp rates and a
new federal agency for marketing and transmission. One Oregon official
split from his state's Congressional delegation, supporting independence
from private power monopolies and accusing the Corps of Engineers
in the region of being dominated by the utilities.[32]

A Corps witness at a Senate hearing in May seemed to confirm
this accusation by agreeing with the Portland Chamber of Commerce
and the utilities on four key points: Power production and transmission
at Bonneville should be left to private utilities; the recommendations
in the Regional Planning Commission's report were "too visionary;" a
transmission system without lower rates for nearby private utilities

and industries was not practical; and a system using uniform rates would not repay the investment in the project.[33]

Like the private utilities' position on rural electrification a year earlier, the Corps report gave no weight to the social benefits of broader electrification, and Secretary of War George Dern summarized the opposition to the belief in low rates to stimulate demand: "If you superimpose an enormous transmission system or grid over that country with its present small populations, relatively speaking, and large distance that you have to cover, and average up the cost so that it is the same all over, it will make your cost so much that you will never be able to sell to industry, and if you don't get industry, you don't get people, and if you don't get people, you can't sell power."[34] The Senate and House committees reported out legislation based on the Corps recommendations, but the bills died in the end-of-session logjam as Congress rushed to adjournment in June to campaign for the 1936 elections.

As the battle over marketing raged, the struggle in the courts about the constitutionality of federal involvement in the industry continued apace. The heavy majority of conservative appointees on federal courts, a legacy of twelve years of Republican presidents, had frustrated Roosevelt from the beginning. Early in his first term, a few decisions allowing a broader exercise of government power in the light of the economic emergency gave him some slight hope that the Supreme Court would interpret the Constitution more liberally. Any traces of that optimism had disappeared, though, when starting in 1935 the Court had relied on a narrow view of federal authority to strike down several of his early economic initiatives. Chief Justice Hughes, who had often opposed the conservative majority when he was an associate justice in the 1910s, sought to balance the opposing factions and preserve the stability and reputation of the Court. This sometimes caused him, often along with recently appointed Justice Owen Roberts, to side with the "Four Horsemen," Justices Butler, McReynolds, Sutherland, and Van Devanter, conservatives who consistently voted to preserve private contract and property rights.[35]

Reeling from their legislative defeats in the summer of 1935, the utilities rebounded with another judicial victory. Seventeen days after the Holding Company Act was signed in August, the 1924 Democratic presidential candidate, John W. Davis, representing a dentist with $2,500 of utility stock, petitioned a friendly U.S. district court judge in Baltimore to declare the law and its death sentence unconstitutional. James Landis, who had recently succeeded Joseph Kennedy as SEC chairman, called the proceedings a "sham," but the plaintiffs received a favorable ruling in November 1935, triggering a host of utility suits to block the requirement that they register with the SEC by December 1. At about the same time Ohio Edison, a C&S subsidiary, filed a separate challenge to the law.[36]

The government fought back vigorously. Landis and Benjamin Cohen, the law's principal draftsman, quickly filed a complaint against Bond and Share, highlighting the registration provision of the law, which they thought would more easily withstand scrutiny than the death sentence. Matching the utilities' skill in forum shopping, they chose a friendly court in New York—the judge was a friend of Frankfurter and a former employer of Cohen. The lines were drawn for a multi-faceted battle that was almost certain to go to the Supreme Court.[37]

The prospects for a government victory before the Court seemed dim, but in February 1936 the Court issued a surprising decision in the *Ashwander* challenge to TVA. An 8-1 majority ruled that TVA had the right to acquire transmission lines to sell surplus power from Wilson Dam and compete in the market. Hughes wrote for the majority: "Certainly, the Alabama Power Company had no constitutional right to insist that it shall be the sole purchaser of the energy generated at Wilson Dam; that the energy shall be sold to it or go to waste."[38]

Justice James McReynolds, a virulent racist and anti-Semite who refused to sit next to Justice Brandeis and so hated Roosevelt that he vowed "never [to] resign as long as that crippled son-of-a-bitch is in the White House," captured the conservative opposition to TVA in his lonely dissent: "We should consider the truth of the petitioners' charge that, while pretending to act within their powers to improve navigation, the United States, through corporate agencies, are really seeking to accomplish what they have no right to undertake—the business of developing, distributing, and selling electric power." Hughes drafted his majority opinion narrowly and did not consider this charge. "We express no opinion . . . as to the status of any other dam . . . or as to the validity of the Tennessee Valley Authority Act . . . ." This kept the other three conservative justices from joining McReynolds. It also limited the scope of TVA's victory, leaving the door open for a future constitutional challenge. But for the moment, the victory was sweet. The day after the decision was announced the *New York Times* trumpeted, "Tennessee Valley Shouts With Joy."[39]

Only Justice James McReynolds (r) dissented from the pro-TVA decision written by Chief Justice Charles Evans Hughes (l) in the *Ashwander* case. (*Library of Congress.*)

Utility leaders and members of the business community counting on the Court to limit the government's aggressive interventions in the economy were equally distressed by the verdict. The president of the American Federation of Investors warned that TVA was an "ambitious Marxian scheme" that, if it ultimately prevailed, "will affect every free industry in our country, for those who advocate it have as their goal government ownership and political management of all industry."[40] Heated rhetoric aside, both sides were right in perceiving that the game had changed. The Court had become less predictable.

Wendell Willkie saw the *Ashwander* decision as a serious blow to the C&S companies in the TVA region. The matter was particularly urgent because the constraints on the expansion of TVA's market that Willkie had negotiated in the January 4, 1935, contract would be lifted ninety days after the Norris Dam began operating. The dam was scheduled for completion in March of 1937, but construction was ahead of schedule.

Construction worker with safety belt on Norris Dam in March 1936. Completion of the dam ahead of schedule triggered fierce competition for territory between TVA and Commonwealth & Southern. (*TVA photo K-680, courtesy of National Archives - Atlanta.*)

Willkie undertook a three-pronged counteroffensive: negotiation, litigation, and public relations. He sought to negotiate a more limited territorial agreement with Lilienthal, although he had no success with an adversary who was bent on expanding the area in which he could establish his yardstick rates. He began preparing another lawsuit, in collaboration with other utility heads. And he stepped up his public

attacks on TVA, giving them a sharper edge. In a March radio broadcast he called the authority "the most useless and unnecessary of all
the alphabetical joy-rides." More creatively, in a June article in *The
Financial World,* referring to TVA taking over his markets and local
systems, he compared it to "the Cuckoo Bird [which] is noted for the
fact that it never builds a nest of its own, it lays its eggs in the nests of
other birds."[41]

He also took the fight directly to the president, though in decidedly
less inflammatory language. After a meeting with Roosevelt in May, he
followed up with a letter about TVA's impact, claiming, "The present
status is practically one of open warfare." He argued that the risk of
competition from TVA was preventing his southern companies from
refinancing their debt at the prevailing low interest rates. His northern
companies had reduced their rates to 3.5 percent, but the southern
companies were still paying 5 percent. He warned the president that a
"more comprehensive lawsuit" would "probably . . . be necessary," but he
also asked him to take the lead in achieving a mutually acceptable agreement: "The utilities in that district naturally feel that they are fighting
for their lives . . . . I feel the problems should be settled by agreement
and I am of the opinion that you, and you alone, are the one person who
has the power to bring such a settlement about."[42]

Lilienthal was creative in looking for solutions. That same month
he had proposed to Willkie the idea of C&S and TVA pooling some
of the power they generated and selling it to all buyers at the same
price, but the idea went nowhere. Willkie opposed it, according to
Lilienthal, because it would still allow TVA to sell power directly to
municipal utilities. Willkie offered a counterproposal, that TVA sell
power only within a "ceded area," roughly the Tennessee Valley within
the state of Tennessee, and that power be distributed outside this
area only through Willkie's companies. Lilienthal felt he could not
agree to this because the TVA Act required the agency to give preference to public bodies, which could not be done if C&S controlled
all distribution outside the "ceded area."[43]

But a settlement seemed out of reach because both Willkie and
Lilienthal had drawn lines in the sand. Willkie would not agree to
any direct competition with TVA because, in his view, its rates were

unfairly subsidized, and Lilienthal was determined to broaden such competition because, in his view, the monopoly status of the utilities protected their unduly high rates and inflated valuations.[44]

Eight days after Willkie sent his letter to the president, he went public with his litigation strategy. Nineteen utilities, led by C&S subsidiary TEPCO, filed another major lawsuit against TVA, a full frontal assault on its constitutionality. Private utility appeals for injunctions against municipal utilities or PWA grants and loans followed in most of the cities in the region. The suit, *Tennessee Electric Power Co. et al v. TVA*, which came to be known as "the TEPCO case," built on Justice McReynolds' dissent in the *Ashwander* decision that alleged power production was the principal aim of TVA and that navigation and flood control were merely a cover to make it constitutional.[45]

In the public relations part of Willkie's strategy, C&S companies ran a massive publicity campaign generating letters to Congress and full-page ads in newspapers throughout the South, seeking to undercut support for TVA and to discourage towns and cities from switching to TVA power when the January 4 agreement expired. They also withdrew all advertising from pro-public power newspapers, leading to the bankruptcy of the *Chattanooga News*. Meanwhile, Alabama Power began building a transmission line across northern Alabama in order to hem in TVA. Lilienthal considered the attack a violation of his standstill agreement with Willkie, and the prospects for compromise seemed remote.[46]

TVA's Norris Dam began producing power on August 1, 1936, six months ahead of schedule. (*Courtesy of Franklin D. Roosevelt Library.*)

On August 1, 1936, the Norris Dam began producing power, six months ahead of schedule. The Joe Wheeler Dam, transferred to TVA by Alabama Power in the wake of the *Ashwander* decision, was also approaching completion, and four others were being built. The construction of transmission lines had moved quickly, too, with thirteen hundred miles of lines almost completed, ready to carry power to Memphis, most of Tennessee, and several towns in surrounding states that were building distribution systems.[47]

The speed with which the system was being constructed and its widespread acceptance in the region were due not only to the large sums of money poured into building the system, but also to its "grass-roots" policy. According to historian William Leuchtenberg, "TVA raised the principle of local participation to a fine art." Wherever possible, local agencies were involved in the execution of its program. Some aspects of the grass-roots system, though, were far from optimal. Working through the land-grant colleges, with their emphasis on chemicals and machinery, meant that TVA's agricultural programs tended to provide less help to farmers and tenants with little money to spare, a group that included most African-Americans. Conforming to regional norms also meant accepting Jim Crow. TVA's model town of Norris, for example, initially built to house construction workers for Norris Dam, allowed only white residents.[48]

Many people were also forced off their land. The purchase of land for the Norris Dam and reservoir displaced more than three thousand largely impoverished rural families, many of whom had lived in their isolated, tightly knit communities for generations.[49] While about 69 percent of those displaced were owners and received compensation, the amount they were paid was rarely sufficient to buy a comparable replacement farm. Options to purchase were slim in the immediate area, with few vacant houses and so much land taken out of circulation. Displaced cash tenants or sharecroppers received only temporary financial assistance to move.[50]

A debate took place within TVA between those who favored minimal land acquisition and those who favored "overpurchase"—the acquisition of land beyond the normal level of reservoirs to advance the goals of conservation, afforestation, and retirement of marginal land. Overpurchase prevailed in the early years, meaning more dispossession of farmers, but after 1941 only "flowage easements" were acquired, giving the agency control during periods of periodic flooding but allowing farms to exist and function in normal times.[51]

Reservoir clearance for Wheeler Dam, 1935. During the 1930s, TVA acquired and cleared land beyond the expected normal levels of reservoirs, displacing more farmers than necessary. (*TVA photo K-1094, courtesy of National Archives - Atlanta.*)

Some dams were also built higher than necessary for power production or navigation, resulting in larger reservoirs and more displacement of farmers. A major reason for the extra water storage was to protect Chattanooga from flooding. Critics later argued that flood plain zoning in Chattanooga would have been more cost effective, and that decisions made by elected officials rather than the unelected TVA board would have been less likely to "flood Peter to save Paul."[52]

The rapid progress in construction in 1936 increased the pressure on Willkie, and Lilienthal wasn't about to relieve it. As soon as Norris Dam started producing power on August 1, he sent an official notification to Willkie that their January 4, 1934, agreement would expire in ninety days. As if to rub it in, the TVA board, over Arthur Morgan's objection, passed a resolution on August 4 that "in future contracts the Authority will not agree to territorial restrictions on the sale of Tennessee Valley Authority power to public agencies." If

Willkie's legal attack on TVA ultimately failed, the removal of the constraints in the January 4 contract would likely spell doom for TEPCO and weaken other C&S companies in the region. But Willkie was to be offered a temporary truce from an unlikely source, President Roosevelt.[53]

Roosevelt invited Willkie to the White House on August 25. Willkie brought along the president of Georgia Power, Preston Arkwright, who had won the president's friendship by buying and refurbishing the inefficient municipal utility at Warm Springs ten years earlier. Willkie told Roosevelt that the no-compete agreement would expire on November 3, adding a couple of days to the actual deadline in order to focus the president's attention. The tactic worked. Roosevelt responded, "That is election day," and added, "but I think the contract should be continued just as it is." Willkie said he agreed but that Lilienthal would not. "That is nonsense," Roosevelt replied. "I will see to it that it is done."[54]

Roosevelt had something of a trick up his sleeve. He raised with Willkie an alternative approach to selling TVA power that might resolve the dispute. He had asked Alexander Sachs, a former planner for the National Recovery Administration and the head of Lehman Corporation, an investment firm with an interest in utilities, to develop an idea for the pooling of public and private power similar to Lilienthal's earlier pooling proposal. Instead of competing with each other, TVA and the private companies would sell their power into a common pool, with the cheapest power generated and dispatched first. That was already done among the southern C&S companies and other contiguous holding companies. Rates would be uniform for all customers, and each producer would benefit by having to own less reserve production capacity for emergencies.[55]

Roosevelt often said different things to different people, and it isn't clear whether he wanted a compromise or just wanted to get past the election. In either case, this suggestion appeared like an olive branch, and both sides had reason to consider a compromise. With the Supreme Court's increasingly hostile attitude, Roosevelt and Lilienthal feared the utilities' constitutional challenge, and the industry wanted an end to TVA's territorial expansion and to government grants and loans for building municipal distribution systems.

At the end of September Roosevelt convened a high-level conference on the pool concept that included Willkie, GE Chairman Owen
Young, senior partner Thomas Lamont of J. P. Morgan & Co., and
the presidents of Hartford Electric Light and Georgia Power. Administration representatives included Chairman Arthur Morgan and
Lilienthal of TVA; Chairman McNinch and Vice Chairman Basil
Manly of the Federal Power Commission; Morris Cooke of the REA;
Louis Wehle, nephew of Justice Brandeis and an expert on corporation
law; and Sachs. The prominence of the participants suggested a serious
effort to compromise, and the stock of C&S rose 15 percent on the
announcement of the meeting. Wehle wrote that the president "fully
intends to pursue [pooling] for the purpose of stabilizing conditions
on a fair basis."[56]

Federal Power Commission Chairman Frank McNinch (l), C&S President Wendell
Willkie (c), and presidential advisor Alexander Sachs leave the White House after
meeting on Sachs's power pool proposal. (*Library of Congress.*)

The *New York Times* reported that Willkie called Roosevelt's
convening of the conference "an act of political statesmanship" and
said that only "the die-hards on either side" could cause "cooperation
between private utility interests and the TVA" to fail. But unlike
Willkie, the *Times* noted, "most utility men continue to express

considerable doubt." Willkie clipped and sent the story to Roosevelt.[57]

Lilienthal's private comments indicated that the businessmen's doubts might have been justified. He supported the overture on pooling, he told its critics on the public power side, largely because of the potential to embarrass the utilities when they rejected it. To Senator Robert La Follette Jr., who had expressed alarm, he wrote, "The companies won't accept this proposal now, of course, but it seemed to me important to put them on the record on this really sensible proposal."[58]

Arthur Morgan again took a position more in line with Willkie than with Lilienthal. He saw the pool proposal as a way to deal fairly with Willkie and to eliminate the policy disputes between himself and Lilienthal. But he let his enthusiasm for a truce override his judgment. With the assistance of the former chief engineer of Insull's Middle West Utilities, he prepared a memo and circulated it to the private sector conferees and to the press before the meeting. A TVA consultant complained, "Dr. Morgan, throughout the memorandum, has well stated the position of the Commonwealth and Southern Corporation."[59]

Lilienthal was appalled, and he wrote to Norris that Morgan had listed concessions he was ready to make, even to urge, before the negotiations even got started. Norris immediately wrote to Roosevelt that he was convinced, "against my will," that Morgan had "gone over to the enemy," and Morgan's memo provoked Lilienthal into complete opposition to the pooling proposal. Lilienthal also had doubts about Sachs and Wehle, who were inexperienced in the power wars and, in his opinion, underestimated the need to protect gains already made in the fight against C&S. Wehle, who had known neither Morgan nor Lilienthal before these discussions, came to view Morgan as ineffective, with "the intense yet diffident manner of an introvert, tending to become inarticulate in man-to-man controversy." Lilienthal, on the other hand, struck him as having "a controlled, driving, effective intensity.[60]

The conference was marked by open hostility. Wehle wrote, "Weapons did not seem to have been left outside." After Roosevelt suggested that cooperation between public and private power in many

European countries could serve as a model, the discussion degenerated into a rehash of Willkie's complaints about the yardstick and
TVA "stealing" his customers followed by Lilienthal's vigorous rebut-
tals. As for the immediate matter of the expiration of the January 4
contract, Lilienthal recommended a one-month extension with no
reference to limits on territorial expansion. Willkie suggested six
months with the same territorial restrictions as before. Roosevelt
directed that the agencies involved should continue with engineering
studies about pooling, a step that would push the controversial issue
past the November election. He also asked Wehle to work out the
details of the terms and duration of the contract extension with
Lilienthal and Willkie.[61]

Much to Roosevelt's relief, he and the Democratic Party scored an
enormous victory on election day. After following the returns by telephone and teletype in his mother's dining room at Hyde Park, the
"laughing and happy" president, leaning on his son's arm, told a crowd
of celebrating supporters on the front lawn, "It looks as though this
sweep has carried every single section of the country."[62] The turnout
was exceptionally high, and he won 46 of 48 states, defeating Governor
Alf Landon of Kansas with the highest popular and electoral vote
totals since President James Monroe ran virtually unopposed in 1820.
Democrats won overwhelming majorities in Congress and reduced
the Republicans to seven governorships.

Liberals were ecstatic. Reporter and columnist Heywood Broun
claimed the returns "suggest that the people of America want the
President to proceed along progressive or liberal lines." Political writer
Max Lerner wrote, "Roosevelt is now, as never before, a colossus
bestriding the American world."[63] *Fortune*, however, drew a less
ideological conclusion. Arguing that Roosevelt's actions were based
more on preserving capitalism than on promoting socialism, the
magazine concluded, "Prosperity is still the best election argument."[64]
Such post-election optimism on the part of business would prove in
the coming year to be as unfounded as Roosevelt's worries before the
election.

After a week of intense negotiations moderated by Wehle, Willkie
and Lilienthal signed a three-month contract extension with no

agreement on territory except one reluctant concession by Lilienthal, at Roosevelt's direction. TVA was to stay out of TEPCO's home base of Chattanooga, despite the city's signed contract with TVA. At Lilienthal's insistence there was also no explicit agreement to a pause in Public Works Administration grants and loans, which Wehle and Morgan had proposed.

The skepticism of many utilities about Roosevelt's motivation seemed justified when Lilienthal and Ickes signaled a lack of interest in improving the atmosphere for future compromise. On November 10, the day the contract extension was announced, the Public Works Administration allotted $3 million to Memphis for a new power system to be connected with a TVA transmission line.[65]

While Roosevelt seemed to have moved in Willkie's direction, he moved back once the election was over. Norris was worried about the continuing negotiations over the power pool and wrote to Roosevelt ten days after the election that C&S was "an outfit who would destroy you in a minute if it had the power." He urged him "not [to] give up the advantage this national victory has given us in this power fight . . . for God's sake, do not give our laurels of victory to those whom we have defeated." Roosevelt replied, "I agree with you. Don't worry."[66]

The election seemed to have set Willkie back, but in December a court gave him what he could not achieve in negotiations. Judge John J. Gore of the U.S. district court in Tennessee issued a sweeping injunction in the TEPCO case that blocked TVA from extending its territory for six months. Although the request for the injunction had been filed before the October negotiations, Lilienthal told Roosevelt he thought it was a breach of faith and recommended termination of the power pool discussions. Over the objections of Wehle and Sachs, the president concurred. *Business Week* reported, "Hopes for peace between utilities and the government in the Tennessee Valley were all but crushed this week," and "many say a fight to the finish in the courts is the industry's only salvation." Congressman Rankin proposed to impeach Judge Gore.[67]

Willkie took Roosevelt's decision as confirmation that the pool proposal had been politically motivated all along. Historian Thomas K. McCraw disagreed, arguing that the president pulled the plug because the injunction "ruined the government's negotiating position." Whichever was the truth, Willkie's favorable statement about Roosevelt's statesmanship in the White House conference marked the last time in the long struggle over the future of the industry that Willkie took a position different from that of most other utility leaders.[68]

With progress being made on many fronts of the push for public power, Willkie and his industry brethren looked to be winning isolated battles while losing the war. The REA in particular was making great strides. That was in part due to innovations that were bringing the costs of line construction down considerably. Simpler, sturdier rural distribution lines and the introduction of competitive bidding for construction led to costs under $900 per mile, compared to private costs of $1,500 to $2,000. The new lines relied on stronger conductors, lighter construction materials, mass production methods, smaller transformers, greater distance between poles, and the absence of cross arms. All of these factors made transmission to rural areas with lower customer density more cost-effective. Morris Cooke took full advantage of the opportunity. While some large suppliers of poles and wire refused to sell to co-ops to preserve their relationships with private utilities, Cooke found others that were happy for the business.[69]

Cooke was also masterful in finding ways to speed the formation of co-ops. He had his staff draft a model state law that eased the typical legal obstacles, and the REA began to win almost all its cases in the courts. The REA also found ways to fight back on the high wholesale rates that private companies charged co-ops. In areas where the rates were unreasonably high, the agency offered loans to co-ops to build their own small power plants. Often just the possibility that a co-op might do so caused the private utility to offer a lower rate. So effective was the threat that in its first five years, the REA had to actually finance plants for only four percent of its borrowers.[70]

With momentum building, by 1937 the REA was in the field actively supporting applicants. One of the outreach activities was the "farm equipment tour," known colloquially as "the REA circus." In some places, organizers attempting to set up a cooperative were not able to find enough members. In others, they just weren't able to project sufficient demand for electricity. And so the REA sometimes brought in a caravan with several tents. Manufacturers demonstrated equipment for grinding, lifting, pumping, heating, and refrigeration, while home economists gave talks on electric cooking and deep freezing. The agency also negotiated with manufacturers for lower priced appliances, sometimes offered in combinations at even lower prices, and in some instances they negotiated a fixed price with qualified wiring contractors in an area and divided the business among them. This reduced the cost of wiring farms by as much as 35 percent.[71]

Early farm use of electricity indoors mirrored that of city dwellers. After electric lights, a radio and an iron were typically the first household purchases, and washing machines and vacuum cleaners usually followed. In addition, electric pumps were a high priority on the farm, where they made indoor plumbing possible and replaced hand pumping of water for livestock. The coming of electricity lengthened the day, saved labor, and improved health. Within three years of the founding of the pioneering Alcorn County Electric Co-op in Mississippi, average monthly electricity consumption by its member-owners rose 180 percent as rates fell by two-thirds.[72]

Cooperatives usually held a ceremony when they were first "energized." Elected officials were eager to be associated with the events, which often included the burial of a kerosene lamp in a mock funeral. Publicity for the events frequently included photos of workers setting poles or stringing wires, a powerful message at a time of high unemployment.[73]

Cooke's policy had been that REA would not go into a territory where a private company had set up its poles. But the length of time between establishing a cooperative and constructing its lines sometimes made it unclear whether a utility was deliberately trying to destroy a cooperative or just happened to set poles in its likely territory. In January 1937, Cooke wrote to Groesbeck about one of Bond and Share's subsidiaries in North Carolina that had started building lines after the farmers had formed their cooperative and applied for an REA loan. He could not prove hostile intent without examining the company's records. "But I would be falling down on my job," he wrote, "if

I did not from time to time remind you higher ups what is going on in certain areas . . . ."[74]

In February 1937, Cooke resigned. He pleaded poor health, but he told a friend, "The thing has become routine . . . . I feel the challenge is gone." He had prepared the ground well, and the pace of rural electrification would continue to accelerate under his successor. But in the larger arena, legal challenges to TVA and the Holding Company Act still loomed large. Flush from his election triumph, Roosevelt decided to make a bold move to turn the fight in his favor. He would come to regret it.[75]

CHAPTER 8

POWER LOSS

The overwhelming Democratic victory in the 1936 election brought the United States closer to one-party government than it had been at any time since Reconstruction, and Roosevelt had received a resounding mandate to push ahead with his New Deal initiatives in his second term. He thus moved quickly to resolve the dispute over how to distribute the large quantities of power that would soon be generated by the Bonneville and Grand Coulee dams.

In January, General Edward Markham, head of the Army Corps of Engineers, wrote Roosevelt to warn that the Bonneville Dam was close to completion and the distribution issue had to be settled soon. With renewed confidence from the landslide, Roosevelt reconstituted the Committee on National Power Policy, chaired again by Ickes, and gave them only two weeks to develop legislation that included a regional framework and postage-stamp rates—"a pretty tall order," thought Ickes. Reflecting the view of public power advocates that the Corps of Engineers was too closely aligned with private utilities, Ickes insisted that a new civilian government agency should control generation, build transmission lines, and set rates. Though the strongest public power advocates on the committee preferred a TVA-like independent government structure, they went along with the proposal for a more typical government agency because they understood this to be a temporary arrangement for Bonneville alone. With Secretary Ickes chairing the committee, it was no surprise that their legislation proposed to house the new agency in the Interior Department rather than in the War Department, as Senator McNary's bill provided, or in a new Department of Conservation that was being discussed.[1]

Roosevelt left little doubt that he also favored the TVA model as the long-term solution when he proposed to some members of the committee that the country be divided into eight districts, each with an organization that could develop and market hydroelectric power as well as manage other aspects of river valley development such as reforestation, soil conservation, and flood control. The organizations would be housed in the proposed new Department of Conservation, though, giving them less independence than TVA. He said he had enlisted the support of Senator Norris and wanted the committee to draft legislation, which would become known as the "Seven Little TVAs" bill. On February 5, Norris publicly proposed what the *Washington Star* called "enough TVAs to cover the entire country."[2]

The fate of that ambitious vision for national public power and planning, like other Roosevelt initiatives, was to be influenced by a miscalculation that seriously undermined the momentum of the New Deal. He wanted to address the opposition of the courts to New Deal initiatives, with particular focus on the Supreme Court, and he decided to test just how strong his hand was with a brash attempt to turn the Court in his favor.

For at least two years he had been considering ways to deal with the unsympathetic Court. These included radical ideas for constitutional amendments, such as to nullify the Court's power of judicial review of legislation and to give Congress the right to override Court decisions. He had ducked questions about his intentions during the campaign, but he began to make his determination clear immediately after the election. He raised his concerns about Court obstructionism at the next cabinet meeting, joking that he expected McReynolds to still be on the Court at the age of a hundred and five. In his January 6 State of the Union address, best known for the ringing phrase, "I see one-third of a nation ill-housed, ill-clad, ill-nourished," he also alluded to the Court. "There is little fault to be found with the Constitution

.... Rightly considered, it can be used as an instrument of progress, and not as a device for prevention of action." None of the justices attended the address, and he noticed. Reflecting on the snub, he wrote to a friend, "I have received some intimation that they at least read the remarks that pertained to them. I hope so!"[3]

Facing a sea of black umbrellas in the pouring rain at his inauguration two weeks later, the president gave certain words extra emphasis as he repeated the oath of office after Chief Justice Hughes: "I do solemnly swear that I will . . . *preserve* . . . *protect* . . . *and defend* the *Constitution* of the United States. *So help me God!*" In his inaugural address, with Hughes sitting a few feet away, he hinted again that he believed the Court was thwarting the democratic process. "The essential democracy of our Nation and the safety of our people depend . . . upon lodging [power] with those whom the people can change or continue at stated intervals . . . . The Constitution of 1789 did not make our democracy impotent." A few days later Ickes noted in his diary that the president had to rein in the Court or face "judicial tyranny."[4]

On February 2, at the annual White House dinner honoring the Supreme Court, an undercurrent of tension ran beneath the surface conviviality. In a radio broadcast the previous night Republican Senator William Borah had sharply criticized those who attacked the Court. During the dinner, Borah noticed the president in a friendly conversation with two of the justices and commented, "That reminds me of the Roman Emperor who looked around his dinner table and began to laugh when he thought how many of those heads would be rolling on the morrow." Only a few insiders, though, knew about the plan Roosevelt had conceived.[5]

Three days later the president offered his audacious legislation. He had relied primarily on his attorney general, Homer Cummings, in preparing the bill, and he briefed the rest of his cabinet and key Congressional leaders just two hours before his message was delivered to Congress. The bill would allow him to appoint a new federal judge, up to a total of six on the Supreme Court and two on any lower court, for every sitting judge who failed to retire within six months of turning seventy.[6]

The idea had its origin in 1913, when Woodrow Wilson's attorney general criticized judges "who have remained on the bench long beyond the time that they are able to adequately discharge their duties." He proposed legislation providing that whenever a judge, other than a justice of the Supreme Court, reached the age of 70, the president could appoint a younger judge to join the elder on the court. Nothing came of the suggestion then, and a year later the attorney general, James McReynolds, was appointed to the Supreme Court, where he still sat at age 74. Although Roosevelt did not publicly attribute the idea to him, he and his advisers took delight in the irony.[7]

The average age of the nine Supreme Court justices in 1937 was the oldest in history, with six over age 70; under his plan, if none retired, Roosevelt would be able to appoint six new justices. A recent hard-hitting bestseller, *The Nine Old Men*, called the justices "aloof from all reality."[8] Roosevelt hoped to take advantage of this perception and couched his proposal in terms of efficiency, workload, and the need for new blood. But that was a thin disguise. The clear purpose of the bill was to shift the balance of the Court in favor of his agenda.

His Court-reform plan—to critics it was always the "Court-packing scheme"—dominated the news throughout the late winter and spring. Opposition from Congressional Republicans was to be expected, but many Democrats withheld their support or gave it only tepidly. Heading back to the Capitol after Roosevelt's last-minute briefing of Democratic leaders, Hatton Summers of Texas, chairman of the House Judiciary Committee, said to his colleagues, "Boys, here's where I cash in my chips." As the president's message was being read to the Senate a couple of hours later, Vice President Garner stood in the doorway of the cloakroom holding his nose and making a thumbs-down gesture.[9]

The press had a field day. Walter Lippmann called it "a bloodless coup d'état," and surveys indicated that more than two-thirds of the newspapers that had supported Roosevelt in the 1936 election opposed the bill. But no one underestimated Roosevelt's power. The *New York Times* predicted that the bill "will be moved steadily to passage," and the *Baltimore Sun* believed "the President happens to have too much power for the opposition to overcome."[10]

Majority Leader Joseph Robinson of Arkansas was widely believed to have been promised Roosevelt's first Court nomination. Although more conservative than many in his caucus, he loyally if unenthusiastically led the fight for the bill. Many in Congress waited to express their views until the public turned decisively one way or the other. Public opinion polling was in its infancy, and George Gallup reported shortly after the bill was introduced that 51 percent of the people opposed it.[11]

The battle in Congress was uphill, thanks in part to the opposition of Roosevelt's Republican allies on public power, George Norris and Hiram Johnson. Even more damaging, he lost the progressive Democrat Burt Wheeler, who had been his first prominent endorser for the presidency and had championed the fight for the Holding Company Act.[12] As Robert La Follette's running mate on the Progressive Party ticket in 1924, Wheeler had sought a Congressional veto over Court decisions in 1924. But he had been disappointed that Franklin Roosevelt had not picked him for vice president, felt he was aggrandizing the power of the presidency at the expense of Congress, and saw a betrayal of progressive views and creeping conservatism in every legislative compromise the president made. Before he announced his opposition publicly, he berated Roosevelt aide Thomas Corcoran at a private lunch, slamming his fist on the table and insisting the bill would not pass. Saying that Roosevelt was "on the way to destroy" his early liberal supporters, he added, "He's made the mistake we've been waiting for a long time—and this is our chance to cut him down to size." A shaken Corcoran told Roosevelt, "From now on this isn't a legislative fight about the Court; this is a baron's revolt against you."[13]

Wheeler soon joined a diverse group of senators opposed to the bill at the home of Maryland Democratic Senator Millard Tydings. Sensing that their cause would be more successful if led by a progressive Democrat, they selected Wheeler as their leader. But Roosevelt wasn't about to back down. When Vice President Garner brought a delegation of Congressional Democrats to the White House to urge him to accept two or three new justices instead of six, he rebuffed them.[14]

On March 3, 1937, Eleanor Roosevelt wrote to their daughter, Anna, "Pa is both nervous and tired. The court hue and cry has got under his skin."[15] The next evening, after a month of silence, Roosevelt restored his own energy with a rousing speech at a Democratic fund-raising dinner at Washington's Mayflower Hotel. He hearkened back to his first inauguration on March 4 four years earlier, a day "that represented the death of one era and the birth of another." Reminding the Democratic faithful that the Court had created "doubts and difficulties for almost everything for which we have promised to fight," he added, "I defy anyone to read the opinions in the TVA case . . . and tell us exactly what we can do as a National Government . . . to control flood and drought and generate cheap power with any reasonable certainty that what we do will not be nullified as unconstitutional." Warning that he could only hope for the future of democracy in America, he compared the three branches of government to a three-horse team plowing a field "where the going is heavy." Vocally underlining and spacing the key words as he rhythmically bobbed his head, he insisted, "If the team of three pull as one, the *field . . . will . . . be . . . plowed*. If one horse lies down in the traces or plunges off in another direction, the *field . . . will . . . not . . . be . . . plowed*."[16]

On March 8, he delivered his first post-election "fireside chat," his preferred way of explaining important policies or decisions, addressing the public directly and in simple terms. At 10:30 in the evening, following Fred Astaire on the NBC Red network and a young Judy Garland on CBS, he settled into parlors all over America for a relaxed conversation.[17] He reminded the people about his fireside chat on the banking crisis four years earlier and of the recovery that had begun. "We are only part-way through," he asserted. "The courts, however, have cast doubts on the ability of the elected Congress to protect us against catastrophe." He argued not that his bill would improve the efficiency of the Court but, more credibly, that it "will provide a reinvigorated, liberal-minded judiciary" and "federal courts willing to enforce the Constitution as written." A week later he headed to Warm Springs, with Congressional mail counts indicating that the fireside chat had caused a spike in support for the bill.[18]

Senator Wheeler asked Chief Justice Hughes to enter the fray. Hughes wrote a narrowly framed letter refuting with detailed statistics the charge that the Court was behind in its work. Wheeler read the letter at a March 22 Senate Judiciary Committee hearing then segued into an attack on Roosevelt's plan, associating Hughes by implication with the opposition. He did not attack Roosevelt personally but rather blamed the staff who had given him bad advice.[19]

Hughes delivered another blow to the bill on March 29 when he read from the bench a 5-4 decision upholding a state minimum wage law that Roosevelt supported. Justice Owen J. Roberts, who had voted with the conservative Four Horsemen in many cases striking down New Deal legislation, here voted against them. Although the confidential vote had been taken in January, when Roosevelt had only been hinting at his plans, his switch was perceived by many to be an effort to undercut the image of an unyielding, anti-New Deal Court.[20]

As the impact of his fireside chat faded, it became increasingly clear that the president had misjudged support he could muster for the bill. Key Democratic leaders had hardened in their opposition, but he was unyielding. At the beginning of April, when Senator Hugo Black reported on the opposition's determination, including refusal to schedule early hearings, he responded, "We'll smoke 'em out. If delay helps them, we must press for an early vote."[21]

Two more important decisions, this time in cases directly challenging New Deal legislation, followed the minimum wage decision. The Court upheld the Wagner Labor Relations Act in April and the Social Security Act in May. Historian Alan Brinkley argues that the Court's change in course was "almost certainly" in response to the bill's introduction. After these decisions, Wheeler declared, "The Court bill is dead." Democratic Senator James Byrnes of South Carolina asked in private, "Why run for a train after you've caught it?" Majority Leader Robinson sent word to the White House: "If the President wants a compromise I can get him a couple of extra justices tomorrow. What he ought to do is say he's won . . . and wind the whole business up."[22]

In early April, Roosevelt had told Ickes that he thought Garner's "defeatist attitude" was the bill's chief problem. The vice president reinforced that impression when he left for Texas on June 13 to go fishing, the first time in his thirty-five years in Washington he had left town while Congress was in session. "He is almost in open revolt," complained Ickes. But Garner was far from the only problem. Public opinion had shifted by June, with Gallup polling showing 59 percent opposed to the bill. The president's standing with Congress was at its lowest ebb, his favorability rating had dropped from 65 to 60 percent, and White House vote counters continued to bring discouraging reports back from the Senate.[23]

A day after Garner left town a report from the Senate Judiciary Committee, which weeks earlier had voted 10-8 to report the bill with a recommendation against passage, described it in stunningly vituperative language as "a needless, futile, and utterly dangerous abandonment of constitutional principle . . . . without precedent and without justification . . . . [that] would subjugate the courts to the will of Congress and the President . . . ." Arthur Krock of the *Times* considered the report's attack on Roosevelt, which was signed by seven Democrats, as an effort to seize control of the party rather than to defeat the bill.[24]

Roosevelt already knew he had another opportunity to declare victory. In mid-May, Justice Willis Van Devanter had announced that he would retire at the end of the current term. His decision was apparently motivated by Roosevelt's signing in May of a relatively non-controversial bill that reversed a 1932 cut in the justices' pensions. With the opportunity to appoint a new justice, and with the Court not having struck down a single New Deal law in its 1936-37 term, Roosevelt could have declared victory and withdrawn his proposal. But in this case the supreme confidence that had served him well all his life led him astray, and he fought on.

When the news reached the Capitol of Van Devanter's planned retirement, senators clustered around Robinson to congratulate him on his anticipated nomination to the Court. His popularity was a major factor in keeping the emerging conservative coalition at bay. He diligently continued to lead the fight for the bill, and he struggled to find a compromise when it was clear one would be necessary. But any slim hope of salvaging the plan died in July when he succumbed to a heart attack two weeks into the contentious Senate debate. The next day the bill's opponents announced that they had the votes to send the bill back to committee. Roosevelt's press office indicated that he was not giving in, and four first-term senators visited him at the White House to beseech him not to tear the party apart. When he lectured them in return, one said, "Mr. President, it's the hardest thing in the world to tell you something you don't want to hear."[25]

When later in July Roosevelt sent the vice president to the Capitol to see whether there was still a chance for any kind of compromise, Garner returned and asked if he wanted the news "with the bark on or the bark off?" Roosevelt wanted it straight, and Garner complied. "You are beat," he declared. "You haven't got the votes."[26] In a minor face-saving gesture toward the president, the Senate voted not on the bill itself but on a motion to send it back to committee, which it did, 70–20. Justice Roberts' unexpected vote in March, which had undercut the case for change, came to be known, in a major oversimplification, as "the switch in time that saved nine."[27]

At his weekly press conference the next morning, Roosevelt was his usual jovial self, showing little disappointment and implying that his purpose in proposing the bill had been to influence the Court's decisions. He noted the favorable decisions handed down after February 5 and compared them with the anti-New Deal decisions handed down before, claiming that he had achieved his goal. But with his staff his anger showed. Postmaster General and Democratic Party Chairman James Farley recorded in his diary, "He isn't going to take his defeat lying down .... He has been double-crossed ... by people who should have been loyal supporters."[28]

In August Roosevelt signed a gutted bill, without the central provision allowing for new judges, and when Van Devanter retired at the end of the Court term, the president nominated Senator Hugo Black to the seat. Despite widespread opposition—the *Washington Post* cited Black's "lack of training . . . and extreme partisanship"—the Senate followed its longstanding custom of courtesy to a colleague and confirmed him 63 to 16 five days later, before evidence of his former Ku Klux Klan membership surfaced. Black took his seat in October and, in an irony that was not lost on critics of Roosevelt's public rationale for his bill, served until 1971, when he resigned eight days before his death at the age of eighty-five.[29]

In another irony, one of the surviving provisions in the decimated court reform bill proved critical in the fight for TVA. In May, during the height of the debate, a circuit court had voided Judge Gore's

December injunction in the TEPCO case and remanded it to the district court for trial. TVA supporters, pessimistic about the outcome of a trial presided over by Gore, inserted in the revised Court-reform bill a requirement that a three-judge panel would be required to hear applications for injunctive relief in constitutional cases. When the new trial began in Chattanooga in November, Gore was just one member of the panel.[30]

As the Court controversy had heated up, a second issue that would badly bruise Roosevelt in 1937 unfolded over responsibility for what became known as "the recession within the Depression" or, to New Deal opponents, "the Roosevelt recession."[31] This conflict would lead to a vitriolic public debate about monopolistic business practices and New Deal interference with private business that would bring Wendell Willkie and his criticism of the TVA to more prominent national attention.

The improving economy had been Roosevelt's greatest political asset. Average annual unemployment had dropped from 24.9 percent in 1933 to 14.3 percent in 1937, and production and wages had reached levels not seen since the 1929 Crash. But the fear of inflation and the absence of significant new private investment led to renewed calls to reduce the federal deficit.[32]

The most influential advocate of this argument was Treasury Secretary Henry Morgenthau. He had supported deficit spending during the first few years of the administration because of the critical need to help the unemployed and shore up the fragile economy, but by late 1936 he believed a balanced budget would increase business confidence and stimulate investment. Using an incredibly insensitive metaphor, given the person he was trying to persuade, he said it was time to "throw away the crutches" and see if the economy "could stand on its own two feet." Whatever Roosevelt thought of the image, if he was even aware of it, in an April 1937 message to Congress he called for "eliminating or deferring all expenditures not absolutely necessary" and "[eliminating] this deficit during the coming fiscal year."[33]

The budget-cutting effort magnified the impact of a technical decision by the Treasury relating to gold supplies and complementary decisions by the Federal Reserve. European investors had become nervous about the stability of their governments during Roosevelt's first term, and gold flows to the United States had increased. The early result was a highly expansionary monetary policy that contributed greatly to the recovery. But the Treasury had reversed this policy in December 1936, "sterilizing" new gold supplies by sequestering them in a special account where they would not increase the money supply. The Federal Reserve had further tightened the money supply by increasing the reserve requirements for banks by 50 percent in late 1936 and by another third in early 1937. The result was a dramatic monetary shock, and unemployment began to rise.[34]

Roosevelt's staff disagreed on how to respond. Jesse Jones, the Hoover holdover who chaired the Reconstruction Finance Corporation, and Donald Richberg, former General Counsel of the National Recovery Administration and Chairman of the National Industrial Recovery Board, joined Morgenthau in supporting more pro-business and conservative fiscal policies. The president's more progressive advisers, including Corcoran, Cohen, Ickes, and Harry Hopkins, by now the head of the Works Progress Administration, sought more government planning and social programs. But Roosevelt was aware of a Gallup poll showing that 63 percent of the public largely sided with the deficit hawks and opposed a big program of deficit spending.[35]

In a reaction common to leaders before and since, he blamed his enemies for the downturn. He told his cabinet on October 8, as the stock market was declining from its August peak, "The present situation is the result of a concerted effort by big business and concentrated wealth to drive the market down just to create a situation unfavorable to me."[36] Although he vacillated over the deficit reduction decision, he avoided public attacks on business. He had called Congress into special session in mid-November to deal with legislation deferred during the Court fight, and he told them that the first step toward halting the recession should be increasing investment of private capital. But he encouraged the progressives in the administration to undertake a campaign to blame business leaders for the recession. The key speakers were Ickes and Assistant Attorney General Robert H. Jackson, a brilliant orator who was considered a possible future nominee for governor of New York. In the last week of December, Jackson aggressively attacked business in a nationwide radio speech: "By profiteering, monopolists and those so near monopoly as to control their prices have simply priced themselves into a slump." Several nights later both Ickes and Jackson made widely covered speeches on the concentration of wealth in America.[37]

The producer of a popular weekly public affairs program, "America's Town Meeting of the Air," noted the widespread interest and invited Jackson to debate Willkie on the evening of January 6, 1938. Four million households tuned in for Willkie's first national radio broadcast—and even some early New Dealers thought he triumphed. Raymond Moley, a member of the Brain Trust during the 1932 campaign and an early speechwriter, said that Jackson and Willkie were evenly matched in their prepared remarks, but "in the rough-and-tumble that followed," the former debating champion and courtroom lawyer "utterly outclassed" Jackson. General Hugh Johnson, the first head of the National Recovery Administration, who had moved to the right, was equally critical, saying that Willkie had made "a perfect monkey" of Jackson.[38]

Willkie's prepared speeches were rarely as effective as his extemporaneous comments. At the end of February, before the Economic Club of Detroit, he used the example of utilities to castigate the New Deal's treatment of business: "I know very well what happens to those individuals who defend their causes against government attack . . . . You may be called an economic royalist. You may be chastised in official speeches . . . . You may have your name dragged into political investigations . . . . You may suffer and your families may suffer by having your reputation smeared." Willkie biographer Joseph Barnes called his language "full-blown, sounding unhappily like what the New Deal wanted the public to believe economic royalists sounded like."[39]

Willkie and the utilities did not have a monopoly on sharp edges. The public power side had received a boost in early 1937 when the play *Power* debuted in New York. Sponsored by the Federal Theater Project, which funded live artistic performances as part of the New Deal's emergency relief program, the play was written in a new, documentary style called the "Living Newspaper," in which writers incorporated news clippings into plays. *Power* criticized high electricity rates, praised TVA, and caricatured a utility baron named Wendell Willkie. It sold more than 60,000 tickets even before it opened. After seeing it, Roosevelt confidant Harry Hopkins, whose Works Progress Administration had funded the project, went backstage and told the company, "People will say it's propaganda. Well, I say, what of it? It's propaganda to educate the consumer who is paying for power."[40]

The degree to which the president's power over Congress had been diminished by the Court bill and the beginning of the recession was evident in June 1937 when Senator Norris introduced his "Seven Little TVAs" legislation. Though Roosevelt was expected to support the Norris bill, which insiders knew reflected his own ideas, the proposal ran into fierce opposition from private utility interests as well as from both the Department of Agriculture and the Corps of Engineers, whose role in the Tennessee Valley had been greatly diminished by TVA. Likely in recognition that he would not be able to persuade Congress to pass such a bold new piece of legislation and not wanting to provoke them during the Court fight, Roosevelt's June 3 message to Congress equivocated. While he still endorsed regional planning agencies, he didn't indicate whether he thought they should have administrative authority, including over power development, as Norris's bill provided. In the absence of strong Presidential support, the House Rivers and Harbors Committee voted unanimously for a substitute bill that allowed for regional planning but otherwise maintained the traditional agency division of responsibilities.[41]

The president's plans for the power industry took a significant step forward when he signed the Bonneville Project Act in August 1937. Harold Ickes and his Committee on National Power Policy had made good progress despite squabbling between the Army Corps of Engineers and Ickes over responsibility for distribution of the power. Their compromise called for the Corps to take charge of the operation of the dam and its power facility, while the new Bonneville Project Administration (BPA) had authority to market the power and to build or buy transmission lines. In truth it was no real compromise, as the BPA administrator could even order the Corps to operate or shut down the generators, but the Corps accepted the terms because it was widely understood that the battle would be re-fought when Grand Coulee was completed.[42]

By 1937 thousands of refugees from the Dust Bowl were seeking work or farmland in Washington and Oregon. When Roosevelt dedicated Bonneville Dam and pushed a button to start its first generator on September 28, the refugees' presence in these states inspired his forceful argument for government planning and conservation, which he asserted could have prevented the destitution, the abandonment of farms, and the migration of thousands of families from the center of the country. He challenged those who "take the point of view that it is not the concern of Federal or State or local government to interfere with what they miscall 'the liberty of the individual.'. . . My conception of liberty does not permit an individual citizen or group of citizens to commit acts of depredation against nature . . . ."[43] The next day the *New York Times* endorsed planning to conserve natural resources but expressed reservations about Roosevelt's embrace of "'planning' in the sense of attempting to substitute governmental control for the processes of free competition and the open market."[44]

Public power advocates scored a victory in Roosevelt's appointment of the BPA administrator. J. D. Ross, an SEC commissioner, was an electrical engineer who had been head of the Seattle municipal utility for thirty-six years. More recently he had been a member of Roosevelt's New York Power Authority and the chief engineer for electricity projects at the Public Works Administration. An enthusiastic advocate of hydropower, he often said, "a great river is a coal mine that never thins out."[45] When his name first surfaced for BPA, business organizations and private utilities sought to undermine his candidacy, charging him with "municipal socialism" in Seattle and alleging that he would favor Washington over Oregon.[46] But with no strong alternative candidate, Ross's friendship with the president, roots in the region, and knowledge of the industry prevailed. Public power advocates saw his appointment as strong affirmation of Roosevelt's commitment to low rates and broader electrification.[47]

Several days later, at the Grand Coulee construction site, Roosevelt praised the progress that had been made and bragged about "the largest structure ... that has ever been undertaken by man in one place." The nearly mile-wide dam would have no fish ladders, and it would eliminate salmon from vast reaches of the upper Columbia and destroy ecosystems vital to several Native American tribes. But the president, who hoped for a conservation legacy like that of "Cousin Teddy," did not on this or any other public occasion discuss the environmental impact of the Columbia River dams.[48]

Both Bonneville and Grand Coulee severely limited the passage of salmon and steelhead trout in both directions between their upstream spawning grounds and the ocean. The fish-kill problem was not unknown in the 1930s, when the dams were planned. But the impacts were unclear and not widely known outside the scientific and environmental communities at the time, while the benefits of cheap hydropower were obvious and highly popular.[49]

Despite a seventy-foot vertical fish ladder at Bonneville, large numbers of juvenile fish were carried into the turbines on their way downstream. Based on research conducted in the early 1950s, biologists estimated that 10 to 15 percent of juvenile fish passing though turbine chambers at any one dam would be killed. At the time, though, fish researchers thought the passage was safe.[50]

Grand Coulee was even more deadly, extinguishing all salmon runs that spawned in the upper Columbia and the tributaries that flowed into it above the dam. The Bureau of Reclamation knew that adult fish would not be able to pass the dam, and they contracted with the Washington Department of Fisheries to develop an ambitious plan to preserve and relocate these runs. Returning fish would be trapped below the first dam on the river and carried in tank trucks to release points in streams below Grand Coulee and to a hatchery. Juvenile fish from the hatchery would be taken to release sites above the dam. It was not a perfect plan, and the director of the department noted in the introduction to the 1938 report, "There was a feeling that the best economic gains to be derived from this project should not be endangered by consideration of the fish."[51]

Private utilities in the Northwest continued to argue that there would not be sufficient demand for the new power from Bonneville and Grand

Coulee. Ross and the other proponents, however, believed the Tupelo example proved that the availability of cheap power would stimulate demand. After all, average household consumption in Tupelo more than tripled in the first three years of access to TVA power. To achieve a similar result, Ross had to develop a marketing strategy that would allow rates low enough to attract adequate customers and promote social and economic development while still generating enough revenue to pay back the investment in the dam. When he postponed issuing a rate schedule for several weeks to allow the Federal Power Commission to review it, as Roosevelt had requested, public power supporters feared he might be considering preferential rates for industry. In fact, as Insull had demonstrated and the municipal utilities in Seattle, Tacoma, and Los Angeles had confirmed, low residential rates were made possible only by selling large blocks of power to industry at even lower rates. Ross was willing to sell up to 20 percent of Bonneville's power to industry, he wrote to Norris, but social and economic development goals would not be completely subordinated to utility economics. He would insist that industry buyers hire large numbers of the unemployed.[52]

In mid-October of 1937, in the middle of the recession, panic selling turned the stock market's slow decline into a precipitous fall. Willkie argued that the Holding Company Act was partly responsible because it was preventing new construction by making it hard for utilities to attract investors.[53] Along similar lines, in November the *New York Times* contended that, "For the sake of punishing certain culprits who deserved it, the Government has pursued policies from which the whole industry has suffered." The editorial urged the administration "to modify laws which are punitive in spirit, and to rid the public utility industry of the fear that through unfair competition the government is seeking to destroy it."[54]

At a press conference focused on measures to offset the recession, Roosevelt floated another compromise. Because state commissions set electricity rates based on the value of a utility's assets, the method of establishing that value was contentious. The president suggested that if utilities would accept the idea that rates should be set based on the actual or original cost of the assets rather than the more common and typically higher replacement cost, an argument he had advanced in his first term as governor, they "might expect less competition from the Federal government."[55]

Willkie responded to Roosevelt's offer with another request for a negotiated solution on TVA and the Holding Company Act. He and the president met for two hours on November 23, agreeing only on the desirability of spending $1.5 billion for utility expansion. Still not willing to concede defeat on the death sentence clause, Willkie left a memorandum suggesting that if the clause were eliminated, and if TVA would agree not to compete with private utilities, the industry would eliminate all write-ups of assets criticized by the Federal Trade Commission in its investigation of holding companies. He said the industry would also agree to the original cost method of ratemaking from this date forward.[56]

The Court-packing scheme and the attacks on business in 1937 had driven a wedge into the Democratic Party and made it easier for Republicans and conservative Democrats to work together. A series of sit-down strikes and labor-management violence also contributed to Roosevelt's loss of political power, since his critics linked them to his encouragement of unionism in the 1935 Labor Relations Act.[57] To give coherence to the growing cross-party alliance, in December Democratic senator Josiah Bailey of North Carolina and Republican Arthur Vandenberg of Michigan secretly drafted a "conservative manifesto" for members of both parties warning of the dangers of the New Deal regulatory-welfare state. It was leaked by Senate Republican Leader McNary, who feared it might jeopardize Republican electoral chances, but Arthur Krock concluded in the *New York Times* that the alliance would make the passage of progressive legislation as difficult as "pulling hippopotamus teeth."[58]

While the TVA battle was being waged on several fronts, the challenges to the Holding Company Act continued to work their way through the courts. Because the Supreme Court had previously struck down regulations that were much less invasive than the death sentence, the administration had decided to concentrate its argument on the registration requirement, hoping to avoid a broader ruling. And it sought to delay the case, hoping for the retirement of one or more of the conservative justices. The narrow focus had led to a preliminary success in January 1937, when Judge Julian Mack of the district court in New York upheld two sections of the law in *Electric Bond and Share Company v. SEC*, ruling that companies must register and disclose their financial holdings. The SEC could then conduct administrative proceedings to limit them to a single, geographically integrated system.[59]

The ruling was upheld on appeal to the circuit court, and Willkie was dealt a new blow when in March 1938 the Supreme Court issued a resounding decision upholding the registration requirement in the Holding Company Act. In a decision written and read by Chief Justice Hughes, the Court upheld the lower court decisions in *Bond and Share* by a 6-1 vote. The *Times* called it "a striking victory" for the New Deal. Assistant Attorney General Jackson, who had argued the *Bond and Share* case, wrote, "Even great aggregations of financial power must be made to operate under the law."[60]

As in the *Ashwander* case involving TVA, the Court decided *Bond and Share* narrowly, postponing a decision on the constitutionality of the death sentence. Hughes wrote for the majority, "All that the defendants have to do is to register . . . . All their rights and remedies with respect to other provisions of the statute remain without prejudice."[61] Justice Benjamin Cardozo, a Hoover appointee who typically voted with the liberal bloc, did not participate in the case due to ill health, and the second Roosevelt-appointed justice, Stanley Reed, recused himself because he had signed briefs in the case while he was Solicitor General. But, the *Times* noted, "Justice Black, who three years ago . . . attacked holding companies as 'rattlesnakes' and urged their destruction as 'networks of chicanery, deceit, fraud and graft,' took part."[62]

C&S had thus far refused to register with the SEC, but within a few hours of the decision Willkie announced that it would. He looked to be heading into the fight of his career over the fate of C&S, and by the end of the year he was working to integrate the northern half of C&S into a single contiguous system, largely by buying the utilities located between his Michigan and Ohio operations.[63]

Willkie also took a beating on the TVA front at the start of 1938.

On January 3, in *Alabama Power v. Ickes*, the Supreme Court refused to permit utilities to use injunctions to stop Public Works Administration funding. "Mr. Ickes's delight over the court verdict was unconcealed," the *Times* reported, and he promptly announced plans to fund sixty-one municipal power projects, including several in Tennessee, Alabama, and Mississippi. In a second decision, a California rate case, the Court allowed, although it did not require, utility regulators to use Roosevelt's preferred replacement cost method. On January 14 Roosevelt announced his flat rejection of Willkie's proposed compromise from November.[64]

Willkie could feel the ground shifting beneath him. He had testified in the rehearing of the TEPCO case that had been remanded to the district court in Eastern Tennessee, and he could not have been optimistic about the outcome. The court, now a three-judge panel thanks to what remained of the Court-reform bill, had ruled out any discussion of rates or of alleged TVA propaganda. TVA counsel confidently declined even to cross-examine Willkie. The day following Roosevelt's rejection of his proposal, he dramatically urged TVA to buy out TEPCO completely, "as a last resort in a desperate situation," with the price to be set by negotiation or determined by arbitrators. Almost anti-climactically, the district court gave Willkie a crippling defeat on January 21, 1938, upholding the constitutionality of the TVA Act and deciding every factual issue in TVA's favor. Only Judge Gore dissented. In a reflection of the hostility pervading the battle, the court noted that the utilities' filing contained "much that is argumentative, repetitious and immaterial to the legal questions presented."[65]

Willkie announced he would appeal the TEPCO decision to the Supreme Court, but he and Lilienthal began negotiations over a sale. Although there was little comity or humility in the room when the two sat down to talk, both wanted a deal. TVA still needed more markets for the power it would soon generate, and TEPCO would be a huge prize. Willkie needed to prevent the destruction of his shareholders' value, and a fair price for TEPCO would achieve that. But in the interim, Alabama Power and Mississippi Power had been losing battles in several towns, and six northeast Mississippi towns

voted for public power even while Willkie and Lilienthal were negotiating. The local manager of a Mississippi Power office said TVA was
taking territory "just like chicken taking corn off the ground." The
negotiators were eventually able to agree on the areas TVA would take
over—Tennessee and parts of Georgia, Mississippi, and Alabama—and
Lilienthal agreed not to compete outside those. But on the question
of price, discussions stalled.[66]

David Lilienthal and Wendell Willkie begin negotiations over the sale of TEPCO
to TVA following a district court decision upholding the constitutionality
of the TVA Act. (*Library of Congress.*)

Once again the issue of original cost versus replacement cost was
the main obstacle. An independent accounting firm hired by TVA with
Willkie's approval gave each side its starting point. The firm calculated
TEPCO's original cost as $81 million, from which Lilienthal deducted
$24 million for depreciation and offered $57 million. Willkie argued
that the TVA should pay a price reflecting the company's market value,
which the accounting firm estimated to be $94 million—itself lower
than the $106 million that Willkie's own consultants had proposed.

Lilienthal raised his offer to $67 million and Willkie came down to $90 million, and then neither would budge further.[67]

Developments in the long-simmering feud between Lilienthal and Morgan made Willkie think he could take advantage of a weakened Lilienthal in fighting for a good price for TEPCO. Two years earlier Morgan had tried to remove the thorn in his side, asking Roosevelt not to reappoint Lilienthal when his term expired in 1936. The president appeared to agree, his frequent method of dealing with contentious issues, but he soon began to backtrack. Morgan began lobbying and told both Norris and Ickes that he would resign if Lilienthal were reappointed. But when the reappointment occurred, he stayed on.[68]

Morgan's support for the private utility viewpoint in the power pool discussions had exacerbated the split, as did his thinly veiled attack on Lilienthal in a *New Republic* article: "A sovereign government should not act in a spirit of retaliation, of getting even for past abuses .... Private power utilities should be looked upon as honorable undertakings ...."[69] Lilienthal in turn had used evidence of Morgan's collaboration with Willkie to seek the chairman's dismissal in early 1937. Roosevelt needed no additional distractions while his battle to reform the Court was escalating, but he did approve a retaliatory *New Republic* article by Morris Cooke attacking Morgan, telling Cooke, "Go the whole hog."[70]

In January 1938, Lilienthal and Harcourt Morgan told the president they thought Arthur Morgan should retire, although he was only fifty-nine years old. On March 7, the chairman released a letter he had sent to Congressman Maury Maverick of Texas accusing Lilienthal of "evasion, intrigue and sharp strategy ... which makes Machiavelli seem open and candid." He called for a Congressional investigation, which he said would uncover "an attitude of conspiracy, secretiveness and bureaucratic manipulation."[71]

Roosevelt could no longer stay above the fray. He summoned the three directors to a six-hour "hearing" and, with the chairman appearing near a nervous breakdown, asked him to substantiate or withdraw his charges. Morgan replied that the venue was unsuitable for a review of the facts, refused to answer questions about his allegations in detail, and insisted on a Congressional investigation. Roosevelt gave him a week to reconsider, then another week, and then dismissed him for "contumacious behavior," making Harcourt Morgan chairman. Arthur Morgan would receive his Congressional investigation, with tedious hearings lasting from May to December, with Democratic and Republican Congressman rehashing their views on TVA, but he was unable to document his charges.[72]

Meanwhile, Lilienthal continued to strengthen his hand in the negotiations with Willkie by working to add customers. Municipal authorities in Chattanooga, Knoxville, and Memphis were building parallel lines with Public Works Administration funds to force TEPCO and Bond and Share to sell them their distribution systems. Some cases were reminiscent of the battles between rival companies in a single city in the late nineteenth century, and the competition sometimes led to burned poles and shootouts. None too subtly, the Chattanooga board wrote Willkie, "You can appreciate that each day this construction program advances the value of your properties to the City of Chattanooga becomes progressively less."[73]

Wendell Willkie proposes to Congress in 1938 that the SEC determine a fair price for the sale of TEPCO to TVA. (*Library of Congress.*)

SEC Chairman William O. Douglas (l) and Solicitor General Robert Jackson, two future Supreme Court justices, leave the White House in June 1938. (*Library of Congress.*)

After Arthur Morgan's dismissal, the feud between him and Lilienthal could not possibly help Willkie in the TEPCO sale negotiations, but at the 1938 Congressional hearings on TVA requested by Morgan he floated another idea for determining a fair price—valuation by the SEC. Lilienthal refused, as did SEC Chairman William O. Douglas, another future Supreme Court Justice who played a role in New Deal power policy. Relying on the SEC might not have helped Willkie in any case. In 1974, the by-then cantankerous Douglas described his reaction to Willkie's frequent visits: "I would always politely rise as he entered and offer him a chair. He never would take my proffered seat; instead he would walk across the room, pull up a chair, sit down with his back to me, put his feet on the window sill, and bellow at me. What interested me most was that he kept his hat on—better to show his contempt."[74]

The administration's push to expand public power also made promising headway in the Pacific Northwest in early 1938. J. D. Ross, head of

BPA, had demonstrated conspicuous political skill with his strategy for overcoming the private companies' opposition to uniform residential rates. In March, he initiated a series of public hearings to allow citizens to weigh in. After hearing state officials in Olympia and Salem, the capitals, he took testimony in Pendleton, Walla Walla, Spokane, and Yakima, where irrigation and reclamation were priorities. By the time the industrial and private utility witnesses in Portland had an opportunity to voice their pleas for rates based on transmission distance, the overwhelming preponderance of testimony already given was against them.

Ross and his advisers agreed on uniform rates throughout the system, with a slight discount for sales within fifteen miles of Bonneville. The rate structure received widespread approval, although not from the Portland Chamber of Commerce, which wanted distance-based rates that would favor its members. The Federal Power Commission approved it in June, and the first generator at Bonneville began producing power for sale on July 9. On the same day areas east of the Cascade Range were opened to ocean shipping. The first ocean-going vessel went through the lock at Bonneville, the highest single-lift sea lock in the world, on its way to The Dalles, Oregon, a town 182 miles from the Pacific.[75]

The principal remaining obstacle to widespread distribution of the Bonneville power was the need to construct many miles of transmission lines. Ross wrote to Norris, "We are certainly going to succeed in making a market here. The trouble is—the one big trouble—lack of funds to get the lines quickly to the people." By late spring in 1938, the previous year's ineffective fiscal restraint and tight monetary policy had been relaxed, and the 1937-38 recession was ending. The stock market bottomed out in May after dropping 48 percent in seven months, a faster fall than in 1929 and 1930, and unemployment started to decline after peaking in June at 19 percent, up from 14.3 percent a year earlier. Congress was again willing to allocate plentiful resources to infrastructure projects, and it promptly appropriated $3.5 million for transmission lines from Bonneville.[76]

Ross moved with remarkable alacrity to build them. He conferred frequently with Roosevelt about a tie line to connect Bonneville and

Grand Coulee and immediately began surveys and property acquisition for a high-tension Portland-Puget Sound-Tacoma transmission loop. The terrain and the need for speed resulted in some unusual survey methods. Automobile headlights were pressed into service for night surveys, and on one line, surveyors observed rockets at night to obtain a sight over a hill.[77]

By mid-1938 the pressure on both sides to reach an agreement was strong. Roosevelt was eager to revive industrial investment in the wake of the recession, and he was increasingly occupied with the prospect of a European war. But then he made another political miscalculation, strengthening the hand of the conservative alliance and making further reforms even more difficult. He campaigned in person for the liberal primary opponents of three conservative Democratic senators— "Cotton Ed" Smith of South Carolina, Walter George of Georgia, and Millard Tydings of Maryland, who had voted against New Deal initiatives an astonishing 77 percent of the time. He also signaled his support for the challengers of other Congressional Democrats who had opposed him, including House Rules Committee Chairman John J. O'Connor. Critics dubbed his effort a purge, with all of its Stalinist associations. But all three senators won their primaries and were re-elected. Roosevelt did savor O'Connor's defeat, but it was small consolation in November as the Democrats suffered a big reversal. Republicans gained eight Senate seats, 81 House seats, and thirteen governorships.[78]

Although the Democrats still had large majorities, political commentator Arthur Krock wrote, "The New Deal has been halted; the Republican party is large enough for effective opposition; the moderate Democrats in Congress can guide legislation." Roosevelt's 1936 election had been the high-water mark of the Democratic coalition forged in 1932. Washington newsman Raymond Clapper held that "President Roosevelt could not run for a third term even if he so desired," and liberal Democrats began searching for a possible candidate for 1940.[79]

But the strength of the court decisions on TVA and the Holding Company Act meant that Roosevelt's electricity policies continued to move forward. Some utilities still argued adamantly that they had been unjustly attacked. The head of the Association of Edison Illuminating Companies, for example, bemoaned their plight in January 1939, saying, "We have been beset with government interference, in many instances reaching the point of real persecution; government competition amounting almost to confiscation; a set-up of government regulation so severe that it borders on actual management."[80] But the united front opposing TVA was splintering, and some utilities not affiliated with C&S withdrew from the TEPCO case. Then on January 31, 1939, the Supreme Court ruled 5-2 that TEPCO and the other remaining utilities did not have standing to bring the suit against TVA's constitutionality.[81]

Willkie conceded defeat. It was time to resolve the sale of TEPCO. At this crucial point, Lilienthal became seriously ill from drinking unpasteurized milk and had to withdraw from the negotiations. Joseph Swidler, a thirty-two-year-old TVA attorney and former law partner of Lilienthal, and Julius Krug, a thirty-one-year-old TVA economist, took his place.[82] Willkie managed to persuade them to agree to a price of $78.6 million, splitting the difference between the last offers on the table. TVA would buy TEPCO's generation and transmission facilities, and the municipalities would buy its local distribution systems. Negotiations would continue on the sale of C&S properties in Mississippi and Alabama.[83]

Although Willkie wanted an ironclad agreement against further TVA expansion, Krug gave him only a mildly reassuring statement: "We have offered to purchase facilities in an area which will absorb our entire output." Lilienthal insisted in subsequent years that TVA could not completely commit to this territorial limitation due to the requirement in the original TVA Act that it give preference to public power distributors and co-ops within transmission distance. The private utilities, though, welcomed the implied demarcation, which they gradually formalized as the Gentlemen's Agreement. As it happened, the huge demand for power during World War II and the Korean War and for uranium enrichment in the 1950s made the question of TVA expansion outside its initial boundaries moot. Not for two decades, though, would the boundaries be written into law.[84]

In August 1939, at a ceremony at the First National Bank in New York, Lilienthal presented Willkie with a check from the federal government. A jovial Willkie said for the newsreel cameras, "Thanks, Dave. This is a lot of money for a couple of Indiana farmers to be kicking around." But off camera his bitterness came through. In a press release he said, "We sell these properties with regret. We do so because we could not stay in business against this subsidized government competition . . . . This sale does not represent the true value of this investment . . . ." Lilienthal responded in kind. "(Willkie's) statement does violence to the fact recognized in all quarters that the terms of the settlement with Commonwealth and Southern were eminently fair . . . ." SEC Chairman Douglas agreed, but Lilienthal would not have liked his reason: "At the SEC, we always thought Willkie outsmarted David Lilienthal."[85]

While investment by private utilities was sluggish, the federal dams were starting to make a difference. TVA more than doubled its power production from 1938 to 1939, from 766 to 1,723 million kilowatt hours, and Bonneville Dam, which only started commercial power sales in 1938, reached 35 million kilowatt hours in 1939. This growth would continue apace and would become crucial to the buildup of military power as America's entry into World War II loomed.[86]

CHAPTER 9

POWERING THE WAR EFFORT

All through 1938 German aggression in Europe increased fear that the U.S. might be drawn into a European war, the second in most Americans' lifetimes. With only the 18th largest army in the world at the time and the "recession within the Depression" nearing its depths, the United States was in no position to become directly involved in the brewing conflict, but Roosevelt began promoting the need for increased readiness. He directed Secretary of State Cordell Hull to speak about the need for naval rearmament, and in August the president insisted to a Canadian audience, "We are no longer a far away continent to which the eddies of controversies beyond the seas could bring no harm." In a radio address in October, he warned that, "ordinary rules of national prudence and common sense require that we be prepared."[1]

Roosevelt also took steps to assess the ability of the country's electrical system to support a substantial war buildup. He had experienced the World War I coal shortages and the difficulties an unprepared and divided America had faced then in ramping up industrially and militarily. He was loath to give any indication that he was preparing the nation for war, but he directed the Federal Power Commission and the War Department in March to confidentially review the status of the nation's power facilities. The National

Association of Railroad and Utility Commissioners also weighed in, noting the time required to take a new plant from design to operation and cautioning, "It would be disastrous to await the actual coming of a war crisis to take necessary steps."[2]

The federal report concluded that war mobilization, in combination with growing demand for power as the recession waned, would lead to "widespread and critical shortages of generating capacity." The agencies recommended giving immediate "pump-priming" orders to GE, Westinghouse, and Allis-Chalmers. The three companies that manufactured 95 percent of the country's steam turbines and generators had been hard hit by the cancellation of orders during the recession and had been laying off workers. The proposed purchases would be financed with Reconstruction Finance Corporation loans to a new government corporation, which would lease the equipment to utilities.[3]

As an alternative, the report suggested that the RFC could loan the money directly to utilities, opening a new public-private front in the battle over the future of the electrical system. Private power interests favored this alternative, saying they would use the funds to finance vital expansion. But Harold Ickes was opposed, anticipating that in the wake of the crisis the industry would undermine the administration's power program. Other officials, notably in the Federal Power Commission and TVA, were less adamant, believing that a potential wartime power shortage affecting defense industries was a greater risk.[4]

Additional controversy developed when the Federal Power Commission and the War and Navy Departments disagreed on strategies for meeting wartime power needs. The FPC recommended the construction of an interconnected, higher voltage power grid, building new transmission lines and upgrading existing ones in order to link the regional grids of various utilities and holding companies more efficiently. "The network," it asserted, "should be constructed, maintained and operated by the Federal Government as a national defense measure and operate as a common carrier during peacetime," available for all sellers and buyers of electricity. The FPC also proposed that the federal and state governments cooperate in building larger hydroelectric plants, leaving to private utilities, financed by low-interest loans, the construction of steam plants.[5]

The War and Navy Departments recommended, by contrast, forgoing the expense of the expanded high-tension grid and building additional generating capacity in the fifteen major industrial centers, primarily in the Northeast and Midwest. The money saved, they asserted, could be better used on armaments. The FPC responded that the military's failure to adequately build up its armaments was no justification for failing to build the network. Both sides understood that either proposal would take up to five years to complete and urged the president to submit legislation to Congress promptly.[6]

To reconcile the differing views and establish a more formal planning process, Roosevelt convened a conference on September 1, 1938. Based on its discussions he created a National Defense Power Committee to evaluate the proposals, to prepare legislation to carry out whichever strategy was chosen, and to recommend appropriations. He appointed Louis Johnson, the assistant secretary of war and a former corporate lawyer, as its chair and included Ickes, SEC Chairman Douglas, and FPC Commissioner Manly among its members.[7] Newspaper reports on the conference and speculation about a power shortage raised a red flag for public power supporters. Judson King, director of the National Popular Government League and a consultant to the REA, wrote to Senator Norris that he had heard from a source at the meeting that the government planned to contract with private utilities to sell the new, government generated power, which would "put a hell of a crimp" in the public power movement. He cautioned Norris that the national defense power network "has equal possibility for good and for evil." He wondered how the transmission network would be used if there was no war, arguing that states, municipalities, and cooperatives should have a "preferential right" to use a government-financed grid. Worried about the committee's close cooperation with industry, he warned Norris that there was "enough queer stuff going on to put us on guard" and to watch out for a power grab.[8]

The committee eventually adopted the proposal for an enhanced national grid as more responsive to long run needs, and in October the PWA provided $200,000 to study the feasibility of a government-built network. As expected, private industry leaders argued against the expansion of public power capacity. They also made yet another attempt to stop the SEC from breaking up holding companies. They had lost the fight against the requirement to register with the SEC in the Supreme Court's *Bond and Share* decision in March, but that didn't stop them from lobbying to weaken the SEC's implementation of the law. They made their case in a meeting of the new Power Committee at the end of September. Only utility leaders who were recommended by the SEC and who might be expected to negotiate in good faith received invitations. Neither Willkie nor C. F. Groesbeck of Bond and Share was included. To prevent the attendees from coordinating on an industry position, they were contacted only a day in advance. [9]

Nonetheless, the utilities were generally in agreement about their concerns. They feared that government regulatory powers would be expanded under the guise of defense preparedness. Mirroring the concern of public power advocates about private utilities, they objected that the cloak of national security might protect the growth of public power programs—primarily TVA and BPA. They further worried that huge expenditures to add capacity in anticipation of demand could be a financial liability for utilities if demand failed to grow as much as expected and regulatory commissions refused to let them pass their costs through to consumers. They advocated the alternative recommendation of the FTC-War and Navy Department report, that the government build the new plants and then lease them to the utilities. Then, if demand increased and made the purchase of the facilities viable for the companies, the government should sell them. Thomas Corcoran, representing the president, was able to tell them that the Reconstruction Finance Corporation was considering just such a proposal. [10]

As for the breakup of holding companies, the utilities' views echoed Willkie's argument the previous November that the government's attacks were making it hard for them to raise capital. These views were reflected in a September 13 *Washington Times* article reporting that a survey of power resources for an emergency was expected to "force a sharp change in SEC efforts to impose the 'death sentence' on scattered utility groups." This expectation forced Johnson, already distrusted by public power advocates for his close cooperation with private utilities, to assure Ickes that "any plan by which the government would aid in

providing new generating capacity" would not undermine implementation of the Holding Company Act.[11]

At the same time, development of public power capacity in both the
Northwest and the Tennessee Valley moved forward with dispatch.
BPA head J. D. Ross was keenly aware of how vital the power from
the Bonneville and Grand Coulee dams would be if war should come.
In his first annual report to Congress in 1938, he alluded to wartime
demand. "In the hydroelectric streams of the Pacific Northwest is
potential power far in excess of that available in other regions of the
nation. It should be developed at an economic rate to meet mounting
peacetime needs and the equally important possibilities of emergency
drains. Preparedness requires foresight."[12]

His plan for marketing BPA's power called for multiple wholesale
customers, but there were only thirty-one municipal electric utilities
in Washington and Oregon, and the largest—Seattle, Tacoma, and
Eugene—already generated a large portion of their own power. Both
states, though, had authorized the establishment of public utility districts (PUDs) to market hydropower. These elected units of government,
with boundaries that were generally the same as rural counties, had
authority to borrow money and collect taxes and the power of eminent
domain to acquire private systems. Although Ross instructed his staff
to stay out of politics, he encouraged them to assist PUDs when they
asked. By the end of 1938, Bonneville customers in Washington
included Seattle and Tacoma, several smaller municipalities, and
twenty-five PUDs. In Oregon, where private power was more influential, only two PUDs and six municipalities had sought BPA's
power.[13]

Ross wanted to ensure that BPA's capacity rapidly grew. He supported BPA purchase of private systems and sale of their assets to the
PUDs in which they were located. The private owners were not eager
to sell, and Ross was urged by public power allies to adopt tough tactics. In a threatening letter, he advised the president of Stone and
Webster, one of the earliest utility holding companies as well as a
construction company, that a long and costly battle could be avoided
by "the disposal of your property as soon as possible."[14]

John C. Fischer, BPA's general counsel, referred to Ross's "usual very cagy tactics" in making repeated offers to buy Washington's largest private utility, Puget Sound Power and Light, while he encouraged the rapid organization of PUDs that would be ready to acquire its properties. This, Fischer noted, would not only provide markets for the power Bonneville would soon produce but would bring "the power companies of Oregon to their knees."[15]

Ickes, though, was initially skeptical of the PUDs because of their principal bond salesman's close Wall Street connections, and he was slow to release Public Works Administration funds for them to acquire properties. But while the PUDs were struggling to get started, Ross wanted customers other than the private utilities serving industry in the Portland area. He did convince Ickes to provide a PWA loan for clearing rights-of-way and persuaded the Reconstruction Finance Corporation to back the construction of transmission lines. With these commitments in hand he was able to borrow enough money from banks to finance a high-voltage line to sell power to a large new customer, the Grand Coulee construction contractor.[16]

In 1938 Ross developed a six-year plan for generation and transmission facilities. With the end of the recession, he urged accelerated completion of the power facilities at Bonneville and received increased appropriations. Tragically, he died in March 1939 due to complications following abdominal surgery. In just under a year and a half he had dramatically increased BPA's appropriations, both for dams and for transmission lines. Roosevelt, who had become a friend, called him "one of the greatest Americans of our generation." The Portland *Oregonian*, no friend of public power, editorialized that his strategy had effectively guaranteed BPA's future. "It is certain that the Administration at Washington, D.C., and the power bloc in Congress—affrighted at the idea of having Bonneville a failure after such huge expenditures for distribution lines—will bring tremendous pressure upon the Bonneville administrator to force adequate sales at any and all costs, and by any and all means."[17]

Although not as directly related to the preparation for war, progress was also vigorous on the rural electrification front. John Carmody, who had been Morris Cooke's deputy at the REA and took over from him in early 1937, enthusiastically embraced the concentration on cooperatives that Cooke had initiated and took full advantage of the methods he had developed to increase growth and support for the program. He had an extensive corporate background, but that didn't stop him from going after what he perceived as abuses by the industry. He later boasted, "I gave recalcitrant private utilities no quarter." In 1937, 140 new co-ops were incorporated, up from one hundred the previous year.[18]

A great assist came from the RFC's Jesse Jones, who didn't dislike Carmody as he had Cooke. Funds from the RFC's Electric Home and Farm Authority began to flow more liberally to REA cooperatives, and by the middle of 1938 over half of the utilities working with the Authority were cooperatives. In Carmody's first year, the Authority supported more than 39,000 loan contracts. Twenty different types of appliances were on its approved list, with the most popular being water pumps, water heaters, washing machines, irons, radios, vacuum cleaners, refrigerators, ranges, and various types of electric farm equipment.[19]

Carmody was a skillful political operator, mobilizing the press and local political leaders against the tactics of private utilities, especially snake lines. In June 1938 he singled out the worst offender, Bond and Share, for ordering its subsidiaries in several states to build competing lines in co-op territory, shrewdly timing his criticism to coincide with the start of the SEC's investigation of the company for violations of the Holding Company Act. He also made sure the REA kept Congress well apprised of its rapid growth, flooding Congressional offices with announcements of contracts in their states and districts. Acknowledging the popularity of the program, Congress in 1938 increased the REA's appropriation to $140 million for the 1939 fiscal year, more than triple the $40 million initially authorized.[20]

The rates and terms of service offered by private utilities to rural customers improved after the REA was created, and there is no doubt that the competition was a major factor. All providers benefited, though, from growing farm income, cheaper appliances, and the declining cost of generation. Although many were unlikely to acknowledge it, the reduction in holding company abuses also helped to bring down the costs and rates of private operating utilities they controlled.

Despite his success—a record 172 co-ops had been incorporated in 1938— Carmody abruptly resigned after Roosevelt surprised him in May 1939 by deciding to move the REA into the Department of Agriculture as part of a larger effort to streamline government. Ickes had wanted REA in the Interior Department, but others strongly resisted. Agriculture Secretary Henry Wallace, himself no slouch at empire building, triumphed. A last-minute appeal by Norris to preserve REA's independence failed, and Carmody didn't want to stay as the agency got "thrashed around by people who know nothing of the history of the enterprise and who see in it only something with which to exploit or to enhance their own official and personal prestige." In his two years in office he had doubled the number of electrified farms.[21]

REA Administrator John Carmody accelerated rural electrification from 1937 to 1939 but resigned when Roosevelt decided to move the REA into the Department of Agriculture. (*Library of Congress.*)

Roosevelt offered the REA directorship to a thirty-year-old Texas congressman who had managed to support the New Deal while mollifying his conservative constituents by bringing home the federal bacon. Lyndon Johnson seemed perfect for the job. His first big project in Congress had been to obtain funding for the Lower Colorado River Authority, a public-private organization created to complete a dam started by Middle West Utilities before Insull's empire collapsed. He secured the appropriation and persuaded local farmers to establish a co-op to receive REA loans, winning the plaudits of his constituents, public power supporters, his senior colleague Sam Rayburn, and the president himself. The resulting cheap power made his name in Texas. When conservatives criticized him for accepting federal money, he responded that Texans wanted "some electric power which doesn't have to run through the cash register of a New York power and light company before it gets to our lamps."[22]

While flattered by the offer, Johnson was not ready to sacrifice his promising congressional career for a job reporting to someone else late in the president's second term.[23] Roosevelt then appointed Undersecretary of the Interior Harry Slattery, who kept up the quick pace of growth, with another ninety-eight co-ops formed in 1939.[24]

TVA did not remain idle during this period. Five years after TVA's home city had passed a pro-TVA referendum, a Bond and Share subsidiary conceded defeat and sold its local properties to the city of Knoxville and TVA in 1938. A similar story played out in Memphis. Five years after its citizens had voted to buy out the local utility, years filled with litigation and negotiations over price, a PWA grant allowed the city to begin building its own system. The utility, another subsidiary of Bond and Share, then surrendered, and Memphis went into the power business with TVA-supplied current in the summer of 1939.[25]

The most hard-fought battle took place in Chattanooga, an important industrial market, the hub of TEPCO's network, and its headquarters city. Although Lilienthal could not sign a contract with the city while his agreement with Willkie, including its territorial limitations, remained in place, or before the circuit court vacated Judge Gore's injunction, the city's engineers proceeded with plans for a new power system and PWA made two grants to the city to build a system.

When the injunction was lifted and Willkie acknowledged the need to sell TEPCO, the imminent loss of Chattanooga was a major factor in his decision.[26]

In contrast to the steady additions of regional capacity by BPA and TVA, progress in developing a national defense power plan was hampered by bureaucratic infighting in Washington. Ickes still feared that the effort to work with private utilities could undermine the administration's power policies, including forceful implementation of the Holding Company Act, and he decided to challenge Assistant Secretary of War Johnson's control of the process. In July 1939 he persuaded Roosevelt to reconstitute the National Power Policy Committee, which he had chaired before it was suspended in 1936, to rename it the National Power Policy and Defense Committee, and to centralize in the Interior Department all government work on peacetime and wartime power planning. Ickes' self-aggrandizement raised hackles throughout the administration. He sought not only to become the government "power czar"—his rivals' term—but also to use the defense emergency to protect and promote public power. He wanted to prevent compromises with the industry that he feared some of his allies, including even Lilienthal and Norris, would be willing to make due to the urgency of increasing capacity.[27]

Interior Secretary Harold Ickes testifies in 1939 in favor of giving his department control of the Bonneville project. His rivals accused him of seeking to become the nation's "power czar." (*Library of Congress.*)

Through the summer of 1939, as the federal government put plans for mobilization in place, isolationist sentiment remained strong in Congress. But after Germany and the Soviet Union signed a non-aggression pact in August and Germany invaded Poland on September 1, public opinion shifted toward preparing for war. In November *Kristallnacht*, the widespread destruction of Jewish synagogues, businesses, and homes throughout Germany, further strengthened public opposition to Hitler. Four days later Roosevelt told a group of top officials to set in motion a hefty expansion of American airpower, saying, "Hitler would not have dared to take the stand he did . . . if the United States had five thousand warplanes and the capacity to produce ten thousand more within the next few months."[28]

For the next several months, festering distrust prevented Ickes' expanded committee from making much progress. In frustration, Roosevelt in June 1940 turned to Leland Olds, the recently appointed chair of the Federal Power Commission and a more collaborative leader than Ickes, asking him to move forward with plans for supplying adequate power to the war-material industries.[29]

The argument for accelerating the growth of public power capacity was not lost, however. Congress in 1939 had appropriated funds for six of the ten planned generators in the Bonneville powerhouse, and the benefit of TVA and BPA having expansion plans in place came into sharp focus when Roosevelt proclaimed a national emergency after Germany invaded Poland. The 234-mile high-tension line from Bonneville to Grand Coulee, begun in 1939, was rushed to completion in July 1940. The first two generators at Grand Coulee, relatively small, ten-megawatt units, began producing power and shipping it to a bomber plant in Seattle and shipyards in Tacoma in March 1941, two years ahead of schedule. By 1940 TVA completed construction of its first four dams, Norris, Pickwick, Wheeler, and Hiwassee, adding 794 megawatts to the power provided by Wilson Dam, by far the largest in its system with 640 megawatts.[30]

Foreign policy and military preparedness had overtaken economic recovery and reform as Roosevelt's principal concerns, and he pulled back from the bold reform initiatives that had characterized his first six years in office. The new coalition of southern Democrats and business Republicans in Congress generally supported his changed priorities while some progressives in both parties resisted. Even so, the SEC was making steady progress in evaluating which holding companies should be broken up. Though the *North American Company* case on the constitutionality of the death sentence clause was still pending, in March 1940 the agency turned its sights on C&S, as was long anticipated, sending notices to the company and its subsidiaries that it was in violation of the law. The president of Georgia Power forwarded the papers to his assistant with the note, "They are shooting at the Commonwealth & Southern. If they kill it, we'll have to scratch for ourselves or get another mama." Willkie wrote his shareholders, "We expect to do all in our power . . . to prevent the forced sale of our properties . . . ." But others would have to lead that battle when Willkie resigned to run for president.[31]

By June 1940, 144 holding companies had registered with the SEC, but few had filed voluntary plans for compliance. The SEC presented C&S with three unattractive choices for dissolution in March 1941. Shocked, the new president, Justin R. Whiting, submitted an alternative plan that conceded the loss of the northern companies but kept the southern group together. By the end of the year, the SEC had started dissolution proceedings against the fourteen largest holding companies, representing two-thirds of all the assets of those who had registered. The process was time-consuming, but it was working.[32]

The growing likelihood of U.S. involvement in the war in Europe was largely responsible for Roosevelt running for an unprecedented third term, although anti-New Deal conservatives, many of whom were isolationists, would portray the 1940 election as a showdown over Roosevelt's "socialist" policies. At the start of his second term in 1937 Roosevelt had probably not planned to run again, although he understood that ruling it out publicly would make him a lame duck. He had won re-election in a landslide, but he faced the strong no-third-term tradition. A month after his victory, 69 percent of voters, including a majority of Democrats, said they opposed a third term.[33] The president's equivocating about whether he would run had sparked a chorus of criticism, even from some Democrats. "We have seen the examples of dictatorship in Europe," said Senator Wheeler, his erst-while ally, in early 1938, "and I think the vast majority of our people are very apprehensive lest some one get in power here and continue in power."[34]

But the setbacks the party had suffered in the 1938 Congressional elections and the ominous developments in Europe raised concerns among party leaders, progressive Democrats, administration insiders, and the party faithful at large about nominating a new candidate. When Hitler invaded Poland on September 1, 1939, and Britain and France declared war two days later, the pressure on Roosevelt to run escalated. But he remained enigmatic.[35]

Whether or not he ran, Roosevelt was determined to protect the achievements of the New Deal. At one time he had his eye on Robert H. Jackson, head of the Justice Department's anti-trust division, as his successor. Later, he favored his close adviser Harry Hopkins, who was best known for heading the Works Progress Administration and was most criticized for the falsely attributed mantra, "Tax and tax, spend and spend, elect and elect." Roosevelt even appointed Hopkins as secretary of commerce in 1938 to give the former social worker a patina of familiarity with business. But Hopkins' viability as a candidate declined beginning in 1939 as he fought an increasingly difficult and ultimately fatal battle with stomach cancer.[36]

Expectations that Roosevelt would ultimately run were high enough that no rival Democratic candidate mounted a serious public campaign. Meanwhile, on the Republican side, three leading competitors were gunning for the nomination. Senator Robert Taft of Ohio, Senator Arthur Vandenberg of Michigan, and Governor Thomas Dewey of New York were all isolationists, but Willkie had caught the attention of several influential Republicans seeking a candidate who shared their views on economic and foreign policy. His internationalist perspective appealed to moderates, and his leadership of the utility industry in its battles against TVA and the Holding Company Act had made him the most visible business opponent of the New Deal.

The private talk had begun in earnest after Willkie had trounced Assistant Attorney General Jackson in the January 1938 national radio debate, and the first significant public mention of a possible Willkie candidacy appeared in the February 23, 1939, *New York Times*. Columnist Arthur Krock imagined a conversation among politicians setting the odds on candidates. One asked, "How about that utilities chap, Wendell Willkie? He managed to talk himself into a good deal with the TVA." Another replied, "If he's a Republican—is he?—you can't wholly count out Willkie . . . . 1940 will be a little early to bring out a utilities man. But if anyone like that can be put over, I'd watch Willkie. He still has his haircuts country style."[37]

Willkie quietly changed his voter registration to Republican,[38] and in early 1940 he broadened his attacks on the New Deal to issues beyond utilities and began to discuss foreign affairs. A coterie of moderate Republicans from the Eastern Establishment, including influential editors and publishers, actively promoted him and his ideas.

Then in March 1940, a young Wall Street lawyer, Oren Root, drafted a Willkie-for-president petition, and within three weeks he received more than 200,000 signatures. With the covert support of the Edison Electric Institute and local utilities, he began to organize Willkie clubs around the country. All the while Willkie, like Roosevelt, remained coy about whether he would run. Throughout the spring he advanced rapidly in the polls of Republican voters, from a mere one percent in March to 29 percent just before the convention, outpolling Taft and Vandenberg combined but lagging well behind Dewey. In June, a week after the German army occupied Paris and a week before the convention in Philadelphia, he declared his candidacy. His sudden rise precipitated attacks from within the party. Senator John Thomas of Idaho said the utility interests have "done enough . . . without wishing their man Willkie on us." His Democratic background also made him a bête noire to the old guard. Former Senate Majority Leader James Watson, still the unofficial leader of the Indiana Republican party, told Willkie to his face at the convention, "Back home in Indiana it's all right if the town whore joins the church, but they don't let her lead the choir the first night."[39]

As the delegates were assembling in Philadelphia, the Philadelphia *Evening Public Ledger* and the Scripps-Howard newspapers endorsed Willkie. Journalist William Allen White reported, "Dewey has most of the delegates, Taft has most of the king-makers, and Willkie has most of the enthusiasm." On the day the balloting began the *New York Herald Tribune,* in an unprecedented front-page endorsement of Willkie, declared, "Such timing of the man and the hour does not come often in history." Willkie's staff had a copy placed on every delegate's seat.[40]

Willkie's odds of gaining the nomination were also improved by some old-fashioned political skullduggery. When the chair of the arrangements committee died just before the convention, control of seating and tickets fell into the hands of a Willkie supporter. Delegates supporting Taft, Vandenberg, and Dewey found it difficult to get gallery passes for friends because 90 percent of them had been given to the Willkie forces, many of them used by young Ivy League graduates who rained down chants of "We want Willkie" throughout the convention.[41]

Through the first five ballots, Willkie gained on and then passed Dewey and Taft. On the sixth ballot states began switching over to him until he had a majority, and the convention voted to make it unanimous. Willkie took the podium to accept the nomination and to thank the delegates. He concluded by shouting, "So, you Republicans, I call upon you to join me, help me"; the "you Republicans" annoyed many of the old guard.[42] A few days later Willkie resigned from C&S.

Roosevelt had still not declared his candidacy when the Democrats gathered for their convention two weeks later in Chicago, but his nomination was widely anticipated. Yet he held off an announcement because, as an antidote to the third-term poison, he wanted to be drafted, and his political team devised a ploy to make the conventioneers appear to be demanding just that. When the convention chairman, Senator Alben Barkley, read a statement from the White House saying "the President has never had, and has not today, any desire . . . to continue in the office of President" and that "all delegates . . . are free to vote for any candidate," a planned pro-Roosevelt demonstration began. Delegates marched down the aisles with Roosevelt signs. But there was a hitch. The galleries were controlled by Democratic Party Chairman James Farley, who was a candidate himself, and they went ominously silent. Then a voice from the loudspeakers began shouting "Illinois wants Roosevelt . . . . America wants Roosevelt . . . ," and delegates picked up the chant. As the demonstration continued for nearly an hour, a reporter tracked the source to the basement of the convention center, where Mayor Edward Kelly, a Roosevelt ally, had ensconced his superintendent of sewers for just this purpose. Roosevelt won easily on the first ballot, and "the voice from the sewer" became as much a symbol of the influence of urban bosses in Chicago as Willkie's Ivy Leaguers in the galleries symbolized the ascendance of the Eastern Establishment in the Republican Party.[43]

Willkie was so well respected by many in the business community and could be so persuasive that he was to give Roosevelt—who did eventually win the Democratic nomination—a much more serious challenge than anticipated. Though advocates of rolling back New Deal power policies expected him to vigorously campaign on that issue, he pragmatically tailored his message to a range of constituencies. When it came to electricity, in California he praised the isolationist Senator Hiram Johnson, the progressive Republican sponsor of Boulder Dam, and in the Northwest he pledged to complete Grand Coulee. Late in the campaign, though, he sought to appeal to the party's isolationist base with reckless charges, including that Roosevelt had agreed to "sell Czechoslovakia down the river." In a speech in Baltimore he said, "On the basis of his past performances with pledges to the people, you may expect we will be at war by April, 1941, if [Roosevelt] is re-elected."[44]

Roosevelt, meanwhile, refused to debate Willkie. He spent his time inspecting military installations, breaking ground for armaments factories, and speaking at nonpolitical events. As *New York Times* correspondent Turner Catledge noted, "Mr. Roosevelt can act while Mr. Willkie can only talk, and talk for the most part about the President's acts." As for the battle over electricity policies, Roosevelt understood that the urgent need to ramp up capacity must be the overriding factor. In August he signed a bill to initiate a $68.5 million defense program at the TVA, simultaneously calling attention to one of his signature programs and to his defense preparation, saying, "This tremendous amount of low cost energy is strategically located for the manufacture of material essential to the national defense."[45]

As a record number of voters prepared to vote on November 5, the polls showed Willkie closing in on Roosevelt. Gallup reported that Roosevelt was "in a precarious position" with 52 percent, adding that "when a Democratic candidate has 52 percent of the popular vote it is an even race because of the surplus Democratic popular majorities in the South.[46] Early returns on election night were mixed, and when Willkie showed some strength in key states, Roosevelt broke into a sweat, giving orders to his Secret Service detail at Hyde Park not to let anyone into the room where he was following the returns. When the Democratic National Committee chair called to assure him he'd won, Roosevelt invited others back in. At about midnight he greeted a torchlight parade of several hundred supporters that arrived from town, and he took particular delight in seeing a repurposed Willkie campaign sign with "Out Stealing Third" crossed out and replaced with "Safe on Third." In the final tally, Roosevelt won nearly 55 percent of the popular vote and an overwhelming 449 to 82 electoral vote margin.[47]

By 1941, the war in Europe created steep demands on the power sector. With entry into the war now considered nearly inevitable, a number of holding companies, led by Bond and Share and C&S, made another plea to delay further action by the SEC to ensure that their performance in the war effort would not be hindered. "We've got a bear by the tail," the vice president of C&S's South Carolina Power subsidiary wrote to Roosevelt. "By the grace of God, we will handle the bear, but let us give him our undivided attention until he's handled." Edward C. Eicher, newly appointed chairman of the SEC, strongly disagreed. "The present scattered systems have 'Balkanized' the utility assets of this country. The resultant hodgepodge utility operations require the surgery of Section 11 [the law's provision for the 'death sentence'] in order that integrated utility properties may be developed in accordance with the power needs of the area served."[48]

During SEC hearings, various holding company officials argued that efficiencies dictated the structure of their organizations and professed not to know about any inflated valuations involved in their mergers, acquisitions, and restructurings. But any hopes they may have had of forestalling SEC action were dashed after the discovery of a damaging memorandum in the files of a Bond and Share subsidiary.

The five-page document had been written in 1927 by a staff attorney, Samuel W. Murphy, who wrote candidly of ways to deceive regulators on transactions that would be embarrassing if disclosed: "I again wish to impress upon you the importance, in my opinion, of scrambling all these reorganizations together so that about the only thing the Pennsylvania Commission will be able to understand will be the result and not how the result was reached." The "Murphy Memo" undercut many of the holding company claims. It carried particular weight because Murphy was now president of Bond and Share, the industry's largest holding company. The writing was on the wall.[49]

Despite the industry's argument that breaking up the holding companies would hamper their ability to support the war effort, they were not prepared to expand capacity before demand actually increased. Under Federal Power Commission directives, however, they did begin to plan for new power plants and interconnections. TVA and BPA, on the other hand, already had extensive plans on the shelf, and TVA was best positioned to increase supply rapidly. It added several tributary dams to its construction program in 1940 and completed them in record time.[50]

An additional incentive came from a drought in the Southeast in the spring of 1941, reducing reservoir levels to 60 percent below normal and resulting in a voluntary campaign to cut electricity use by 20 to 30 percent. That focused attention on the fact that the system was vulnerable to shortages, and FPC Chairman Olds brought TVA leaders and private utility officials together to finally work out a power pooling arrangement similar to the one Roosevelt had dangled before Willkie in 1936. With TVA's purchase of TEPCO complete and his concern about markets allayed, Lilienthal acquiesced.[51]

Ickes contended in 1941 that "there is a power shortage now and a greater one in prospect," and one vital need was to provide the power necessary to increase aluminum production, largely for the manufacture of aircraft. The wartime Office of Production Management (OPM) estimated that producing the increased supply of aluminum alone would require an additional 1,000 megawatts of electrical capacity, or seven Norris Dams. The aluminum production process was highly energy-intensive, requiring about 10-12 kilowatt hours of electricity per pound of aluminum. Roosevelt had set a target of manufacturing

50,000 planes, but neither the airplane manufacturers nor the military nor Alcoa, the country's only aluminum manufacturer, knew how much aluminum would go into the planes, which were just being designed. The president of the Edison Electric Institute, though, working for OPM, argued that utilities had a 20 percent reserve margin, which was adequate for all needs. Like many other business executives who helped the government manage industrial production during the war, he was working for a token $1 a year, and Ickes grumbled, "He's worth all of the $1 a year he's being paid."[52]

Alcoa had resisted pressure from the administration for years to add capacity in anticipation of increased wartime demand, denying there would be an aluminum shortage. Based on information from the Justice Department, which had been investigating Alcoa for antitrust violations, Ickes called Alcoa "one of the worst monopolies that has ever been able to fasten itself upon American life." According to one of his aides, "Everything they did was calculated to keep supply down and prices up." Now, the public power from TVA and BPA would allow an upstart producer to break Alcoa's stranglehold.[53]

A young customer of Alcoa, Richard S. Reynolds, a nephew of tobacco producer R. J. Reynolds, ran a firm that made aluminum foil for cigarette packs. He doubted Alcoa's confident projections of supply, and he obtained backing from the Reconstruction Finance Corporation to build aluminum plants in the Southeast and Northwest where they would have access to cheap TVA and BPA power. In response, Alcoa sought power from Bonneville for a plant of its own. Ickes denied the request at first, but as the feared shortage transpired and began to hamper the military buildup—aircraft manufacturer Northrup, for example, had to cut its work shifts by 20 percent because of a six-month delay in receiving aluminum—he changed tack. He negotiated for Alcoa to build three plants and lease them to the government for five years. That made Alcoa BPA's largest industrial customer. The company's initial assertion that it had been prepared to meet demand had been remarkably shortsighted; by the end of the war, demand for aluminum had increased 600 percent.[54]

As for the initial hopes of the administration to create a TVA-like Columbia Valley Authority, the demands of war and politics induced

Roosevelt to change course. He no longer had a compliant Congress, and C&S's unhappy experience with TVA had intensified the opposition of private utilities. During the presidential campaign, Willkie had given a full airing to the utility side of the argument, and extensive public relations campaigns by utilities in the Northwest characterized the Columbia Valley Authority idea as unnecessary and un-American. It was not a fight Roosevelt needed.

In August 1940 he made the Bonneville Project Administration the transmission and marketing agency for power from Grand Coulee as well as Bonneville, changing its name to the Bonneville *Power* Administration. The expanded authority triggered renewed struggles over pricing. BPA, reflecting Roosevelt's priorities, wanted to sell the power as cheaply as possible to encourage further electrification of homes and farms. The Bureau of Reclamation, which still operated Grand Coulee, wanted high rates to help subsidize its irrigation projects in the region. The private utilities wanted even higher rates for BPA power, knowing that the public preference requirement would direct much of it to their competitors. Eventually BPA and the Bureau agreed to a rate structure providing some subsidies for irrigation, but the rates were still low enough to give the Pacific Northwest some of the cheapest power in the country.[55]

The existence of J. D. Ross's six-year plan, according to one of the construction managers, cut two years from BPA's wartime expansion. A private report on the nation's power supply issued during the war made a subtler but equally strong case for the importance of the advance work on developing government dams. It noted that hydroelectric plants in operation make few demands on the nation's manpower or transportation during wartime and "represent a reservoir of 'human labor' largely stored up at the time of construction during peacetime. But private industry as now constituted cannot be expected to take account of these considerations."[56]

The War Production Board, successor to the Office of Production Management, accelerated capacity additions at Grand Coulee Dam when it directed in 1942 that two 75-megawatt generators built for Shasta Dam in California be transferred to Grand Coulee to meet growing demand. They began operation in the spring of 1943, serving an integrated power and defense materials network—including aluminum, aircraft, and shipbuilding—that was growing in the Northwest on the foundation of Columbia River power.[57]

Worker looks up at water rushing over Grand Coulee Dam in 1942. Two generators built for Shasta Dam in California were transferred to Grand Coulee to meet wartime demand for power. (*Library of Congress.*)

TVA was building nine more dams and a coal-fired plant by 1943, and by 1945 it doubled its pre-war capacity and tripled its production to 11.9 billion kilowatt hours, eventually generating ten percent of the power produced for war purposes and making it the largest integrated system in the country. Its rapid wartime buildup vindicated the 1936 *Ashwander* decision, which cited the war powers clause of the Constitution and the national defense origins of the Wilson Dam at Muscle Shoals in upholding TVA's right to sell and transmit power in competition with private utilities.[58]

TVA war posters made employees aware of their role in the war effort.
(*TVA photo K-2665, courtesy of National Archives - Atlanta.*)

BPA sold 5.6 billion kilowatt hours in 1943 and over 9 billion in 1945—3.4 billion from Bonneville Dam and 5.7 billion from Grand Coulee.[59] It powered smelters that produced over a third of the nation's aluminum and the raw material for over 10,000 combat aircraft, and shipyards that produced almost 750 large ships for the war effort. Its master grid of 2,737 circuit miles of transmission lines, planned as a ten-year project, had been completed in five years.[60]

In addition, TVA and BPA were essential to the secret Manhattan Project to develop an atomic bomb. Two huge facilities requiring massive quantities of electricity were built near these sources of abundant power. One, in Oak Ridge, Tennessee, produced enriched uranium, which was used in the bomb dropped on Hiroshima on August 6, 1945. The other, in Hanford, Washington, produced plutonium, which was used in the one dropped on Nagasaki three days later.

The REA, by contrast, had difficulty sustaining its rate of progress during the war. The War Production Board set strict priorities for the allocation of critical materials, including copper for distribution lines, and the shortage of materials set limits on rural electrification. Private utilities often received priority because they had industrial customers producing war material, creating bitterness among many co-ops.[61]

With the help of Sam Rayburn, who had become Speaker of the House in 1940, the newly formed National Rural Electric Cooperative Association persuaded the War Production Board to allow extension of lines to some farmers, those who could most enhance food production. By 1942, nearly 40 percent of farms had been electrified, but for the remaining war years the pace of connecting new farms dropped to about half that of the immediate pre-war years.

The overriding imperative of mobilizing the country for the war led to accommodation between Roosevelt and Willkie. A few weeks after the election, when Roosevelt proposed his controversial Lend-Lease program to allow the United States to provide Britain with defense materials without violating the Neutrality Act of 1939, Willkie came out in support. Other prominent Republicans, notably Herbert Hoover, Alf Landon, Robert Taft, and Arthur Vandenberg, vigorously opposed it. Shortly thereafter Roosevelt and Secretary of War Henry Stimson asked Willkie to travel to Britain to observe and report back on London's valiant resistance to the Luftwaffe's intense aerial bombardment in the recent Battle of Britain. Willkie carried a letter from Roosevelt to Winston Churchill stating that Willkie was "being a true help in keeping politics out of things." On his return in February, he testified in the Senate in favor of Lend-Lease, and Roosevelt later acknowledged that Willkie's help was essential to the bill's passage in March.[62] During the hearing isolationist Senator Gerald Nye of North Dakota asked whether, with Roosevelt having been elected, Willkie still thought the United States would be at war by April 1941. Grinning, Willkie replied that his statement "had been "a bit of campaign oratory."[63]

In late 1941 the prime minister of Australia invited Willkie to make an official visit, and Roosevelt followed up on December 5, "It would give me very great pleasure if you would care to make a short trip . . . . The situation is definitely serious." Two days later Japan bombed Pearl Harbor. The next day, after Roosevelt's powerful "day that will live in infamy" speech, Congress declared war on Japan, and four days later on Germany and Italy. In a national radio broadcast Willkie said, "We go to war because, if we do not, freedom will die with us and with all men."[64]

Roosevelt signs declaration of war against Japan two days after the bombing of Pearl Harbor. (*Library of Congress.*)

Roosevelt called on Willkie again in 1942, asking him to make a trip to the Middle East, Russia, and China as his personal representative to demonstrate American unity and to discuss plans for the postwar future with key world leaders. After visiting the North African front he met with General Charles DeGaulle, leader of the Free French, in Beirut, with Jews and Arabs in Jerusalem, with Joseph Stalin in the USSR, and with Chiang Kai-shek in China. After his return in October, he reported on his seven-week trip in a nationwide radio broadcast.

While Willkie had essentially lost the fight over TVA and the breakup of holding companies, he had gained stature in the process and his non-partisan contributions to war diplomacy further enhanced his reputation with the American public. They flocked to his 1943 book on his journey, *One World,* in which he put forward many progressive views, calling for World Federalism, racial equality in the United States, and an end to Old World colonial empires. The book became the best-selling non-fiction book in the United States to that time.[65]

While Willkie's fervent opposition to Roosevelt's power policies had gained him admiration from Republicans and catapulted him to national prominence, his later support for Roosevelt, especially during the 1942 mid-term Congressional elections, turned the Republican party leadership against him. In 1941, polls had shown he was the leading contender for the Republican nomination for president in 1944, but by 1943 that lead had slipped away. In April 1944, after decisively losing a make-or-break primary election in Wisconsin, he withdrew from contention.

Roosevelt saw in Willkie's fall from Republican grace a tantalizing prospect to create a powerful new political coalition unified around the pragmatic progressivism that had prevailed in the wartime political struggle. In July 1944 he sent word to Willkie that he would like to talk about joining forces in "the somewhat distant future" to form a new political party that would encompass progressive Republicans and force out conservative Democrats. This intriguing possibility died with Willkie in October, when he succumbed to a strep infection that had spread to his heart.[66] Whether Roosevelt would have pushed ahead with such an overture after war's end is a mere ponderable, as the president died in April of 1945 with the final push for victory still underway. What we do know about their high-tension struggle over the national power system is that it forged a distinctive combination of public and private enterprise that had served the country well.

EPILOGUE

The Securities and Exchange Commission ruled in 1945 that Commonwealth & Southern would not be allowed to exist even as the parent of the five utilities in its southern group, and in 1946 the Supreme Court upheld the death sentence in the *North American Company* case. Multistate holding companies were forced to seek the best deal they could from the SEC. C&S proposed to sell its northern subsidiaries as independent companies and to create a new, more limited holding company over its southern utilities. In 1947 the SEC agreed to this plan subject to the sale of South Carolina Power and of all the holding company's gas and transit properties. C&S complied and went out of existence in 1949, as Southern Company was formed as a contiguous, integrated, multi-state holding company. Most other large, multi-state holding companies fared no better. Between 1938 and 1950, non-contiguous or multi-layered companies were forced to dispose of 759 subsidiary companies. Huge companies like Bond and Share and the Insull holdings were fragmented. Only eighteen registered interstate companies remained by 1958. Utilities continued to lobby to repeal the Holding Company Act for years, finally succeeding in 2005.[1]

The Rural Electrification Administration's initial ten-year authorization was due to expire in 1945, and private utilities led the opposition to its renewal. With about 45 percent of farms connected, they argued, the REA was no longer necessary. The program's political popularity, though, guaranteed its survival, and connections surged in the post-war years. By 1949 the number of electrified farms reached 78 percent, with about three out of four newly connected farms served by REA-financed systems. By the mid-1950s, almost all farms had electricity, and in 1998, rural cooperatives served 11 percent of electricity customers in the country.[2]

Rural electrification in TVA's service area grew from about one-third of the national average in 1930 to slightly above the average in 1954,[3] but the liberal-conservative split that characterized views about public power during the Roosevelt years continued into the 1950s. President Dwight Eisenhower told his cabinet in 1953, "By God, if we ever could do it before we leave, I'd like to see us *sell* the whole thing, but I suppose we can't go that far."[4] He did propose in 1954 to allow a consortium of private utilities to construct power plants and sell TVA the power it needed to enrich uranium for nuclear weapons, nuclear submarines and, prospectively, civilian nuclear power plants. He failed following the disclosure that a Bureau of Budget employee who drafted the plan was also a vice-president of a major financial backer of the deal, a fact that Eisenhower denied and then had to admit. In reaction to the scandal, called the Dixon-Yates affair after the presidents of the consortium companies, the Democratic Congress in 1959 amended the law to give TVA even more autonomy.

By the 1960s, the arguments became more complicated than public vs. private, and TVA and BPA were subjected to more varied criticism. As stronger environmental and consumer movements arose, liberals who had little sympathy for industry complaints of unfair treatment were more responsive to claims that the environment or customers were harmed.

The Corps of Engineers and the Bureau of Reclamation continued to build dams and add capacity on the Columbia River and its tributaries in the 1950s, including two Corps dams, Chief Joseph and The Dalles, which had greater capacity than Bonneville. By 1974, Bonneville reached a capacity of 1,190 megawatts and Grand Coulee 6,809 megawatts. By 2017, 274 hydropower dams in the Columbia

River Basin, including some in British Columbia and many small private dams, had 16,254 megawatts of capacity and provided over 55 percent of the total energy produced in the Northwest. Fish kills remained a greater concern as increased efforts to mitigate the problem were matched or surpassed by increased public awareness and concern.

The Roosevelt administration never laid out an integrated, comprehensive power policy. Policies were developed in an ad hoc fashion, influenced at different times by economic conditions, real or perceived abuses, politics, the interplay of specific advisers, and, eventually, the war effort. Because the goals were not always well defined, the policies frightened utility executives and investors and were sometimes subject to exaggerated criticism. Roosevelt's general goals for the sector, though, primarily developed while he was governor of New York, were constant. They were best described in his 1932 Portland speech, which is the yardstick, so to speak, against which one can measure his achievements.[5]

In that speech he set out several principles: Private ownership of the production, transmission, and distribution of electricity is generally desirable. Municipal utilities, when desired by the citizens, and federal government hydroelectric projects are exceptions to this rule. These exceptions also encourage price competition by providing a comparison with the rates of private utilities. In addition, federal power development can encourage greater use of electricity, the "servant of the people." Where necessary to obtain reasonable service, the government also has the right to transmit and distribute the power from these projects. Electricity is a social good, a necessity rather than a luxury, and by implication universal service is a critical objective. The federal government must rein in holding companies and limit manipulation of their securities, and rate regulation should be based on original cost, not replacement cost.[6]

Roosevelt was more specific about rural electrification in 1934 when he directed his National Power Policy Committee to "develop a plan . . . whereby . . . electricity may be made more broadly available at cheaper rates . . . particularly, to agricultural consumers." He also directed the committee to develop "legislation . . . for the regulation of electric current in interstate commerce," a charge that led to the Federal Power Act.[7]

His four major electricity initiatives—TVA, the Public Utility Holding Company Act (including the Federal Power Act), the REA, and the BPA—largely achieved these goals. It may not have seemed obvious to his critics, but the Holding Company Act may have allowed private utilities to survive. In the wake of the scandals reported by the Federal Trade Commission and the investor losses resulting from the collapse of many of the pyramids, there was some sentiment for municipalizing or nationalizing the industry as had been done in other countries. Roosevelt offered no support for such a radical solution. After private utility interests weakened the more draconian draft of the Holding Company Act in the legislative process, the law allowed federal regulation of interstate electricity sales and eliminated the worst of the financial abuses, both without seriously damaging the operating utilities. Economic historian Harold Underwood Faulkner concluded, "No company died that seemed to have the slightest excuse for living."[8]

In the struggle for TVA, each of the combatants won a partial victory. Historian Henry Steele Commager sided with Roosevelt and Lilienthal, calling TVA "probably the greatest peacetime achievement of twentieth-century America."[9] TVA built sixteen dams in its first twelve years, provided thousands of jobs during the Depression, made rivers navigable and controlled floods, brought affordable electricity and appliances to thousands, lifted the standard of living of one of the poorest areas of the country, and showed regulators and private utilities that low rates could increase consumption.

The TVA example also encouraged advocates of federal dams elsewhere, primarily in the Northwest and Southwest. But Willkie's political skills were largely responsible for limiting TVA's territorial expansion, for the generous payment to TEPCO investors, for calling into question the yardstick theory, and for thwarting other river valley developments with comprehensive planning authority like that of TVA.[10]

Both Willkie and Lilienthal emerged with enhanced reputations. Willkie's leadership of the utility industry in its battles against TVA and the Holding Company Act made him the most visible business opponent of the New Deal, which in turn put the 1940 Republican presidential nomination within his reach. Lilienthal's stature in the public power community and within the administration led to his appointment as chairman of TVA in 1941 and chairman of the new Atomic Energy Commission in 1946.

Victory in the larger battle, although not total, goes to Roosevelt. He could not eliminate all holding companies or replicate TVA, but the Supreme Court eventually upheld TVA's constitutionality, supervision of the capital structure of holding companies, and regulation of interstate power sales. The Holding Company Act and its implementation by the SEC largely eliminated multi-layered, multi-state holding companies while allowing operating utilities to survive and thrive. Additional multi-purpose federal dams contributed to regional economic development and rural electrification. Even though Willkie and his allies discredited the idea of a precise yardstick, the "birch rod in the cupboard" provided by government competition was real. From 1920 to 1932, when holding companies claimed to be providing efficiencies through management and system integration, inflation-adjusted residential rates were flat. From 1933 to 1942, with growing competition from public power, rates declined by about 40 percent in real terms.[11]

The large federal hydroelectric projects epitomized by TVA and BPA represented another Roosevelt success. The economics of multiple purpose dams—power, irrigation, flood control, and navigation— brought large amounts of cheap power to less developed regions of the country. Although conceived and justified in terms of economic development and healthy competition for private utilities, they also proved to be critical to winning the war.

The REA showed that relatively small subsidies, combined with a strategy similar to Samuel Insull's gospel of consumption, could bring electricity to underserved rural areas. As economic historian Gavin Wright has written, "The social implications of electrification for rural households can scarcely be overstated."[12] In the short run, it affected the lives of more Americans more dramatically than any other New Deal program. It extended electric service directly to millions of farms and indirectly to many more by pressuring private utilities to compete.

It brought appliance costs down and increased sales, added manufacturing jobs, and helped raise rural property values by up to 20 percent a year during the Depression. Almost every dollar of its loans was repaid. Even the private utilities may have benefited. The large amount of wholesale power they sold to co-ops was new business that added to their demand, increased their efficiency, and reduced their costs.[13]

With all of these achievements, however, the New Deal did surprisingly little to restructure operating utilities as a whole. The system created by Edison and expanded by Insull, the most important technological achievement of the twentieth century, remained basically intact. The relative roles played by private and public power in the nation's blended system remained nearly constant after public power's surge beginning in the Roosevelt administration. The public share of utility generation, including both federally and municipally owned power plants, grew from about 6 percent in 1932 to nearly 19 percent in 1945. As government power plants planned before or during the war continued to come on line in the next decade, the public share increased to about 23 percent in 1955. And there it remained, give or take a percentage point or two, through 25 years of rapid economic growth, until the advent of independent power producers who began selling power to utilities in the 1980s.[14]

The high-tension struggle between Roosevelt and Willkie and between private and public utilities established the distinctive hybrid system that fueled the country's global economic supremacy during the remainder of the twentieth century. It also provided an enduring example for other industries critical to people's daily lives, including health care, telecommunications, and infrastructure. The private sector is a powerful source for innovation and growth, but government has a role to play in shaping and policing these industries, not only by preventing abuses but also by catalyzing growth directly when incentives for private action are insufficient. Finding the right balance between these competing realities is a continuing challenge for the American political system.

HOW TO BUILD A HOLDING COMPANY PYRAMID

Suppose operating utilities A, B, and C are each capitalized with $50 million of bonds, $50 million of preferred stock, and $50 million par value of common stock.* (Bonds are loans made by an investor to a borrower such as a corporation or government, usually at fixed interest rates for a specific term. Stocks represent ownership in a corporation in proportion to the number of shares, and they can fluctuate in value. Preferred stock has priority over common stock for dividends and typically receives a higher rate of return. Usually only common stock has voting rights.) An investor can purchase control of each $150 million company with half of the common stock, or $25 million, less than 17 percent of the company's value. (In reality, control of a widely held company normally requires much less than half of its common stock.)

The controlling investors prefer not to tie up even that much money, so they form holding company X and transfer to it, as its sole assets, their $75 million in common stock in utilities A, B, and C. They receive in exchange $45 million in bonds, $15 million in preferred stock, and $15 million in common stock of the holding company. They

---

* Hypothetical example based on Bonbright & Means, 18-9; Sidney A. Mitchell, 80; FTC, Part 72A, 87.

then sell the bonds, the preferred stock, and half of the common stock, maintaining their control of the holding company with their remaining 50 percent of its common stock, worth $7.5 million. They now control the three operating utilities, collectively worth $450 million, with an investment of less than 2 percent of their value.

The investors buy a controlling interest in three similarly financed operating utilities D, E and F, and transfer their holdings to holding company Y. Again retaining only $7.5 million in common stock of the holding company, as in the previous example, they control another three utilities worth $450 million for under 2 percent of their value.

Now suppose that the investors want to control all six of these companies with an even smaller investment than $15 million. They form super-holding company S and transfer to it the $7.5 million controlling interest in the common stock of each holding company, X and Y, or a total of $15 million. If super-holding company S is financed with the same proportion of bonds, preferred stock, and common stock as holding companies X and Y, the investors can control it by retaining 50 percent of the $6 million in common stock. They now control the six operating utilities, worth $900 million, with an investment of $3 million, or one-third of one percent of their value.

Each additional layer of the pyramid would increase the leverage of the common stock owners at the top. Some holding companies by the late 1920s had as many as ten layers. A higher ratio of debt to equity, more common among utilities than most other industries, would also increase the leverage of common stock owners, as would the ability to control companies with less than 50 percent of the common stock. Unfortunately, as many owners learned during the stock market crash, higher leverage magnifies risk as well as returns.

APPENDIX B:

HOW TO MAKE DIVIDENDS FLOW UPHILL

Holding company X purchases a controlling share of the common stock of an operating utility. For each $100 it buys, it earns $8 as a dividend. The holding company raises the $100 for the purchase by marketing its own securities: 60 percent in bonds, 20 percent in preferred stock, and 20 percent in common stock. At 6 percent interest, it pays $3.60 on the bonds. With a 7 percent dividend, it pays $1.40 on the preferred stock. This amounts to $5 of the $8 it receives in common stock dividends from the operating company, leaving $3 that can be paid as a dividend on the holding company's $20 worth of common stock, a generous dividend rate of 15 percent.*

Super-holding company S is then formed to control holding company X. To pay for the $100 in common stock of X that it buys, S also sells $60 in bonds, $20 in preferred stock, and $20 in common stock. It receives the 15 percent dividend on the common stock of holding company X, or $20. It pays $3.60 of this in interest on the $60 in bonds it has issued and $1.40 in dividends on the $20 in preferred

---

* Based on Syndey A. Mitchell, 80. The proportion of bonds, preferred stock, and common stock used in the example is within the target range of Electric Bond and Share, i.e., 50-60% bonds, 20-25% preferred, and 20-25% common. FTC, 72A, 87.

stock, leaving $15 that can be paid in dividends on its $20 worth of common stock – a rate of return of 75 percent.

The big benefit to the controlling interests is the way the returns multiply as they move up the layers of the pyramid. Few outsiders owned any common stock in the higher levels. Most small investors were satisfied with the interest rates on bonds and preferred stock and with the appreciation in the value of utility common stock during the steady rise in the stock market during the 1920s.

Although this is a hypothetical example, a 1927 Federal Trade Commission report noted that the organizers of actual holding companies frequently kept ownership of their common stock, and that in 1924 their intercorporate dividends gave them rates of return on this stock ranging from 19 to 55 percent.*

---

* FTC, "Control of Power Companies," Feb. 22, 1927, xxiv.

ACKNOWLEDGMENTS

Writing a book can at times be a solitary trek, but one of its rewards is the help and encouragement that comes from many directions. I salute the following people for their assistance.

My agent, Rita Rosenkranz, showed immediate enthusiasm for the book I envisioned, and her encouragement and patience never faltered as the book's shape and focus changed. She was my indispensable guide in navigating the world of publishing.

Keith Wallman, my editor at Diversion Books, is an enthusiast of presidential history and biography, and his excitement about my topic and his generosity with compliments during the editing process made his suggestions for changes easy to accept. The team of consummate professionals at Diversion Books was helpful in numerous ways, including some of which I am only vaguely aware.

Emily Loose provided invaluable advice for reshaping the book after a sprawling first draft proved too large in scope for a popular history, and she helped me enliven the prose style that I had honed in decades of government work. She also encouraged me to glance to the sides as I traveled the narrow road of my story, adding color and context.

I am grateful to authors who shared their wisdom and experience when my project was still just an idea or as I was feeling my way through the process. Among them are Bruce Babbitt, Robert Dallek, Mickey Edwards, Clark Ervin, Walter Isaacson, Betsy Kraft, Marty Sherwin, Jim Srodes, and David Stewart.

Several people read large or small parts of the manuscript at various stages, in some cases offering their knowledge of the subject, in others their suggestions for clarity or felicity of language. All provided insights and recommendations that improved the final product. Among them are Steve Cole, Charlie Curtis, Peter Fox-Penner, Dave Freeman, Jeff Lott, Everett Mattlin, John Maxson, John Morrison, Barbara Patocka, John Rowe, and Gavin Wright. To the extent that the final version does not meet their standards, the failing is mine.

Numerous friends and family members bolstered my spirit and my resolve with friendly questions or encouraging comments. They include Win Arias, Duffy Campbell, Charlie Firestone, Wilson Jones, Larry Kellerman, Frank Loy, David Monsma, John Nutter, Carol Parker, Jed Rakoff, Toivo Raun, Julie Riggs, Phil Sharp, Jim Spiegelman, Sue Tierney, Susan Wade, Conrad Weiler, and Dan West.

Several people provided assistance beyond the ordinary when I asked for information from their organizations, including Ed Comer of the Edison Electric Institute, Pat Ezzell of TVA, Andrew Gahan of the Bureau of Reclamation, Maureen Hill of the National Archives at Atlanta, Martin Lowery of the American Public Power Association, Jennifer Muller of the Army Corps of Engineers, Jim Nanney and Christy Hinton of the Alcorn County Electric Power Association, and Bill Zimmerman and Rob Diffely at the Bonneville Power Administration.

Thanks, too, to the many librarians whose knowledge and enthusiasm for their work made my work easier. In particular I appreciate those at the Franklin D. Roosevelt Presidential Library, the Information Resources Center of the Edison Electric Institute, the Lilly Library at Indiana University, and the Library of Congress, especially in its Business and Science Reading Room and its Law Library.

By far the most important support came from my wife Judy and my son Mike. Both are skilled writers and gave useful critiques of various drafts, and Mike helped me understand some of the physical mysteries of electricity before the technical sections of the book ended up on the cutting room floor. I would have given up long ago without Judy's unfailing love and support and her endless patience with the encroachment on family time. I promise to make up for the missed hikes, bike rides, and vacations.

BIBLIOGRAPHY

Abel, Amy. "Electricity Restructuring Background: Public Utility Holding Company Act of 1935 (PUHCA)." Congressional Research Service, RS20015 (Jan. 7, 1999).

Adams, Edward Dean. *Niagara Power: History of the Niagara Falls Power Company, 1886–1918; Evolution of its Central Power Station and Alternating Current System* (2 vols). Niagara Falls, NY: The Niagara Falls Power Company, 1927.

Agran, Edward Gale. *Herbert Hoover and the Commodification of Middle-Class America: An American Promise.* Lanham: Lexington Books, 2016.

Allen, Frederick Lewis. *Lords of Creation.* New York: Harper & Brothers, 1935.

Alsop, Joseph and Turner Catledge. *168 Days.* Garden City, NY: Doubleday, Doran, 1938.

Alter, Jonathan. *Defining Moment: FDR's Hundred Days and the Triumph of Hope.* New York: Simon & Schuster, 2006.

Anderson, Douglas D. *Regulatory Politics and Electric Utilities: A Case Study in Political Economy.* Boston: Auburn House, 1981.

Asbell, Bernard. *The F.D.R. Memoirs.* New York: Doubleday, 1973.

Ashwander et al. v. Tennessee Valley Authority et al. 297 U.S. 288 (1936).

Badger, Anthony J. *FDR: The First Hundred Days.* New York: Hill and Wang (Farrar, Straus and Giroux), 2008.

Baldwin, Neil. *Edison: Inventing the Century.* Chicago: University of Chicago Press, 2001.

Barnard, Ellsworth. *Wendell Willkie: Fighter for Freedom.* Marquette, MI: Northern Michigan University Press, 1966.

Barnes, Irston R. *Cases on Public Utility Regulation.* New York: F.S. Crofts & Co., 1938.

Barnes, Joseph. *Willkie.* New York: Simon & Schuster, 1952.

Barron, Clarence W. *More They Told Barron*. New York: Arno Press, 1973.

Baum, Robert. *The Federal Power Commission and State Utility Regulation*. Washington, DC: American Council on Public Affairs, 1942.

Beard, Charles A. "The New Deal's Rough Road." *Current History*, 42 (Sept. 1935): 625-32.

Behling, Burton. *Competition and Monopoly in Public Utility Industries*. Urbana, IL: University of Illinois Press, 1938.

Bellush, Bernard. *Franklin D. Roosevelt as Governor of New York*. New York: Columbia University Press, 1955.

Bergman, Michael. "Electric Utility Statistics: 1882-1982." *Public Power* 40, no. 5 (Sept.-Oct. 1982): 65-68.

Berle, Adoph A. and Gardiner C. Means. *The Modern Corporation and Private Property*. New York: Macmillan Co., 1933.

Bernstein, Theodore. "A Grand Success." *IEEE Spectrum*, 10, no. 2 (Feb. 1973): 54-58.

Beschloss, Michael. *Kennedy and Roosevelt: The Uneasy Alliance*. New York: Norton, 1980.

Billington, David P. and Donald C. Jackson. *Big Dams of the New Deal Era: A Confluence of Engineering and Politics*. Norman: University of Oklahoma Press, 2006.

Blackford, Mansel G. "Businessmen and the Regulation of Railroads and Public Utilities in California During the Progressive Era." *Business History Review* 44, no. 3 (Autumn, 1970): 7-19.

Bloch, Marc. *The Historian's Craft*. New York: Random House, 1953.

Blum, Robert. "SEC Integration of Holding Company Systems." *Journal of Land and Public Utility Economics,* 17 (Nov. 1941): 423-39.

Bonbright, James C. *Principles of Public Utility Rates*. New York: Columbia University Press, 1961.

Bonbright, James C. *Public Utilities and the National Power Policies*. New York: Columbia University Press, 1940.

Bonbright, James C. and Gardiner Means. *The Holding Company: Its Public Significance and Its Regulation*. New York: McGraw-Hill, 1932.

Bonneville Power Administration. "BPA Powered the Industry That Helped Win World War II." Oct. 31, 2012. https://www.bpa.gov/news/newsroom

Bonneville Power Administration. "Woody Guthrie & BPA: An Unlikely Collaboration." https://www.bpa.gov/news/aboutus/history/Guthrie

Bowers, Brian. *Lengthening The Day*. New York: Oxford University Press, 1998.

Bradley, Robert L., Jr. *Edison to Enron: Energy Markets and Political Strategies*. New York: Wiley & Sons, 2011.

Brandeis, Louis D. *Other People's Money, and How the Bankers Use It*. New York: A. M. Kelley, 1971.

Brands, H.W. *Traitor to His Class: The Privileged Life and Radical Presidency of Franklin Delano Roosevelt*. New York: Doubleday, 2008.

Brigham, Jay. *Empowering the West: Electrical Politics Before FDR*. Lawrence: University Press of Kansas, 1998.

Bright, Arthur Aaron, Jr. *The Electric Lamp Industry: Technological Change and Economic Development, 1880-1947*. New York: Macmillan, 1949.

Brinkley, Alan. *The End of Reform: New Deal Liberalism in Recession and War*. New York: Alfred A. Knopf, 1995.

Brinkley, Douglas. *The Wilderness Warrior: Theodore Roosevelt and the Crusade for America*. New York: HarperCollins, 2009.

Brown, D. Clayton. *Electricity for Rural America: The Fight for the REA*. Westport, CT: Greenwood Press, 1980.

Brown, D. Clayton. "Farm Life: Before and After Electrification." *Proceedings of the Annual Meeting, Association for Living Historical Farms and Agricultural Museums*, 1975. Washington, DC: Smithsonian Institution.

Bryan, William Jennings. Speech, in *Chicago Conference on Trusts: Speeches, Debates . . . Sept. 1899*. Chicago: The Civic Federation of Chicago, 1900.

Buchanan, Norman S. "The Origin and Development of the Public Utility Holding Company." *The Journal of Political Economy*, 44, No.1 (Feb. 1936): 31-53.

Bureau of the Census. *Census of Electrical Industries: 1902, 1907, 1912, 1917, 1922, 1927*. Washington: Government Printing Office.

Bureau of the Census. *Historical Statistics of the United States, Colonial Times to 1970.* Washington: U.S. Dept. of Commerce, Bureau of the Census, 1975.

Bureau of the Census, *Historical Statistics of the United States 1789-1945.* Washington: U.S. Government Printing Office, 1949.

Bureau of Reclamation, Phoenix Area Office. "A Brief History of Roosevelt Dam." Last updated June 25, 2015. https://www.usbr.gov/lc/phoenix/projects

Burns, James MacGregor. *Roosevelt: The Lion and the Fox.* Norwalk, CT: Easton Press, 1989.

Busch, Andrew E. "1930 Midterms Heralded New Deal." April 2006. Ashbrook Center. www.ashbrook.org/publicat/oped/busch/06/1930.html

Busch, Andrew E. "The New Deal Comes to a Screeching Halt in 1938." May 2006. Ashbrook Center. https://ashbrook.org/publications/oped-busch-06-1938/

"Business: "Bond and Share Defense." *Time,* Nov. 23, 1936.

Business Week. "Insull Crisis Dramatizes Plight of Investment Holding Groups." April 20, 1932.

Callahan, North. *TVA: Bridge Over Troubled Waters,* New York: A.S. Barnes and Company, 1980.

Carlisle, Floyd L. "The Control of Public Utility Corporations." *National Electric Light Association Bulletin* 17 (Nov. 1930): 679-81.

Carlson, W. Bernard. *Innovation as a Social Process: Elihu Thomson and the Rise of General Electric, 1870-1900.* Cambridge: Cambridge University Press, 1991.

Carlson, W. Bernard. *Tesla: Inventor of the Electrical Age.* Princeton: Princeton University Press, 2013.

Carmody, John M. "Rural Electrification in the United States." *Annals of the American Academy of Political and Social Science* 201, no. 1 (Jan. 1939): 82-88.

Caro, Robert A. *The Path to Power.* New York: Vintage Books, 1983.

Carter, Susan B. et al. *Historical statistics of the United States: Earliest Times to the Present.* New York: Cambridge University Press, 2006.

Chandler, Alfred D., and Richard S. Tedlow. *The Coming of Managerial Capitalism.* Homewood, IL: Richard D. Irwin, 1985.

Chandler, Alfred D. *The Visible Hand: The Managerial Revolution in American Business*. Cambridge, MA: Belknap Press, 1977.

Chandler, William U. *The Myth of TVA: Conservation and Development in the Tennessee Valley, 1933-1983*. Cambridge, MA: Ballinger Publishing, 1983.

Chernow, Ron. *The House of Morgan: An American Banking Dynasty and the Rise of Modern Finance*. New York: Grove Press, 2001.

Chessman, G. Wallace. *Governor Theodore Roosevelt: The Albany Apprenticeship, 1898-1900*. Cambridge: Harvard University Press, 1965.

Chessman, G. Wallace. *Theodore Roosevelt and the Politics of Power*. Boston: Little, Brown, 1969.

Childs, Marquis W. "Samuel Insull, III: The Collapse." *The New Republic* (Oct. 5, 1932): 201-3.

Christie, Jean. "Giant Power: A Progressive Proposal of the Nineteen-Twenties." *Pennsylvania Magazine of History and Biography*, 96 (Oct. 1972): 480-507.

Christie, Jean. *Morris Llewellyn Cooke, Progressive Engineer*. New York: Garland, 1983.

Civil Works Administration. "A Comprehensive Survey of Behavior Patterns of the People of a Single Community and of the Social, Cultural, Intellectual and Economic Forces that Influence Them" (aka "The Gorgas Study"). April, 1934. Unpublished document, available in National Archives, Atlanta.

Clemens, Eli Winston. *Economics and Public Utilities*. New York: Appleton-Century-Crofts, 1950.

Cohen, Adam. *Nothing to Fear: FDR's Inner Circle and the Hundred Days that Created Modern America*. New York: Penguin Books, 2009.

Colignon, Richard A. *Power Plays: Critical Events in the Institutionalization of the Tennessee Valley Authority*. Albany: State University of New York Press, 1997.

Commager, Henry Steele. *The American Mind: An Interpretation of American Thought and Character since the 1880's*. New Haven: Yale University Press, 1950.

Commons, John R. *Myself, the Autobiography of John R. Commons*. Madison: University of Wisconsin Press, 1963.

Commons, John R. "The Wisconsin Public-Utilities Law." *Review of Reviews* 36 (1907): 221-24.

Congress, House, Committee on Interstate and Foreign Commerce. *Relation of Holding Companies to Operating Companies in Power and Gas.* House report 827, 73rd Congress, 1st Session, 1933.

Congress, House, Committee on Interstate and Foreign Commerce. *Report on Public Utility Holding Company Act of 1935, H.R. 1318.* 74th Congress, 1st Session, 1935.

Cooke, Morris Llewellyn. "The Early Days of the Rural Electrification Idea: 1914–1936." *American Political Science Review* 42, no. 3 (June 1948): 431-47.

Cooke, Morris Llewellyn. "New Deal Proposed in Rural Electrification." Interview, *Electrical World,* July 6, 1935.

Conot, Robert. *A Streak of Luck.* New York: Seaview Books, 1978.

Coppock, Joseph D. "Organization and Operations of the Electric Home and Farm Authority," in *Government Agencies of Consumer Installment Credit.* Cambridge, MA: National Bureau of Economic Research, 1940.

Coughlin, John P. "Public Utilities and the Public." *National Electric Light Association Bulletin,* 19 (Dec. 1932): 711-14.

Cowan, Ruth Schwartz. "The 'Industrial Revolution' in the Home: Household Technology and Social Change in the 20th Century." *Technology and Culture* 17 (1976): 1-23.

Cowan, Ruth Schwartz. *More Work for Mother: The Ironies of Household Technology from the Open Hearth to the Microwave.* New York: Basic, 1983.

Coyle, David Cushman, ed. *Electric Power on the Farm.* Rural Electrification Administration. Washington, DC: U.S. Government Printing Office, 1936.

Crowther, Samuel. "He's the Public's Hired Man." *Colliers* 75 (Jan. 17, 1925): 12-3.

Cudahy, Richard D., and William D. Henderson. "From Insull to Enron: Corporate (Re)regulation after the Rise and Fall of Two Energy Icons." *Energy Law Journal* 26, no. 35 (2005): 35-110. http://ssrn.com/abstract+716321.

Culvahouse, Tim, ed. *The Tennessee Valley Authority: Design and Persuasion.* New York: Princeton Architectural Press, 2007.

Cushman, Robert E. *The Independent Regulatory Commissions.* New York: Quorum Books, 1941.

Danielian, N. R. "From Insull to Injury: A Study in Financial Jugglery." *Atlantic Monthly* 115 (April 1933): 497-508.

Daniels, Jonathan. "Banner on a Yardstick," *The New Republic* 96 (Aug. 24, 1938): 67-9.

Daniels, Josephus. *The Wilson Era: Years of War and After, 1917-1923.* Chapel Hill: The University of North Carolina Press, 1946.

Daniels, Roger, *Franklin D. Roosevelt: Road to the New Deal, 1882-1939.* Urbana: University of Illinois Press, 2015.

Davidson, Donald *The Tennessee, vol. 2: The New River, Civil War to TVA.* New York: Rinehart & Co., 1948.

Davis, Kenneth S. *FDR: The Beckoning of Destiny 1882-1928.* New York: Random House, 1986.

Davis, Kenneth S. *FDR: The New Deal Years 1933-1937.* New York: Random House, 1986.

Davis, Kenneth S. *FDR: The New York Years 1928-1932.* New York: Putnam, 1971.

DeGraaf, Leonard. "Corporate Liberalism and Electric Power System Planning in the 1920s," *Business History Review* 64, no. 1 (Spring 1990): 1-31.

Dillon, May Earhart. *Wendell Willkie.* New York: Lippincott, 1952.

Dorau, Herbert B. *The Changing Character and Extent of Municipal Ownership in the Electric Light and Power Industry.* Chicago: Institute for Research in Land Economics & Public Utilities, 1929.

Douglas, William O. *Go East, Young Man.* New York: Random House, 1974.

Doyle, Jack. *Lines Across the Land: Rural Electric Cooperatives.* Washington: Environmental Policy Institute, 1979.

Dreher, Carl. "J. D. Ross, Public Power Magnate," *Harper's Magazine* 181 (June 1940): 46-60.

Droze, Wilmon H. *High Dams and Slack Waters: TVA Rebuilds a River.* Baton Rouge: Louisiana State University Press, 1965.

Edison Electric Institute. "History of the Electric Power Industry." http://www.eei.org/industry_issues/industry_overview_and_statistics/history/index. htm

Edison Electric Institute. *Pocketbook of Electric Utility Statistics,* 30th Ed. Washington, DC: Edison Electric Institute, 1984.

Eldot, Paula. *Governor Alfred E. Smith: The Politician as Reformer*. New York: Garland, 1983.

Ellis, Clyde T. *A Giant Step*. New York: Random House, 1966.

Elsbree, Hugh L. *Interstate Transmission of Electric Power: A Study in the Conflict of State and Federal Jurisdictions*. Cambridge, MA: Harvard University Press, 1931.

Emmons, William M., III. "Franklin D. Roosevelt, Electric Utilities, and the Power of Competition," *The Journal of Economic History* 53, no. 4 (Dec. 1993): 880-907.

Energy Information Administration, Department of Energy. "History of the U.S. Electric Power Industry, 1882-1991," in *The Changing Structure of the Electricity Industry*, 1996.

Energy Information Administration, Department of Energy. "Public Utility Holding Company Act of 1935: 1935-1992." Jan. 1993.

Energy Information Administration, Department of Energy. "United States Energy History," in *Annual Energy Review 2001*, Report No. DOE/EIA-0384, 2001. www.eia. doe.gov/aer/eh/eh.html.

Engler, Robert. *America's Energy: Reports from The Nation on 100 Years of Struggles for the Democratic Control of our Resources*. New York: Pantheon Books, 1980.

Essig, Mark. *Edison and the Electric Chair: A Story of Light and Death*. New York: Walker & Company, 2003.

"Executives Storm House Committee to Stop Bill." *Newsweek* 5 (Apr. 13, 1935): 32-3.

Farley, James A. *Jim Farley's Story: The Roosevelt Years*. New York: Whittlesey House, 1948.

Farley, James A. *Governor Al Smith*. New York: Vision Books, Farrar, Straus & Cudahy, 1959.

Federal Trade Commission. *Control of Power Companies*. Government Printing Office, 1927.

Federal Trade Commission. *Supply of Electrical Equipment and Competitive Conditions*, Part 2. Government Printing Office, 1928.

Federal Trade Commission. *Utility Corporations: Report on Publicity and Propaganda Activities by Utilities Groups and Companies* No. 81-A. Government Printing Office, 1935.

Federal Trade Commission. *Utility Corporations: Summary Report on Economic, Financial, and Corporate Phases of Holding and Operating Companies of Electric and Gas Utilities* Part 72-A. Government Printing Office, 1935.

Federal Trade Commission. *Utility Corporations: Summary Report on Efforts by Associations and Agencies of Electric and Gas Utilities to Influence Public Opinion* Part 71-A. Government Printing Office, 1934.

Feldman, Noah. *Scorpions: The Battles and Triumphs of FDR's Great Supreme Court Justices.* New York: Twelve, 2010.

Field, Gregory B. "'Electricity for All': The Electric Home and Farm Authority and the Politics of Mass Consumption, 1932-1935," *Business History Review* 64, no. 1, (Spring, 1990): 32-60.

Finlayson, Ranald A. "The Public Utility Holding Company Under Federal Regulation," *The Journal of Business of the University of Chicago* 16, supp. (July 1946): 1-41.

Finney, Ruth. "A Pyramid of Profit," *Nation* 136 (May 10, 1933): 524-5.

Flynn, John T. "Up and Down with Sam Insull," 4 installments, *Collier's Magazine,* Dec. 3 to 27, 1932.

Forbes, John Douglas. *J. P. Morgan, Jr., 1867-1943.* Charlottesville: University Press of Virginia, 1981.

Fortune 15. "Commonwealth and Southern." (May 1937): 82-7, 180-200.

Fortune 15. "Wendell Lewis Willkie." (May, 1937): 89-90, 202-209.

Frank, Jeffrey. "The Willkie What-If: FDR's Hybrid Party Plot," *The New Yorker,* July 28, 2015.

Fuhrman, Peter. "Do It Big, Sammy." *Forbes* (July 13, 1987): 278-280.

Franch, John. *Robber Baron: The Life of Charles Tyson Yerkes.* Urbana: University of Illinois Press, 2006.

Freeberg, Ernest. *The Age of Edison: Electric Light and the Invention of Modern America.* New York: Penguin Press, 2013.

Freidel, Frank Burt. *Franklin D. Roosevelt: A Rendezvous with Destiny.* Boston: Little, Brown, 1990.

Friedel, Robert and Paul Israel, with Bernard S. Finn. *Edison's Electric Light: Biography of an Invention.* New Brunswick, NJ: Rutgers University Press, 1987.

Funigiello, Philip J. *Toward a National Power Policy; the New Deal and the Electric Utility Industry, 1933-1941.* Pittsburgh: University of Pittsburgh Press, 1973.

Fusfield, Daniel R. *The Economic Thought of Franklin D. Roosevelt and the Origins of the New Deal.* New York: Columbia University Press, 1956.

Gallagher, Hugh Gregory. *FDR's Splendid Deception.* New York: Dodd, Mead & Company, 1985.

Garland, J.V. and Charles F. Phillips. *The Crisis in the Electric Utilities.* New York: H.W. Wilson, 1936.

Geisst, Charles R. *Monopolies in America: Empire Builders and Their Enemies, from Jay Gould to Bill Gates.* New York: Oxford University Press, 2000.

Glaeser, Martin G. *Public Utilities in American Capitalism.* New York: Macmillan, 1957.

Goldman, Eric F. *Rendezvous with Destiny: A History of Modern American Reform.* New York: Knopf, 1952.

Golway, Terry. *Frank and Al: FDR, Al Smith, and the Unlikely Alliance that Created the Modern Democratic Party.* New York: St. Martin's Press, 2018.

Gould, Jacob Martin. *Output and Productivity in the Electric and Gas Utilities: 1899-1942.* Cambridge: National Bureau of Economic Research, 1946.

Greenwood, Ernest. "The Three Water Witches—Boulder Dam, St. Lawrence and Muscle Shoals—Brew a Political Broth." *Public Utilities Fortnightly* 8, pt. 1. (Sept. 17, 1931): 331-39.

Gulick, Charles A. "Holding Companies in Power." *The New Republic* 47 (May 26, 1926): 25-8.

Hagenah, W. J. "Soundness of Regulation Proved." *Electrical World* 93 (June 8, 1929): 1170.

Hamilton, Gordon. "Wendell Willkie of C & S." *Current History* 51, no. 6 (Feb. 1940).

Handlin, Oscar. *Al Smith and His America.* Boston: Little, Brown and Co., 1958.

Hargrove, Erwin C. *Prisoners of Myth: The Leadership of the Tennessee Valley Authority, 1933-1990.* Princeton: Princeton University Press, 1994.

Harris, Douglas B. and Lonce H. Bailey. *The Republican Party: Documents Decoded.* Santa Barbara: ABC-CLIO, 2014.

Hawley, Ellis W. "The New Deal and Business." In *The New Deal*, v.1, edited by John Braeman, Robert H. Bremner, and David Brody. Columbus: Ohio State University Press, 1975.

Hawley, Ellis W. *The New Deal and the Problem of Monopoly.* Princeton: Princeton University Press, 1966.

Hayes, Henry R. "Public Confidence in the Power Industry." *National Electric Light Association Bulletin* 18 (Feb. 1931): 77-80.

Hays, Samuel P. *Conservation and the Gospel of Efficiency: The Progressive Conservation Movement, 1890-1920.* Cambridge: Harvard University Press, 1959.

Hellman, Richard. "The TVA and the Utilities." *Harpers* 178 (Jan. 1939): 164-74 .

Hellman, Richard. *Government Competition in the Electric Utility Industry: A Theoretical and Empirical Study.* New York: Praeger, 1972.

Herman, Arthur. *Freedom's Forge: How American Business Produced Victory in World War II.* New York: Random House, 2012.

Hilton, George W. and John F. Due. *The Electric Interurban Railways in America.* Stanford: Stanford University Press, 1960.

Hirsh, Richard F. *Power Loss: The Origins of Deregulation and Restructuring in the American Electric Utility System.* Cambridge: MIT Press, 1999.

Hirsh, Richard F. *Technology and Transformation in the American Electric Utility Industry.* Cambridge: Cambridge University Press, 1989.

Hodge, William H. "A Defense of the Holding Company." *The Annals of the American Academy of Political and Social Science,* 159, pt. 1 (1932): 7-14.

Hodgins, Eric and F. Alexander Magoun. *Behemoth: The Story of Power.* Garden City, NY: Doubleday, Doran & Co., 1932.

Hogan, John. *A Spirit Capable: The Story of Commonwealth Edison.* Chicago: Mobium Press, 1986.

Holstine, Craig. "Power to the People: Construction of the Bonneville Power Administration's 'Master Grid', 1939-1945." *The Pacific Northwest Forum* 1 no. 2 (Spring 1988): 35-46.

Hooker, H. Lester. "The Raid of the Radicals on State Regulation," *Public Utilities Fortnightly* 6 (Dec. 25, 1930): 771-83.

"Hoover and Super-Power." *Time.* Oct. 22, 1923.

Hubbard, Preston J. *Origins of the TVA: The Muscle Shoals Controversy, 1920-1932.* Nashville: Vanderbilt U. Press, 1961.

Hughes, Thomas P. "The Electrification of America: The System Builders." *Technology and Culture* 20 (1979).

Hughes, Thomas P. "Harold Brown and the Executioner's Current: An Incident in the AC-DC Controversy." *Business History Review* 32 (1958): 43-65.

Hughes, Thomas P. *Networks of Power: Electrification in Western Society, 1880-1930.* Baltimore: The Johns Hopkins University Press, 1983.

Hughes, Thomas P. *American Genesis: A Century of Invention and Technological Enthusiasm 1870-1970.* Chicago: University of Chicago Press, 2004.

Hundley, Norris. *Water and the West: The Colorado River Compact and the Politics of Water in the American West.* Berkeley: University of California Press, 1975.

Hunt, Edward Eyre, ed. *The Power Industry and the Public Interest: A Summary of the Results of a Survey of the Relations Between the Government and the Electric Power Industry – The Factual Findings.* New York: The Twentieth Century Fund, 1944.

Hyman, Leonard S. *America's Electric Utilities: Past, Present, and Future,* 4th Edition. Arlington, VA: Public Utilities Reports, 1992.

"Indiana Advocate." *Time,* July 31, 1939.

Ickes, Harold L. *The Autobiography of a Curmudgeon.* Westport, CT: Greenwood Press, 1985.

Ickes, Harold L. *The Secret Diary of Harold L. Ickes: The First Thousand Days 1933-1936.* New York: Simon and Schuster, 1953.

Ickes, Harold L. *The Secret Diary of Harold L. Ickes: The Inside Struggle, 1936-1939.* New York: Simon and Schuster, 1953.

Insull, Martin J. "Is Control of Operating Companies Sufficient?" *Proceedings of the Academy of Political Science* 14 (May 1930): 81-89.

Insull, Martin J. "The Real Power Problem," *Forum* 83 (Feb. 1930): 88-94.

Insull, Samuel. "Economics of the Public Utility Business," *Electrical World* 79 (March 25, 1922).

Insull, Samuel. *The Memoirs of Samuel Insull*. Polo, IL: Transportation Trails, 1992.

Insull, Samuel. "Public-Utility Commissions and Their Relations With Public Utility Companies," speech, Dubuque, Iowa, May 11, 1916. In *Public Utilities in Modern Life*, Keily, ed., private printing, 1924.

Insull Samuel. "Standardization, Cost System of Rates, and Public Control," presidential speech to the National Electric Light Association, Chicago, 1898. In *Central Station Electric Service*, Keily, ed., private printing, 1915.

Israel, Paul. *Edison: A Life of Invention*. New York: John Wiley & Sons, Inc., 1998.

Jacob, Charles E. *Leadership in the New Deal: The Administrative Challenge*. Englewood Cliffs, NJ: Prentice Hall, 1967.

Jacobson, Charles David. *Ties That Bind: Economic and Political Dilemmas of Urban Utility Networks, 1800-1990*. Pittsburgh: University of Pittsburgh Press, 2000.

Jehl, Francis. *Menlo Park Reminiscences*. New York: Dover Publications, in association with Henry Ford Museum & Greenfield Village, 1990.

Jones, W. A. "A National Viewpoint of Utility Problems," *Electrical World* 96 (Oct. 18, 1930): 731-2.

Jonnes, Jill. *Empires of Light: Edison, Tesla, Westinghouse, and the Race to Electrify the World*. New York: Random House, 2003.

Josephson, Matthew. *Edison*. New York: McGraw-Hill, 1959.

Josephson, Matthew, and Hannah Josephson. *Al Smith: Hero of the Cities*. Boston: Houghton Mifflin, 1969.

Keller, Morton. *Regulating a New Economy: Public Policy and Economic Change in America, 1900-1933*. Cambridge: Harvard University Press, 1990.

Kerwin, Jerome G. *Federal Water-power Legislation*. New York: Columbia University, 1926.

Kindleberger, Charles P. and Robert Aliber. *Manias, Panics and Crashes*, 4th ed. Hoboken: John Wiley & Sons, 2005.

King, Judson. *The Conservation Fight, from Theodore Roosevelt to the Tennessee Valley Authority*. Washington: Public Affairs Press, 1959.

King, Judson. "The Need for Public Yardsticks." *The New Republic*, 47 (May 26, 1926).

King, Judson. "The Record of the REA," *The Nation* 159 (July 8, 1944): 41-3.

Kitchens, Carl and Price Fishback. "Flip the Switch: The Spatial Impact of the Rural Electrification Administration 1935-1940." *Journal of Economic History* (Dec. 2015): 1161-1195. https://www.nber.org/papers

Kleeman, Rita Halle. *Gracious Lady: The Life of Sara Delano Roosevelt*. New York: D. Appleton-Century, 1935.

Klein, Maury. *The Power Makers: Steam, Electricity, and the Men Who Invented Modern America*. New York: Bloomsbury Press, 2008.

Kleinsorge, Paul L. *The Boulder Canyon Project: Historical and Economic Aspects*. Stanford:, Stanford University Press, 1941.

Kline, Ronald R. *Steinmetz; Engineer and Socialist*. Balitmore: The Johns Hopkins University Press, 1992.

Kluger, Richard, *The Paper: The Life and Death of the New York Herald Tribune*. New York: Alfred A. Knopf, 1986.

Knox, John C., *A Judge Comes of Age*, New York: Scribner's, 1940.

Kyvig, David E. *Daily Life in the United States, 1920-1940: How Americans Lived Through the Roaring Twenties and the Great Depression*. Chicago: Ivan R. Dee, 2004.

La Follette, Robert, M. Jr. "Address to the State Agricultural Society at Milwaukee," Sept. 1898. In Douglas B. Harris and Lonce H. Bailey. *The Republican Party: Documents Decoded*. Santa Barbara: ABC-CLIO, LLC, 2014.

Lash, Joseph P. *Dealers and Dreamers: A New Look at the New Deal*. New York: Doubleday, 1988.

Lash, Joseph P. *Eleanor and Franklin: The Story of Their Relationship, Based on Eleanor Roosevelt's Private Papers*. New York: W.W. Norton, & Co. 1971.

Lawrence, Robert M. and Norman I. Wengert, eds. *The Energy Crisis: Reality or Myth*. Philadelphia: American Academy of Political and Social Science, 1973.

Layton, Edwin T., Jr. *The Revolt of the Engineers: Social Responsibility and the American Engineering Profession*. Baltimore, MD: Johns Hopkins University Press, 1986.

Lear, Linda J. "The Boulder Canyon Project: A Reexamination of Federal Resource Management," *Materials and Society* 7, nos. 3-4 (1983): 329-37.

Lear, Linda J. "Boulder Dam: A Crossroads in Natural Resource Policy," *Journal of the West* 24 (October, 1985): 82-94.

Lee, Maurice W. *Economic Fluctuations.* Homewood, IL: R. D. Irwin Inc., 1955.

Leuchtenburg, William E. *Franklin D. Roosevelt and the New Deal, 1932-1940.* New York: Harper & Row, 1963.

Leuchtenburg, William E. "Roosevelt, Norris and the 'Seven Little TVA's'," *The Journal of Politics* 14 (Aug. 1952): 418-41.

Levin, Jack. *Power Ethics.* New York: Alfred Knopf, 1931.

Lewis, David Levering. "The Implausible Wendell Willkie: Leadership Ahead of its Time." In *Profiles in Leadership,* Walter Isaacson, ed. New York: W. W. Norton & Co., 2010.

Lewis, David Levering. *The Improbable Wendell Willkie: The Businessman Who Saved the Republican Party and His Country, and Conceived a New World Order.* New York: W.W. Norton, 2018.

Lilienthal, David E. "Birchrods? Legislative Suggestions for Regulating the Public Utility Industry and Its Alter Ego, the Holding Company," *State Government,* 5 (Feb. 1934): 39-41.

Lilienthal, David E. "Electricity: The People's Business," *Annals of the American Academy of Political and Social Science* 201, Jan. 1939.

Lilienthal, David E. "Four Point Program for Legislation," *Electrical World,* 101, Apr. 1, 1933.

Lilienthal, David E. *The Journals of David E. Lilienthal,* v. 1, *The TVA Years.* New York, Harper & Row, 1964.

Lilienthal, David E. "Reconciling Holding Companies with the Public Interest," *Electrical World,* Oct. 29, 1932.

Lilienthal, David E. "Regulation of Public Utilities During the Depression," *Harvard Law Review.* 46. 745-75. 1933.

Lilienthal, David E. "The Regulation of Public Utility Holding Companies," *Columbia Law Review* 29 (Apr. 1929): 404-40.

Lilienthal, David E. *TVA: Democracy on the March*. New York: Harper & Brothers, 1944.

Lilienthal, David E. "Wisconsin's Latest Steps in Utility Regulation," *Electrical World* 99 (March 12, 1932): 436-88.

Link, Arthur S. and Richard L. McCormick. *Progressivism*. Arlington Heights, IL: Harlan Davidson, Inc., 1983.

Losee, Gordon C. *The Reorganization of the Electric Power Industry into Regional Systems*. Urbana: University of Illinois Press, 1940.

Lowery, Martin. "On the Shoulders of Giants," *Management Quarterly* 51:1 (Spring, 2010): 4-15.

Lowitt, Richard. *George W. Norris: The Persistence of a Progressive, 1913-1933*. Urbana: University of Illinois Press, 1971.

Lowitt, Richard. *George W. Norris: The Triumph of a Progressive, 1933-1934*. Urbana: University of Illinois Press, 1978.

Lyons, James R. "FDR and Environmental Leadership." In *FDR and the Environment*, Henry L. Henderson and David B. Woolner, eds. New York: Palgrave MacMillan, 2005.

Madison, James H., ed. *Wendell Willkie: Hoosier Internationalist*. Bloomington, IN: Indiana University Press, 1992.

Marple, Warren H. "An Appraisal of Edison Electric Institute's Statistics on Farm Electrification," *Journal of Land and Public Utility Economics* 14, no. 4 (March, 1939): 471-6.

Martin, Roscoe C., ed. *TVA: The First Twenty Years: A Staff Report*. Tuscaloosa: University of Alabama Press, 1956.

Maxwell, Robert S., ed. *La Follette*. Englewood Cliffs, NJ: Prentice-Hall, 1969.

Maxwell, Robert S. *La Follette and the Rise of the Progressives in Wisconsin*. Madison: State Historical Society of Wisconsin, 1956.

McCaig, R. *Electric Power in America*. New York: Putnam.

McCraw, Thomas K. *Morgan vs. Lilienthal: The Feud Within the TVA*. Chicago: Loyola University Press, 1970.

McCraw, Thomas K. "Regulation in America: A Review Article." *Business History Review* 49 no. 2 (Summer, 1975):159-183.

McCraw, Thomas K. "Triumph and Irony—The TVA," *Proceedings of the IEEE* 64 (Sept. 1976): 1372-80.

McCraw, Thomas K. *TVA and the Power Fight: 1933-1939*. Philadelphia: Lippencott, 1971.

McDonald, Forrest. *Insull*. Chicago: University of Chicago Press, 1962.

McDonald, Forrest. *Let There Be Light: The History of the Utility Industry in Wisconsin, 1881-1955*. Madison, WI: The American History Research Center, 1957.

McDonald, Forrest. "Samuel Insull and the Movement for State Utility Regulatory Commissions," *Business History Review*, 32 (Autumn 1958): 241-54.

McDonald, Michael J. and John Muldowney. *TVA and the Dispossessed: The Resettlement of Population in the Norris Dam Area*. Knoxville: University of Tennessee Press, 1981.

McKenna, Marian C. *Franklin Roosevelt and the Great Constitutional War: The Court-Packing Crisis of 1937*. New York: Fordham University Press, 2002.

McKinley, Charles. *Uncle Sam in the Pacific Northwest: Federal Management of Natural Resources in the Columbia River Valley*. Berkeley: University of California Press, 1952.

McNichol, Tom. *AC/DC: The Savage Tale of the First Standards War*. San Francisco: Jossey-Bass, 2006.

Messing, Marc, H. Paul Friesema, and David Morell. *Centralized Power: The Politics of Scale in Electricity Generation*. Cambridge, MA: Oelgeschlager, Gunn, and Hain, 1979.

Miller, Char. *Gifford Pinchot and the Making of Modern Environmentalism*. Washington, DC: Island Press, 2001.

Miller, John B. "Pussyfooting with Government Ownership," *Electrical World* 87 (May 8, 1926) 964.

Mitchell, Broadus. *Depression Decade: From New Era through New Deal, 1928-1941*. Armonk, N.Y.: M.E. Sharpe, 1989.

Mitchell, Sidney A. *S.Z. Mitchell and the Electrical Industry*. New York: Farrar, Straus & Cudahy, 1960.

Moe, Richard. *Roosevelt's Second Act: The Election of 1940 and the Politics of War.* New York: Oxford University Press, 2013.

Moeller, Beverly B. *Phil Swing and Boulder Dam.* Berkeley: University of California Press, 1971.

Moore, John Robert. "Senator Josiah W. Bailey and the 'Conservative Manifesto' of 1937," *The Journal of Southern History* 31, no. 1 (Feb. 1965): 21-39.

Moran, Richard. *Executioner's Current: Thomas Edison, George Westinghouse, and the Invention of the Electric Chair.* New York: Knopf, 2002.

Morison, Samuel Eliot and Henry Steele Commager. *The Growth of the American Republic.* New York: Oxford University Press, 1950.

Morgan, Arthur. *The Making of the TVA.* Buffalo: Prometheus Books, 1974.

Moscow, Warren. *Roosevelt and Willkie.* Englewood Cliffs, NJ: Prentice-Hall, 1968.

Mosher, William E. and Finlay G. Crawford. *Public Utility Regulation.* New York: Harper & Brothers, 1933.

Mosher, William E., ed. *Electrical Utilities: The Crisis in Public Control.* New York: Harper & Brothers, 1929.

Munson, Richard. "Electricity after Insull," *Management Quarterly* 47, no. 2 (June 22, 2006).

Munson, Richard. *From Edison to Enron: The Business of Power and What It Means for the Future of Electricity.* Westport, CT: Praeger 2005.

Murray, Vernon M. "Grand Coulee and Bonneville Power in the National War Effort," *Journal of Land and Public Utility Economics*, 18 (May, 1942): 131-42.

Nasaw, David. *The Chief: The Life of William Randolph Hearst.* Boston: Houghton Mifflin, 2000.

Nasaw, David. *The Patriarch: The Remarkable Life and Turbulent Times of Joseph P. Kennedy.* New York: Penguin Press, 2012.

National Civic Federation. *Municipal and Private Operation of Public Utilities.* 3 vols. New York: 1907.

National Electric Light Association. *The Radical Campaign Against American Industry as Shown by the Brief and Exhibits Offered to the Federal Trade Commission in its*

Investigation into Public Utilities. Washington DC: National Electric Light Association, 1930.

Neal, Steve. *Dark Horse: A Biography of Wendell Willkie.* Lawrence KA: University Press of Kansas, 1984.

Neuberger, Richard L. and Stephen B. Kahn. *Integrity: The Life of George W. Norris.* New York: Vanguard Press, 1937.

Neuse, Steven M. *David E. Lilienthal: The Journey of an American Liberal.* Knoxville: University of Tennessee Press, 1996.

Newman, Roger K. *Hugo Black: A Biography.* New York: Pantheon Books, 1994.

Nord, David. "The Experts Versus the Experts: Conflicting Philosophies of Municipal Utility Regulation in the Progressive Era." *Wisconsin Magazine of History* 58 (Spring 1975): 219-36.

Norris, George. *Fighting Liberal: The Autobiography of George W. Norris.* New York: MacMillan, 1945.

Northwest Power and Conservation Council, "Dams: Impacts on Salmon and Steelhead." https://www.nwcouncil.org/

Northwest Power and Conservation Council, "Fish Passage at Dams." https://www.nwcouncil.org/

Northwest Power and Conservation Council, "Grand Coulee Dam: Impacts on Fish." https://www.nwcouncil.org/

Nye, David E. *Electrifying America.* Cambridge: MIT Press, 1990.

Nye, David E. *Consuming Power: A Social History of American Energies.* Cambridge,: MIT Press, 1998.

Nye, David E. "On Writing the History of Technology." *Science, Technology, & Human Values* 9, no. 2 (Spring, 1984), 78-82.

Olds, Leland. "The Age of Giant Power." *Rural Electrification,* Sept. 1956.

Owen, Marguerite. *The Tennessee Valley Authority.* New York: Praeger, 1973.

Passer, Harold C. *The Electrical Manufacturers, 1875-1900,* Cambridge: Harvard University Press, 1953.

Patterson, James T. *Congressional Conservatism and the New Deal: The Growth of the Conservative Coalition, 1933-1939.* Westport, CT: Greenwood Press, 1981.

Pennsylvania Giant Power Survey Board. *Report of the Giant Power Survey Board to the General Assembly of the Commonwealth of Pennsylvania.* Harrisburg, PA: Telegraph Printing Co., 1925.

Perkins, Frances. *The Roosevelt I Knew.* New York: Viking, 1946.

Persico, Joseph E. *Franklin & Lucy: Mrs. Rutherford and the Other Remarkable Women in Roosevelt's Life.* New York: Random House, 2008.

Person, Harlow S. "The Rural Electrification Administration in Perspective." *Agricultural History* 24 (Apr. 1950): 70-88.

Peters, Charles. *Five Days in Philadelphia: The Amazing "We Want Willkie!" Convention of 1940 and How It Freed FDR to Save the Western World.* New York: Public Affairs, 2005.

Phillips, F. R. "Thoughts of an Operating Executive." *Electrical World* 102 (Oct. 7, 1933): 460-64.

Phillips, Charles F., Jr. *The Regulation of Public Utilities: Theory and Practice.* Arlington, VA: Public Utility Reports, 1993.

Phillips, Sarah T. *This Land, This Nation: Conservation, Rural America, and the New Deal.* New York: Cambridge University Press, 2007.

Pinchot, Gifford. "Electric Farm Rival of City, Says Pinchot." *North American,* (Dec 9, 1924).

Pinchot, Gifford. "Giant Power." *Survey Graphic* 51 (March 1924): 561.

"Pinchot Urges Electric Power as Aid to Farms." *North American.* (Jan. 23, 1924).

Pinchot, Gifford. "What the Progressive Conference Committee Proposes to Do About the Utilities." *Public Utilities Fortnightly* 8 (Nov. 26, 1931): 676-83.

Pitzer, Paul C. *Grand Coulee: Harnessing a Dream.* Pullman: Washington State University Press, 1994.

Platt, Harold L. *The Electric City.* Chicago: University of Chicago Press, 1991.

Platt, Harold L. "Samuel Insull and the Electric City," *Chicago History* 15, no. 1 (Spring, 1986): 20-35.

Prendergast, William A. "Has State Regulation Protected the Public's Interest?" *National Electric Light Association Bulletin*, 17 (July 1930): 426-30.

Public Utilities Commission of Rhode Island v. *Attleboro Steam and Electric Co.*, 273 U.S. 83 (1927). http://www.supreme.justia.com.

Public Utilities Fortnightly 8, pt. 1. "Uncle Sam's War Baby, Muscle Shoals, Is Put to Use for the Making of Political Thunder." (Oct. 29, 1931).

Public Utilities Fortnightly 8, pt. 1. "Boulder Dam, the Largest, the Costliest and the Most Uneconomic of Uncle Sam's Business Enterprises." (Nov. 12, 1931): 604.

Radin, Alex. *Public Power–Private Life: A Memoir and History of Public Power in the Twentieth Century.* Washington, DC: American Public Power Association, 2003.

Ramsay, M. L. *Pyramids of Power: The Story of Roosevelt, Insull, and the Utility Wars.* Indianapolis, New York: The Bobbs-Merrill Company, 1937.

Raushenbush, H. S. *High Power Propaganda.* New York: New Republic, 1928.

Raver, Paul J. "Aces in the Hole." *Rural Electrification News* 8, no. 7 (March 1943): 7-9.

Read, Howard J. *Defending the Public: Milo R. Maltbie and Utility Regulation in New York.* Pittsburgh: Dorrance Publishing Co., 1998.

Reich, Leonard S. "Lighting the Path to Profit: GE's Control of the Electric Lamp Industry, 1892-1941." *Business History Review* 66 (Summer 1992): 305-34.

Reisner, Marc. *Cadillac Desert: The American West and Its Disappearing Water.* New York: Penguin Books, 1983.

Reynolds, Terry S., and Theodore Bernstein. "The Damnable Alternating Current." *Proceedings of the IEEE* 64 (1976), 1339-43.

Richberg, Donald R. *My Hero: The Indiscreet Memoirs of an Eventful but Unheroic Life.* New York: Putnam, 1954.

Ripley, William Z. *Main Street and Wall Street.* Boston: Little, Brown and Company, 1927.

Ritchie, Robert F. *Integration of Public Utility Holding Companies.* Ann Arbor: University of Michigan Law School, 1954.

Roosevelt, Franklin D. *F.D.R. His Personal Letters,* 4 vols., Elliott Roosevelt, ed. New York: Duell, Sloan, and Pearce.

Roosevelt, Franklin D. Presidential Library and Museum, Master Speech File. https://fdrlibrary.marist.edu/archives/collections/franklin.

Roosevelt, Franklin D. *The Public Papers and Addresses of Franklin D. Roosevelt*. 13 vols. New York: Russell & Russell, 1969.

Roosevelt, Franklin D. "The Real Meaning of the Power Problem." *Forum* 82 (Dec. 1929): 327-32.

Roosevelt, Theodore. *An Autobiography*. New York: Da Capo Press, 1913.

Rosenman, Samuel I. *Working with Roosevelt*. New York: Da Capo Press, 1972.

Rudolph, Richard, and Scott Ridley. *Power Struggle: The Hundred-Year War over Electricity*. New York: Harper and Row, 1986.

Saloutos, Theodore. *The American Farmer and the New Deal*. Ames: Iowa State University Press, 1982.

Satterlee, Herbert. *J. Pierpont Morgan, An Intimate Portrait*. New York: Arno Press, 1940.

Sayre, Kenneth, ed. *Values in the Electric Power Industry*. Notre Dame, IN: University of Notre Dame Press, 1977.

Schaenzer, J.P. "Rural Electrification Since the Turn of the Century." *Agricultural Engineering* 38 (June 1957): 442-52.

Schap, David. *Municipal Ownership in the Electric Utility Industry: A Centennial View*. New York: Praeger, 1986.

Schlesinger, Arthur M., Jr. *The Crisis of the Old Order, 1919-1933*. Boston: Houghton, Mifflin, 2003.

Schlesinger, Arthur M., Jr. *The Coming of the New Deal, 1933-1935*. Boston: Houghton, Mifflin, 2003.

Schlesinger, Arthur M., Jr. *The Politics of Upheaval, 1935-1936*. Boston: Houghton Mifflin, 2003.

Schurr, Sam, and Bruce Netschert. *Energy in the American Economy, 1850-1975*. Baltimore: Johns Hopkins University Press/Resources for the Future, 1960.

Schwarz, Jordan A. *The New Dealers: Power Politics in the Age of Roosevelt*. New York: A. A. Knopf, Inc., 1993.

SEC Historical Society, "Chasing the Devil Around the Stump: Securities Regulation, the SEC and the Courts." http://www.sechistorical.org.

Seligman, Joel. *The Transformation of Wall Street: A History of the Securities and Exchange Commission and Modern Corporate Finance.* Boston: Houghton Mifflin Co., 1982.

Selznick, Philip. *TVA and the Grass Roots: A Study in the Sociology of Formal Organization.* Berkeley: University of California Press, 1949.

Sharlin, Harold I. "Electrical Generation and Transmission." In *Technology and Western Civilization.* Melvin Kranzberg and Carroll Pursell, Jr., eds. London: Oxford University Press, 1967.

Sharlin, Harold I. "The First Niagara Falls Power Project," *Business History Review* 35 (Spring 1961): 58-74.

Shesol, Jeff. *Supreme Power: Franklin Roosevelt vs. the Supreme Court.* New York: W.W. Norton, 2010.

Shlaes, Amity. *The Forgotten Man: A New History of the Great Depression.* New York: Harper Collins, 2007.

Silverberg, Robert. *Light for the World: Edison and the Power Industry.* Princeton: D. Van Nostrand Company, 1967.

Simon, James F. *FDR and Chief Justice Hughes: The President, the Supreme Court, and the Epic Battle Over the New Deal.* New York: Simon & Schuster, 2012.

Simonds, William Joe, and Toni Rae Linenberger. *The Columbia Basin Project.* Denver: U.S. Bureau of Reclamation History Program, 1998.

Singer, Bayla. "Power Politics." *IEEE Technology and Society Magazine.* Dec. 1988.

Skeel, David. *Icarus in the Boardroom.* New York: Oxford University Press, 2005.

Slattery, Harry. *Rural America Lights Up.* Washington, DC: National Home Library Foundation, 1940.

Slayton, Robert A. *Empire Statesman: The Rise and Redemption of Al Smith.* New York: Free Press, 2001.

Sloan, Mathew S. "Consolidations in the Electric Utility Industry." *National Electric Light Association Bulletin* 16 (Oct. 1929): 629-31.

Smeltzer, Karl C. "Memories from Early Days of the Securities and Exchange Commission," June, 2004. SEC Historical Society, Oral Histories. http://www. sechistorical.org/

Smith, Jean Edward. *FDR*. New York: Random House, 2007.

Smith, Karen. *The Magnificent Experiment: Building the Salt River Reclamation Project, 1890-1917*. Tucson: University of Arizona Press, 1986.

Smith, Richard Norton. *An Uncommon Man: The Triumph of Herbert Hoover*. Worland, WY: High Plains Press, 1984

Sobel, Robert. *The Great Bull Market: Wall Street in the 1920s*. New York, Norton, 1968.

Springer, Vera. *Power and the Pacific Northwest: A History of the Bonneville Power Administration*. Washington: Bonneville Power Administration, 1976.

Steel, Ronald. *Walter Lippman and the American Century*. New York: World Publishing Co., 1954.

Stevens, Joseph E. *Hoover Dam: An American Adventure*. Norman: University of Oklahoma Press, 1988.

Stigler, George J., and Claire Friedland. "What Can Regulators Regulate? The Case of Electricity." *Journal of Law and Economics* 5 (Oct. 1962): 1-16.

Stross, Randall E. *The Wizard of Menlo Park: How Thomas Alva Edison Invented the Modern World*. New York: Crown Publishers, 2008.

Strouse, Jean. *Morgan: American Financier*. New York: Perennial, 2000.

Sundborg, George. *Hail Columbia: The Thirty-year Struggle for Grand Coulee Dam*. New York: Macmillan, 1954.

Swidler, Joseph C. "Legal Foundations." In *TVA: The First Twenty Years: A Staff Report*, Roscoe C. Martin, ed. Tuscaloosa: University of Alabama press, 1956.

Swidler, Joseph C. *Power and the Public Interest: The Memoirs of Joseph C. Swidler*, A. Scott Henderson, ed. Knoxville: University of Tennessee Press, 2002.

Swidler, Joseph C. and Robert Marquis. "TVA in Court: A Study of TVA's Constitutional Litigation." *Iowa Law Review* 32 (Jan. 1947): 296-326.

Swing, Raymond Graham. "So This Is Bureaucracy!" In Robert Engler, ed. *America's Energy: Reports from The Nation on 100 Years of Struggles for the Democratic Control of Our Resources*. New York: Pantheon Books, 1980.

Taft, Dub and Sam Heys. *Big Bets: Decisions and Leaders that Shaped Southern Company*. Atlanta: Southern Company, 2011.

Talbert, Roy. *FDR's Utopian: Arthur Morgan of the TVA*. Jackson: University Press of Mississippi, 1987.

Tate, Alfred O. *Edison's Open Door: The Life Story of Thomas A. Edison, a Great Individualist*. New York: E. P. Dutton, 1938.

Tobey, Ronald C. *Technology as Freedom: The New Deal and the Electrical Modernization of the American Home*. Berkeley: University of California Press, 1996.

Trickey, Erick. "The Grand Coulee Powers On, 75 Years After Its First Surge of Electricity." (March 22, 2016). http://www.smithsonianmag.com/history

Troesken, Werner. "Regime Change and Corruption: A History of Public Utility Regulation." In *Corruption and Reform: Lessons from America's Economic History*, Edward L. Glaeser and Claudia Goldin, eds. Chicago: University of Chicago Press, 2006.

Trombley, Kenneth E. *The Life and Times of a Happy Liberal: A Biography of Morris Llewellyn Cooke*. New York: Harper and Brothers, 1954.

Troxel, Emery. *Economics of Public Utilities*. New York: Rinehart & Company, 1947.

Twentieth Century Fund. *Electric Power and Government Policy: A Survey of the Relations Between the Government and the Electric Power Industry*. New York: Twentieth Century Fund, 1948.

Twentieth Century Fund. *The Power Industry and the Public Interest: A Summary of the Results of a Survey of the Relations Between the Government and the Electric Power Industry*. New York: Twentieth Century Fund, 1944.

Voeltz, Herman C. "Genesis and Development of a Regional Power Agency in the Pacific Northwest, 1933-43." *Pacific Northwest Quarterly* 53, no. 2 (Apr. 1962): 65-78.

Ward, Geoffrey C. *A First-Class Temperament: The Emergence of Franklin Roosevelt*. New York: Harper & Row, 1989.

Warne, Colston E. "The Muted Voice of the Consumer in Regulatory Agencies." In *A Critique of Administrative Regulation of Public Utilities*. Warren J. Samuels and Harry M. Trebing, eds. East Lansing: Michigan State University, 1972.

Wasik, John F. *The Merchant of Power: Samuel Insull, Thomas Edison, and the Creation of the Modern Metropolis*. New York: Palgrave Macmillan, 2006.

Wehle, Louis B. *Hidden Threads of History: Wilson through Roosevelt.* New York: Macmillan, 1953.

Welch, Francis X. "Another Year of Grilling for the Public Utility Companies." *Public Utilities Fortnightly* 8 (Aug. 6, 1931): 169-70.

Welch, Francis X. "The Effect of the Insull Collapse on State Regulation." *Public Utilities Fortnightly* 10 (Nov. 10, 1932): 29-39.

Wendt, Lloyd and Herman Kogan. *Big Bill of Chicago.* Evanston: Northwestern University Press, 2005.

Wessel, O.S. "The Power Program." In *TVA: The First Twenty Years: A Staff Report,* Roscoe C. Martin, ed. Tuscaloosa: University of Alabama Press, 1956.

Wesser, Robert F. *Charles Evans Hughes: Politics and Reform in New York, 1905-1910.* Ithaca, NY: Cornell University Press, 1967.

Whitman, Willson. *David Lilienthal; Public Servant in a Power Age.* New York: H. Holt, 1948.

Wigmore, Barrie A. *Crash and its Aftermath: A History of Securities Markets in the United States, 1929-1933.* Westport, CT: Greenwood Press, 1985.

Wilcox, Clair. *Competition and Monopoly in American Industry: A Study Made for the Investigation of Concentration of Economic Power.* Temporary National Economic Committee. Washington: Government Printing Office, 1940.

Wooddy, Carroll Hill. *The Case of Frank L. Smith: A Study in Representative Government.* Chicago: University of Chicago Press, 1931.

Wright, Gavin, "The New Deal and the Modernization of the South." *Federal History* 2 (2010): 58-73.

Young, Harold H. *Forty Years of Public Utility Finance.* Charlottesville: University Press of Virginia, 1965.

Zarbin, Earl A. *Roosevelt Dam: A History to 1911.* Phoenix: Salt River Project, 1984.

Zucker, Norman L. *George W. Norris: Gentle Knight of American Democracy,* Urbana: U. of Illinois Press, 1966.

NOTES

Abbreviations

CR	*Congressional Record*
EW	*Electrical World*
NYT	*New York Times*
FDR Library	Master Speech File, Franklin D. Roosevelt Presidential Library and Museum

Preface

1. James Fallows, "The 50 Greatest Breakthroughs Since the Wheel," *Atlantic Monthly*, November 2013. https://www.theatlantic.com/magazine/archive/2013/11/innovations list

2. "The conquest," quoted in Marc Bloch, *The Historian's Craft*, 55; Nye, "On Writing the History of Technology," 78.

Chapter 1 – Throwing Down the Gauntlet

1. "Roosevelt Here To Seek Support," *The Morning Oregonian*, Sept. 22, 1932.

2. FDR Library, File No. 490.

3. "The Oregonian" and "Come to," "Roosevelt Here To Seek Support," *The Morning Oregonian*, Sept. 22, 1932; David Greenberg, *Atlantic*, Jan. 24, 2016. https://www.theatlantic.com/politics/archive/2016/01/how-teddy-roosevelt-invented-spin/426699/

4. "Your problems," FDR Library, File No. 517.

5. "Roosevelt Fires At Power Giant," *The Morning Oregonian*, Sept. 22, 1932.

6. Allen, 204.

7. *Edison Round Table*, Dec. 1, 1931, 8.

8. Michelle Pautz, "The Decline in Average Weekly Cinema Attendance, 1930-2000." *Issues in Political Economy* 11 (2002): Appendix.

9. Cowan, "Industrial Revolution in the Home," 5.

10. "19 to 55 percent," Federal Trade Commission, *Control of Power Companies*, (Feb. 22, 1927): xxiv.

11. FDR Library, File No. 518.

12. FDR Library, File No. 518.

13. FDR Library, File No. 518.

14. McDonald, *Insull*, 98.

15. FDR Library, File No. 522.

Chapter 2—The First Wave of Electrification

1. Bradley, 23.

2. *New York Sun*, Sept. 16 and Oct. 20, 1978, quoted in Friedel & Israel, 13 and 8.

3. Strouse, 182.

4. J. Pierpont Morgan to his brother-in-law Walter Burns, Oct. 30, 1878, quoted in Strouse, 181.

5. Josephson, *Edison* 344.

6. Moran, 94; Essig, 143-6.

7. *NYT,* Oct. 12, 1889

8. *New York World,* Oct. 12, 1889, quoted in Essig, 215.

9. Essig, 250-2; *NYT,* Aug. 7, 1890.

10. "Edison and Thomson disliked," Conot, 302; "amateurs" and "boldly appropriated," Edison to Villard, April 1, 1889, in Carlson, 292; "attitude," Coffin to Higginson, May 7, 1891, in Carlson, 298; "very swelled head," Clarence W. Barron, *More They Told Barron*, 38-9, in Klein, 288; "The man," Edison note on Edward D. Adams letter to Edison, February 2, 1889, in Carlson, 290; "irritates his rivals," Fairchild to Higginson, July 24, 1891, in Carlson, 298.

11. Passer, 150; Israel, 336. McDonald, *Insull*, 50, and Silverberg, 257, say the stock of Edison General Electric was watered by Morgan at the time of its organization, which partly explains its lower rate of return.

12. Tate, p. 278, quoted in Josephson, *Edison* 365.

13. Adams, II:222-4, 227-8; Klein, 332; Jonnes, 285.

14. Hughes, *Networks*, 131-5.

15. Jonnes, 296-7; Klein, 343-4; *Electrical World,* Sept. 16, 1893, 208; "part of," Coffin letter to Twombly, May 9, 1893, cited in Jonnes, 297.

16. Passer, *Manufacturers,* 290-2; Jonnes, 304.

17. Nye, 54; "Meet Me in St. Louis" lyrics by Andres B. Sterling, music by Kerry Mills, quoted in Nye, 47.

18. McDonald, *Insull*, 16; "the kind of," Insull, *Memoirs*, 25.

19. Josephson, *Edison*, 253-4; Insull, *Memoirs*, 29-31; McDonald, *Insull*, 20-2.

20. Tate, 264.

21. "If necessary," Insull, *Memoirs*, 48.

22. McDonald, *Insull*, 30; Josephson, *Edison* 270.

23. Klein, 398-9.

24. McDonald, *Insull*, 52-4, "one of the best," 53; Insull, *Memoirs*, 62.

25. Platt, 54-8.

26. McDonald, *Insull*, 59; Flynn, *Colliers's*, Dec.10, 1932.

27. Platt, 109; Wasik, 79-80; McDonald, *Insull*, 98.

28. Platt, 99.

29. Klein, 408.

30. Wasik, 77-8; McDonald, *Insull*, 89; Platt, 81-2.

31. McDonald, *Insull*, 91, 121-4.

32. Platt, 108; Brigham, 6.
33. Platt, 120-1.
34. McDonald, *Insull*, 108.
35. McDonald, *Insull*, 108-9.
36. McDonald, *Insull*, 113-4.
37. Commons, *Myself*, 111-28; McDonald, *Insull*, 120-1.
38. McDonald, *Light*, 119-21; National Civic Federation, *Public Utilities* 1:26; Hirsch, *Power*, 30.
39. Rudoph & Ridley, 40.
40. Anderson, 51; Wesser, 31.
41. "The investment," NY Senate committee report, "Gas and Electricity," quoted in Mosher & Crawford, 22.
42. Hellman, 16-7, "It can doubtless," 16.
43. Hellman, 18; "These commissions," Keller, 60.
44. United States v. E. C. Knight Co., https://supreme.justia.com/cases/federal/us/156/1/case.html; Geisst, 57-8.
45. "corporations and masters," Harris and Bailey, 41.
46. Bryan, *Chicago Conference*, 500.
47. Morison and Commager 2, 81-2.
48. T. Roosevelt, *Autobiography*, 428.
49. "You can ride," Baker, "Great Northern Pacific Deal," *Collier's Weekly*, Nov. 30, 1901, 15.
50. Strouse, 441.
51. T. Roosevelt, *Autobiography*, 209.
52. T. Roosevelt, Presidential Speeches, Miller Center, University of Virginia. https://www.millercenter.org.
53. Zarbin, 37.
54. K. Smith, 79-80, 82.
55. *Arizona Republican*, Nov. 22, 1903, cited in Zarbin, 75-6, 78.
56. Zarbin, 245.

Chapter 3 – The Golden Years
1. Ripley, *Main Street*, 101.
2. McDonald, *Insull*, 103.
3. Ripley, *Main Street*, 143.
4. Ripley, *Main Street*, 87.
5. McDonald, *Insull*, 150-1, "were recorded" 150; Flynn, John, "Up and Down," *Collier's*, Dec. 17, 1932, 21.
6. "left the company…," McDonald, *Insull*, 151. Insull, *Memoirs*, 104, says the holding company was his idea, and simply that he took the common stock in payment for his Southern Indiana properties and sold the preferred stock to friends in Chicago, New York, and London.
7. Allen, *Lords*, 12.
8. Insull, "Public-utility Commissions and their Relations with Public-utility Companies," speech, May 11, 1916, reprinted in Keily, *Public Utilities*, 55.

9. McDonald, *Insull*, 156-7.

10. McDonald, *Insull*, 156-61; Insull, *Memoirs*, 172-5.

11. McDonald, *Insull*, 168-72, "appreciation," *Minutes*, Illinois council meetings, quoted in *Insull*, 170; Wasik, 113.

12. McDonald, *Insull*, 173-5.

13. "Industry during WWI," https://sites.google.com/site/wartoendallwarscom/home/industry-during-ww1.

14. Allen, *Lords*, 177.

15. Hyman, 92.

16. Hughes, 291; Platt, 232-3.

17. *NYT*, Dec. 14, 1917, 1.

18. *Chicago Tribune*, Jan. 18, 1918, 1, quoted in Platt, 204.

19. Platt, 211-3.

20. Hughes, 291-2.

21. *EW*, July 9, 1921, 55.

22. Hughes, 292.

23. Platt, 232-3; Hughes, 291.

24. Ron Grossman, "'Big Bill' Thompson, Chicago's Unfiltered Mayor," *Chicago Tribune*, Feb. 25, 2016.

25. McDonald, *Insull*, 178-82. Platt, 231, gives the year as 1921.

26. "Historical Inflation Rates: 1914-2018," https//www.usinflationcalculator.com/inflation/historical-inflation-rates

27. McDonald, *Insull*, 198-200.

28. Census, *Historical Statistics (1789-1945)*, 159, cited in Hyman, 92.

29. McDonald, *Insull*, 201; McDonald, *Light*, 185.

30. Shlaes, 402.

31. *EW*, Aug. 4, 1923: 247; Wasik, 126-7.

32. McDonald, *Insull*, 182.

33. McDonald, *Insull*, 182-3, "I believe," speech to Illinois Gas Association, March 19, 1919, quoted at 183; Munson, *Power Makers*, 66; Rudolph and Ridley, 49.

34. McDonald, *Insull*, 184.

35. Platt, 243-4; Nye, 304; Allen, *Yesterday*, 142; Public Broadcasting Service http://www.pbs.org/wgbh/aso/databank/entries/dt20ra.html.

36. FTC, 71A, 59.

37. Aylesworth, "National Electrical Development and Its Effect Upon Utility Regulation," speech and NELA pamphlet, March, 1922, cited by McCraw, 11.

38. *EW*, March 19, 1921, 661.

39. Raushenbush, 10.

40. *Editor and Publisher*, July 14, 1928, 14, 36.

41. "had secretly," quoted in Barnes, 47.

42. Nye, 16; Hyman, 91.

43. Hyman, 92.

44. Wasik, 122.

45. "The final brilliance," Schlesinger, *Crisis*, 121.

46. Rudolph & Ridley, 48.

47. McDonald, *Insull*, 202-3.

48. McDonald, *Insull*, 185.

49. Munson, 67.

50. Ramsey, 136.

51. Insull, "Economics of the Public Utility Business," *EW*, March 25, 1922; Wasik, 109; McDonald, *Insull*, 203-5; Munson, *Power Makers*, 67.

52. Rudolph & Ridley, 40; Keller, 64.

53. "can get light" and "those who own," *Riverside Enterprise*, July 26, 1921, 4, quoted in Tobey, 76.

54. Tobey, 72-3, 76-7; "Keep our state clean," *EW*, June 9, 1923, 1357.

55. *EW*, Feb. 24, 1923, 435.

56. McCraw, 7; Tugwell, 79.

57. McDonald, *Light*, 187; Funigiello, xiii-xiv; Hughes, 393, 437.

58. Brigham, 28-9; Funigiello, xv; Cudahy, 51, fn 89.

59. Freidel, *FDR: The Apprenticeship*, 61f.

60. Ripley, *Main Street*, 303.

61. FTC, *Supply of Electrical Equipment*, xviii; *Public Utilities Commission Of Rhode Island v. Attleboro Steam & Electric Co.*, https://supreme.justia.com/cases/federal/us/273/83/

62. "provided opportunities," Twentieth Century Fund, *Electric Power*, 34; Rudolph & Ridley, 54; "so adroitly," Allen, 273-4.

63. FTC, 72A, 847-8; Allen, 275-6, 290-1; Rudolph & Ridley, 53.

64. FTC, 72A, 37; 20th Century Fund, *Power*, 27.

65. New York Power Authority, https://www.nypa.gov/about/timeline

66. Eldot, 236-7.

67. M. & H. Josephson, 276-7.

68. *EW*, Jan. 5, 1924, 60; Slayton, 174; Eldot, 248-9.

69. Handlin, 103; *EW*, March 24, 1923.

70. Miller, *Pinchot*, 251, 258; "We can expect," Pinchot, "Giant Power," 561, quoted in S. Phillips, 25.

71. Miller, *Pinchot*, 266-7; Trombley, 38-45.

72. Neuberger & Kahn, 202-4; Hughes, *American Genesis*, 362.

73. Lowitt, 197-8.

74. Lowitt, 198-9.

75. Hubbard, 12-16, 21-3; Barnes, 43.

76. Lowitt, 210-4; Hubbard, 113; "How did," in "Senate Investigates the 'Teapot Dome' Scandal," U.S. Senate. https://www.senate.gov/artandhistory/history/minute/senate_investigates_the_teapot_dome_scandal/htm

77. Stevens, 11-12.

78. Shlaes, 33; Stevens, 14.

79. Williams, 259, Stevens, 16-18.

Chapter 4 – The Tide Turns

1. "Dow Jones – 100 Year Historical Chart," https://www.macrotrends.net/1319/dow-jones-100-year-historical-chart/

2. "impossible," McCraw, 9.

3. Klein, 435.

4. *EW*, Aug. 15, 1925, 329; "What in hell," Danielian, 502.

5. Allen, *Yesterday*, 162-3.

6. *CR*, Jan. 12, 1922, cited in Wooddy, 20, fn.

7. *CR*, May 19, 1926, 9674.

8. U.S.Senate.gov/Contested Senate elections, "The Election Case of William B. Wilson v. William S. Vare of Pennsylvania (1929)," http://www.senate.gov/artandhistory/history/common/contested_elections/intro.htm; McDonald, *Insull*, 264.

9. *NYT*, June 4, 1926, 6.

10. *CR*, June 26, 1926, 12018-9; *NYT*, June 27, 1926, 1; Wooddy, 24-7, "the opportunity," 27; *Chicago Tribune*, June 28, 1926.

11. 69th Congress, 1st Session, Hearings, Special Committee Investigating Expenditures in Senatorial Primary and General Elections, Part 2, 1536-7.

12. *NYT*, Aug. 5, 1, and Aug. 6, 1; McDonald, *Insull*, 154, 256.

13. Lowitt, 383-91, "the domination," 391.

14. "He was not," Will Rogers, *NYT*, Dec. 17, 1926, 25.

15. *CR*, Jan. 19, 1927, 1911ff.; Wooddy, 233-8.

16. *NYT*, Feb. 19, 1927, 2; *CR*, Feb. 18, 1927, 4227-31, "who believe," 4229.

17. "lion in the path," *NYT*, Feb. 22, 1927.

18. *NYT*, Feb. 22, 1927, 1.

19. *CR*, Mar. 3, 1927, 5483.

20. *NYT*, Feb. 24, 1927, 4.

21. *NYT*, Feb. 25, 1927, 2.

22. *NYT*, Feb. 25, 1927, 29.

23. *NYT*, Feb. 22, 1927, 1, and Mar. 1, 1927, 29, "further," Mar. 1.

24. *CR*, Feb. 26, 1927), 4899.

25. *CR*, Feb. 25, 1927, 4813.

26. *CR*, Feb. 26, 1927, 4900.

27. McDonald, *Insull*, 267; *CR*, Feb. 28, 1927, 4991-3, "more boldly," and "either neutral," 4991.

28. *NYT*, Mar. 5, 1927, 1.

29. *NYT*, Mar. 5, 1927, 2.

30. U.S.Senate.gov/Contested Senate elections, "The Election Case of Frank L. Smith of Illinois (1928)" and "The Election Case of William B. Wilson v. William S. Vare of Pennsylvania (1929)." https://www.senate.gov artandhistory/history/common/contested_elections/intro.htm; "is not a question," Lowitt, 394.

31. McDonald, *Insull*, 266.

32. Stevens, 27. Although the dam had informally been called Boulder Dam throughout the 1920s, the legislation did not mention a name. Hoover's secretary of interior named it Hoover Dam at a ceremony in 1930, citing a precedent of naming dams after presidents, although it had not previously happened while they were still in office. Construction began in 1931. After Roosevelt's election, his interior secretary, Harold Ickes, renamed it Boulder Dam. The names were used

interchangeably until 1947, when Congress unanimously restored the name Hoover Dam.

33. Lovitt, 339-46.

34. Hubbard, 220-1; Funigiello, 7, 16-9, "He is like a tiger," 17.

35. Alter, 16-20.

36. Lash, *Eleanor and Franklin,* 118.

37. Brands, 25; Alter, 24.

38. Lash, *Eleanor and Franklin*, 118; Daniels, Roger, 6; Kleeman, 209.

39. Davis, *New York Years,* 142.

40. J. E. Smith, *FDR*, 47.

41. "thought" and "first," Grenville Clark, *Harvard Alumni Bulletin,* April 28, 1945, 47: 452, quoted in Freidel, *Apprenticeship,* 86.

42. Freidel, *Apprenticeship,* 109-15; "Outwitted," New York *Tribune*, April 1, 1911, quoted in Freidel, 112; Handlin, 43.

43. "the one place," Josephus Daniels, 66, quoted in Freidel, *Apprenticeship,* 155.

44. Dallek, 65; "my partially successful," *FDR Letters*, 2:422; Roger Daniels, 37-8, "I have seen war," 37.

45. Dallek, 70.

46. Perkins, 27.

47. Roosevelt to Langdon Marvin, Dec. 19, 1924, quoted in Schlesinger, 1:374.

48. Brands, 145-7.

49. Alter, 51; "You can say," *NYT*, Sept. 16, 1921; "He has such courage," Ward, 605.

50. Davis, *Beckoning,* 754.

51. Golway, 97-9.

52. Davis, *Beckoning,* 754; "because you're," *The Reminiscences of Joseph Proskauer,* Columbia Center for Oral History, quoted in Golway, 148.

53. Ward, 694-5; Davis, *Beckoning*, 64; "seem[ing]," Perkins, 37.

54. Roger Daniels, 63.

55. "bridged," Golway, 157.

56. Lash, *Eleanor and Franklin,* 291.

57. M. & H. Josephson, 336-7.

58. Smith, J.E., 221; Golway, 182-3.

59. Slayton, 254.

60. Barnes, 53-4.

61. Asbell, 244 and 213, cited in J. E. Smith, 207, fn.; Roger Daniels, 65; Gallagher, 34-52, *passim.*

62. Ward, 788.

63. J. E. Smith, 223; Davis, *New York Years,* 16-18, 24-5; Roger Daniels, 70; "Thanks, Frank," Dallek, 98.

64. Rudolph & Ridley, 64; Davis, *New York Years,* 31-2, 40-2, 57; Hubbard, 256; Shlaes, 56; Platt, 271. "Steal," Davis, 40, "most effective," 42.

65. J. E. Smith, 227-8; Davis, *New York Years,* 47.

66. FTC, 72-A, 37.

67. McDonald, *Insull,* 278; Kindleberger and Aliber, 197.

68. Danielian, 502; FTC, 72-A, 111; Bonbright & Means, 110; McDonald, *Insull*, 252. "Insull studied," McDonald, 252 fn.

69. McDonald, *Insull*, 251-2.

70. Insull, *Memoirs*, 188; McDonald, *Insull*, 280; Wasik, 165-6;

71. McDonald, *Insull*, 283; FTC, 72-A, 565-6. 867.

72. Insull, *Memoirs*, 188-90; McDonald, *Insull*, 281.

73. Cudahy and Henderson, 62-3; Insull, *Memoirs*, 189-91.

74. Insull, *Memoirs*, 191-2; Allen, 283-4.

75. Bonbright & Means, 25, 108-13; Sobel, 80-1.

76. Email, Rowe to author, Dec. 8, 2013.

77. "The year 1929," *Time*, Sept. 23, 1929; "a sure sign," Chernow, 308-9; FTC, *Control of Power Companies*, xxiv; FTC, *Utility Corporations* Part 72-A, 37, 67-7; McDonald, *Insull*, 245-52; Skeel, 87; Funigiello, 13.

78. Commager, Henry Steele, "Introduction," *The Journals of David E. Lilienthal* 1: xxiii.

79. Cudahy and Henderson, 63.

80. Wasik, 187-9; Flynn, Dec. 24, 1932, 40; *EW*, Dec. 14, 1929, 1165.

81. McDonald, *Insull*, 285-6; Wigmore, 344-8.

82. Insull, *Memoirs*, 193-5.

83. Wasik, 190; Insull, *Memoirs*, 196-8, "This was," 198; Cudahy and Henderson, 64-5.

84. McDonald, *Insull*, 290-5; Insull, *Memoirs*, 201.

85. McDonald, *Insull*, 126-7, 296-7.

86. Insull, *Memoirs*, 211; Wasik, 200; McDonald, *Insull*, 298-300, "Does this mean" and "It looks that way," 300.

87. McDonald, *Insull*, 301-4, "Well, gentlemen," 304; Insull, *Memoirs*, 220-3; *EW*, June 11, 1932, 1001.

88. Insull, *Memoirs*, 232-8; "the Ishmael or Insull," FDR Library, File No. 522; McDonald, *Insull*, 308-313.

89. Davis, *New York Years*, 76-7, "if possible," 76, "If not," 77; Burns, 113-4.

90. Davis, *New York Years*, 77-8, 91, "not merely conservative," 77, "see to it," 91.

91. Davis, *New York Years*, 88-9.

92. Bellush, 15

93. *NYT*, July 8, 1929.

94. Twentieth Century Fund, *Electric Power*, 43.

95. Burns, 118.

96. McCraw, *TVA*, 26; McDonald, *Insull*, 272-3.

97. Davis, *New York Years*, 92, 99.

98. "when you pay," FDR Library, File No. 408; Davis, *New York Years*, 189-90.

99. Christie, *Cooke*, 100; Davis, *New York Years*, 99-101.

100. Davis, *New York Years*, 100-1, "initiation," 100-1, "to go," 101, "It will not," 101.

101. Dallek, 106-7, 109.

102. Alter, 76, 88.

103. "The fundamental business," *NYT*, Oct. 26, 1929, 1; "federal aid," Dallek, 109; "not as a matter," Dallek, 105; "48 laboratories," Dallek, 107.

104. Davis, *New York Years*, 256.

105. Alter, 101-2. "Here Roosevelt double-crossed," 101, "there is a difference," 102.

106. Wallace, 174.

107. Roger Daniels, 105.

108. "Unprecedented and unusual," FDR Library, File No 483a; "His blithe spirit," Leuchtenburg, 13.

109. National Popular Government League, *Bulletin No. 156* (Washington, 1932), cited by Leuchtenburg, 13, fn. 33.

Chapter 5 – Creating TVA

1. FDR Library, File No. 57; *NYT*, Nov. 1, 1932.

2. FDR Library, Files No. 603 and 604.

3. James A. Hagerty, "Government Operation of Muscle Shoals Plant Pledged by Roosevelt," *NYT*, Jan. 22, 1933, 1-2, "This ought" and "It is," 2.

4. "A great plant" and "Muscle Shoals gives us," FDR Library, File No. 606.

5. "in this period," Cohen, 148; "Painting rainbows," Callahan, 29.

6. Schwarz, 214-5.

7. Freidel, *Launching*, 190; Leuchtenburg, 38-9.

8. *Barron's*, Feb. 13, 1933, cited in Leuchtenburg, 30.

9. Steel, 299.

10. *Wall Street Journal*, editorial, March 4, 1933, cited in Friedel, *Launching* 195.

11. FDR Library, File No. 610.

12. "The whole country," *NYT*, Mar. 6, 1933, 16.

13. FDR Library, File No. 616a.

14. FDR Library, File No. 616a.

15. Alter, 245-52; Friedel, *Launching*, 214-32.

16. McCraw, *TVA*, 34-5; Cohen, 148.

17. Goldman, 263.

18. FDR Library, File No. 622; *NYT*, Apr. 11, 1933, 4.

19. 20th Century Fund, *Electric Power*, 575; Vennard, 74.

20. *NYT*, April 11, 1933, 4.

21. *NYT*, April 12, 1933, 2.

22. "one of the most," McCraw, *TVA*, 161; J. Barnes, 61; Shlaes, 10; Barnard, 84.

23. Neal, 2-3; Barnard, 8-9; Lewis, 22.

24. "the most radical," Barnard, 46.

25. Lewis, 45.

26. Barnett, 58; Dillon, 30, 33.

27. Dillon, 30-1.

28. Barnes, 33.

29. Neal, 21-2.

30. Neal, 18.

31. Barnes, 35.

32. Taft & Heys, 77-8; Barnard, 80, 83; "I thought," Willkie to Hugh S. Johnson, quoted in *Saturday Evening Post*, June 22, 1940, 114, cited in Neal, 24; Jeffries, 56.

33. Dillon, 39.

34. Neal 28.

35. Taft & Hays, 84-5; McCraw, 50-1; Shlaes, 191. James C. Bonbright, member of the Power Authority and a former Columbia professor, was not affiliated with the investment bank Bonbright and Company that helped form C&S.

36. Barnes, 60; Neal, 28; Barnard, 84; "too damn stuffy," Gordon Hamilton, 21, cited in Barnard.

37. *Time* quip cited by Herman B Wells in Madison, viii.

38. "a man wholly natural," and "Inside this rustic," Burns, 433.

39. *NYT*, Apr. 14, 1933, 29.

40. "I know," Neal, 8.

41. *NYT*, Apr. 14, 1933, 29.

42. McCraw, *TVA,* 36; House Military Affairs Committee, *Muscle Shoals,* 73rd Congress, 1st session, 115, 159, 223, 225.

43. "take our markets," Barnard, 85; Davis, *New Deal Years,* 93.

44. Hellman, 33-4.

45. "patterned," *CR,* 73rd Congress, First Session, 2178-9, cited in Leuchtenburg, *FDR and New Deal,* 55; "Some of you," Callahan, 29; "The power plants," *NYT,* Apr. 26, 1933, 14.

46. Barnard, 85-6; Davis, *New Deal Years,* 93-5.

47. Colignon, 118; Daniels, Roger, 148; Hargrove, 24-5, "into a secular passion," 24.

48. Davis, *New Deal Years,* 91-2; "may have been," Neuse, 39.

49. "designed," Funigiello, 37; Schwarz, 216-7.

50. Colignon, 47; Hargrove, 23, 31, 44, 47; McCraw, *TVA,* 56.

51. Neuse, 1-7, 10-4, "platonic friendship," 10.

52. Neuse, 20-3; Whitman, 5; "I am ambitious," Neuse, 21.

53. Neuse, 27-32.

54. McDonald, *Light,* 317; Neuse, 42-3.

55. *NYT*, Oct. 11, 1931, 1; Neuse, 47-8; *Public Utilities Fortnightly,* May 14, 1931, 635.

56. "If the company," Lilienthal, *Journals* 1, 24-5; Neuse, 49, Whitman, 8-9.

57. Lilienthal, *Journals* 1, 26.

58. Neuse, 58-61.

59. McCraw, *TVA,* 55; Lilienthal, *Journals,* 1, 39; Schwarz, 221-2; Callahan, 41.

60. Lilienthal, Memphis State Oral History Project, Feb. 6, 1970, 4, quoted in Hargrove, 36-7.

61. McCraw, 53.

62. Callahan, 41, 97; Davis, *New Deal Years,* 93-4; Hargrove, 38-41.

63. *NYT,* Aug. 25, 1933: 23.

64. *NYT,* Aug. 25, 1933: 23.

65. Taft & Heys, 111.

66. Hellman, 34; Schwarz, 223; McCraw, 59-61.

67. Barnes, 73; Schwarz, 237; "just the kind of experimentation," McCraw, "Triumph and Irony," 1375-6.

68. Lilienthal to Marvin McIntyre, Nov. 21, 1933, quoted in McCraw, 61-2.

69. Hellman, 437-8.

70. McCraw, *TVA*, 62, 124; Hargrove, 45; Barnes, 65; "shorn," Swing, in Engler, 70; Brown, 38.

71. McCraw, *TVA*, 63.

72. Lilienthal, *Journals* 1, 711-3.

73. Callahan, 64.

74. Taft & Heys, 105-7, "means an armistice," 106, "Everybody was talking," 105.

75. Taft & Heys, 111; "extortionary," Emmons, 886-7.

76. McCraw, *TVA*, 64.

77. McCraw, *TVA*, 64-5.

78. Taft & Heys, 111-2, "It's tough," 112; Neal, 29-30; Barnard, 88; Barnes, 64.

79. Colignon, 187.

80. Jim Nanney, "ACE Power Celebrates 75 Years," *Celebrating 75 Years*, Alcorn County Electric Power Association, 4; Robert Palmer, "The Corinth Experiment Played a Kay Role in Rural Electrification," *50 Years 1934-1984, Alcorn County Electric Power Association* 2A, 3A.

81. Julie Bivens, "The History of ACE Power," *Celebrating 75 Years*, Alcorn County Electric Power Association, 6-8, "People," "really scared," and "It was," 8.

Chapter 6—Enlarging the Battlefield

1. "The next great," FDR Library, File No. 518; Springer, 15-6; Clemens, 630, 636; Billington & Jackson, 155.

2. National Archives at Seattle, "The Great Depression and the New Deal." https://www.archives.gov/seattle/exhibit/picturing-the-century/great-depression.html

3. Springer, 16; Holstine, 35.

4. "Up in the Grand Coulee," and "white elephants," Trickey.

5. Billington & Jackson, 167-8.

6. Billington & Jackson, 167-8.

7. Billington & Jackson, 159, 169-70; "I've got to give," Springer, 16.

8. Funigiello, 129-30; Trombley, 112-3.

9. Cooke, "Early Days," 444; Brown, *Rural America*, 40. "I'll have nothing" and "Then will you," Brown.

10. "impetuous plunge" and "the greatest error," Funigiello, 131; Hughes, 300; *EW*, Sept. 29, 1934.

11. Trombley, 116; "take a rather," Brown, *Rural America*, 41.

12. Trombley, 120.

13. Trombley, 116, 120; Cooke, "Early Days," 445.

14. Trombley, 120; Funigiello, 132-3.

15. Cooke, "Early Days," 445; Funigiello, 132-3.

16. Funigielllo, 133.

17. *NYT*, March 31, 1934, 1; Barnes, 73.

18. Cudahy, 69-70; *NYT*, Mar. 16, 18, 19, 20, 22, 23, 24, 28, 30, 31, April 1, 1934; McDonald, *Insull*, 315; "resented" and "as evidence," *NYT*, Mar. 16; "attempted suicide," *NYT*, Mar. 31.

19. Burton Y. Berry, "Mr. Samuel Insull," (typescript of shipboard conversations), 62, quoted in McDonald, *Insull*, 1-2.

20. Wasik, 216.

21. McDonald, *Insull*, 319.

22. McDonald, 330-1; "on the verge" and "caused many," *NYT*, Nov. 2, 1934, 1.

23. "I beg you," Wasik, 228; McDonald, 331-3, "You son of a bitch," 332, and "Insull and his fellow defendants," *Chicago Times*, Nov. 26, 1934, 332-3.

24. McDonald, 333; Knox, 268-72, "to give people," 272.

25. McDonald, 338-9.

26. McCraw, 74; Brown, 36-7; Schwarz, 432-3; "what you are doing," Taft & Heys, 114; "for the benefit," Lilienthal, *TVA Years*, 43.

27. *NYT*, Nov. 20, 1934, 23.

28. Barnes, 74; "rubber," and "The Tennessee River waters," Callahan, 59; Hyman, 104.

29. "The mask is off," *NYT*, Nov. 26, 1934, 1-2; Colignon, 185.

30. "An absolute," Neal, 30; McCraw, 108-12; Taft & Heys, 113.

31. Taft & Heys, 113-4, "if it would go," 113; "the Hindenburg line," letter, George Fort Milton to Norris, Sept. 27, 1935, McCraw, *TVA*, 128.

32. Barnes, 75, 101; Barnard, 93; McCraw, 111-2; Shlaes, 238; *Ashwander v. TVA*; "The effect," "Business & Finance: Grubb on Surplus," *Time*, March 4, 1935.

33. "Judiciary: Curses & Blessings," *Time*, July 29, 1935; Barnard, 93; Dillon, 46-7.

34. Lilienthal, *Journals* 1, 43-6; Funigiello, 52.

35. Funigiello, 54-5.

36. "were very favorably," Barnard, 110; "Charm exaggerated," Barnes, 77.

37. Funigiello, 58-9.

38. "abolition of the evil," Neal, 30; "there was great truth," Schlesinger, *Politics of Upheaval*, 305; Funigiello, 57-8.

39. Lilienthal, *Journals* 1, 46-7.

40. Lilienthal, *Journals* 1, 47.

41. Schlesinger, *Politics of Upheaval*, 305-6; Funigiello, 62-3; Barnes, 82.

42. Barnes, 84-5, "serious doubt," 85.

43. Taft & Heys, 135; Funigiello, 63-5; Yanney, 1; Tugwell, 89.

44. "essential politics" and "personal conviction," Funigiello, 73; "dangerous" and "revival," Christopher Lasch, "Walter Lippmann Today," *New York Review of Books*, Dec. 9, 1965; Barnes, 90.

45. "raised such a hue and cry," Davis, *New Deal Years*, 531; "Quick death," Taft & Heys, 139; "seriously affects," Funigiello, 67-8.

46. Barnes, 89.

47. Barnes, 86-7; "There is no reason," Taft & Heys, 140; Funigiello, 79; "to see," Barnard, 97.

48. Davis, *New Deal Years*, 532.

49. Willkie, "Why the Rayburn Bill Must Be Stopped," *Forbes* 35, May 1, 1935, 11-2.

50. "We have been relegated," Brinkley, 18.

51. Simon, 267.

52. Funigiello, 84 5; "You can show this," Davis, *New Deal Years*, 532.

53. Davis, *New Deal Years*, 533.

54. Schwarz, 255; Davis, *New Deal Years*, 533-5; Funigiello, 82 91.

55. Schwarz, 255.

56. "richest and most ruthless," Lewis, *Implausible*, 235.

57. Davis, *New Deal Years*, 535; Freidel, *Rendezvous*, 168; Funigiello, 99-100; "a bloodsucking business," Newman, 175.

58. Newman, 178.

59. Newman, 178-9.

60. Newman, 179.

61. "crown prince" and "holding company legerdemain," Ritchie, 3; Newman, 181-3; "Eliza," Newman, 182.

62. Newman, 183-4.

63. Funigiello, 93-4.

64. Funigiello, 95-6.

65. Funigiello, 96-7; "had done nothing," Roosevelt, *Public Papers*, 1935: 328-9, cited in Freidel, 169; Simon, 268.

66. "While a strait-jacket," Lewis, "Implausible," 236; Taft & Heys, 144; Barnard, 101.

Chapter 7—Peak Power

1. Nye, 316; Person, 71.

2. Bonbright, *Public Utilities*, 51.

3. Cooke, "Early Days," 439.

4. Funigiello, 141; Person, 74; 20th Century, *Electric Power*, 445.

5. Person, 71.

6. Clemens, 581; Taft & Heys, 117; Smith, 357.

7. Funigiello, 174-5.

8. Springer, 30; Funigiello, 175.

9. Pitzer, 99-100, 115, 121, 195-7; Billington & Jackson, 174.

10. "the greatest dam" and "the first of four," FDR Library, File No. 84; "four great Government," File No. 518.

11. Cooke, "Early Days," 446; Person, 74; 20th Century, *Electric Power*, 445; Nye, 316.

12. Lilienthal, *Journals* 1, 52-3.

13. Person, 75.

14. Funigiello, 149-50, "prohibitive costs" and "a positive program," Trombley, 154-5.

15. Coppock, 98-9; Funigiello, 158; "this work," Funigiello.

16. Caro, *Path to Power*, 520.

17. Francis X. Welch, "World Wide Electrification," *Public Utilities Fortnightly* Mar. 12, 1936, 389-91, cited in Funigiello, 151-2.

18. Funigiello, 152; Caro, 520-1, "When free enterprise," 521.

19. Caro, 521.

20. Funigiello, 152-3; Carmody, 82.

21. Clemens, 582; Schwarz, 257.
22. "Electric Cooperatives Light Up America," National Rural Electric Cooperative Association. https://www.cooperative.com/content/public/maps/growth/map.html.
23. Person, 75; Carmody, 85; McCraw, 87; Clemens, 588.
24. Funigiello, 154-5.
25. Clemens, 587.
26. "The cooperatives," and "normally," Funigiello, 155.
27. Funigiello, 159.
28. Taft & Heys, 117.
29. Taft & Heys, 117-8.
30. Funigiello, 175-6
31. Funigiello, 176-7; Springer, 30.
32. Springer, 31; Funigiello, 177-9.
33. Funigiello, 178-80, "too visionary," 179.
34. Secretary of War George Dern to National Resources Committee, Apr. 11, 1936, quoted in Funigiello, 180.
35. Simon, 192-204, 248, 252, 299.
36. Schwarz, 150.
37. Schwarz, 150-1; Mitchell, *Depression*, 175.
38. Shlaes, 270-1; Simon, 284-5; "Certainly," Swidler and Marcus, quoted in Colignon, 189.
39. Davis, *New Deal Years*, 611-2; "Never," Shesol, 6; "We should consider," *Ashwander et al v. Tennessee Valley Authority et al*, http://www.loc.gov/law, 357; *NYT*, Feb. 18, 1936, "we express," 11, "Tennessee Valley," 1.
40. "ambitious Marxian," Barnes, 103.
41. Colignon, 189-90; Taft & Heys, 118, Barnes, 103-5, "the most useless," Barnes, 105; "the Cuckoo Bird," Willkie, *Financial World*, June 3, 1936, 557.
42. Barnard, 111.
43. Barnes, 104-5.
44. Barnard, 111.
45. Swidler, "Legal Foundations," 32.
46. Barnes, 106; Colignon, 189-90.
47. Taft & Hays, 119.
48. McCraw, 140-2; Leuchtenburg, 86-7.
49. McDonald and Muldowny, 4.
50. McDonald and Muldowny, 91.
51. McDonald and Muldowny, 128.
52. Chandler, 80-3.
53. "in future contracts," Barnes, 105.
54. Taft & Heys, 120; Barnard, 112. "That is election day," and "That is nonsense," Preston Arkwright, "Memorandum of Conference with President Roosevelt," Georgia Power Co. archives, cited in Taft & Heys.
55. Taft & Heys, 119-20.
56. Taft & Heys, 121: Barnard, 113; McCraw, *TVA*, 96-7 ,"fully intends," 97.

57. *NYT,* Oct. 11, 1936, 117.
58. "The companies," Lilienthal to LaFollete, Sept. 16, 1935, quoted in McCraw, *TVA,* 98.
59. Taft & Heys, 121; McCraw, *TVA,* 98-9, "Dr. Morgan, throughout," 99.
60. McCraw, *TVA,* 99-100, "against my will," 99; Schwarz, 229-30; "the intense" and "a controlled," Wehle, 164.
61. "Weapons," Wehle, 165; McCraw, *TVA,* 100-1.
62. *NYT,* Nov. 4, 1939, 1.
63. "suggest," "The Shape of Things," *Nation,* Nov. 7, 1936; "Roosevelt is" and "The Task for Roosevelt," *Nation,* Nov. 14, 1936, both quoted in Brinkley, 15-6.
64. *Fortune,* Feb. 1937, 67.
65. McCraw, *TVA,* 101-3; Barnes, 107-8.
66. Barnes, 108.
67. Taft & Heys, 122-3; "Hopes for peace," *Business Week,* Jan. 23, 1937; McCraw, 104-6.
68. Taft & Heys, 122-3; "ruined," McCraw, 105.
69. Person, 78; 20th Century, *Electric Power,* 454.
70. Carmody, 84-5; 20th Century, *Electric Power,* 445, 452-3, 469; Trombley, 162; Person, 77-8.
71. Person, 78; 20th Century, *Electric Power,* 456.
72. "How Cheap Electricity Pays Its Way," TVA pamphlet, (Knoxville, 1937), pp. 4, 7, 29-30, cited in McCraw, 74.
73. Nye, 318-25.
74. Trombley, 155; Funigiello, 154; "But I would," Funigiello..
75. McCraw, 87; "The thing has become," Trombley, 173; Schwarz, 258.

Chapter 8—Power Loss

1. Billington & Jackson, 189-90; Funigiello, 182-4; "a pretty tall order," Ickes, *Secret Diaries* 2:50.
2. Funigiello, 182-3; Leuchtenberg, "Roosevelt, Norris and the 'Seven Little TVA's'," 418-9; "enough TVAs," *Washington* (DC) *Star,* Feb. 5, 1937, cited in Leuchtenberg, 418.
3. Burns, 296; "I see one-third" and "There is little fault," FDR Library, File No. 1028; "I have received," Roosevelt to Claude Bowers, quoted in Dallek, 270.
4. Shesol, 281; "The essential democracy," and "The Constitution," FDR Library, File No. 1030; Ickes, *Secret Diaries* 1:524.
5. Burns, 293; "That reminds me," Dallek, 270.
6. Burns, 293.
7. Shesol, 253-4, "who have remained," 253.
8. "Aloof," Shesol 4.
9. Shesol, 293-9, "Boys," 293.
10. Shesol, 300-3, "a bloodless," 303, "will be moved" and "the President," 300.
11. Brands, 473.
12. Heilbrunn, Jacob, "War Torn," *NY Times Book Review,* July 28, 2013, 16; Simon, 319.

13. Shesol, 315-24, "on the way" and "He's made," 322, "From now on," 323.

14. Freidel, 233.

15. "Pa is both," Cook, *Eleanor Roosevelt*, 433, quoted in Shesol, 371.

16. FDR Library, File No. 1040A; "I defy," Shlaes, 304; Burns, 299; Dallek, 271; Shesol, 374.

17. Shesol, 379

18. FDR Library, File No. 1041A.

19. Daniels, 328.

20. Daniels, 328.

21. Burns, 303.

22. Daniels, 328; "almost certainly," Brinkley, 19; "The Court bill," Shesol, 435; "Why run" and "If the President," Alsop and Catledge, 153, quoted in Freidel, 235.

23. "defeatist attitude," Ickes, *Secret Diaries* 2:108; Shesol, 406, 464-5; Brands, 474.

24. Shesol, 468-470, "a needless," 468-9.

25. Burns, 308; "Mr. President," Shesol, 491.

26. Dallek, 276.

27. http://www.judiciary.senate.gov/about/history/CourtPacking.cfm/

28. Shesol, 501-2, "he isn't," Farley diary, July 23, 1937, quoted at 502.

29. McKenna, 35-6, 335-6.

30. Taft & Heys, 123.

31. Brinkley, 28.

32. Stanley Lebergott, "Labor force, employment, and unemployment, 1929-39: estimating methods," *Monthly Labor Review*, April 1948, Bureau of Labor Statistics. https://www.bls.gov/

33. Brinkley, 26-8, "throw away," 27, "eliminating," 28.

34. Douglas Irwin, "What caused the recession of 1937-38?" Center for Economic Policy and Research (CEPR), VoxEU.org; Brinkley, 26.

35. Dallek, 300.

36. Farley, *Jim Farley's Story*, 101.

37. Dillon, 107-8; Lewis, 101; Moore, 27; Brinkley, 48; "By profiteering," Dillon, 108.

38. Dillon, 108; Lewis, *Improbable Willkie*, 101; "in the rough-and-tumble" and "a perfect monkey," Neal, 45.

39. Barnes, 123-4, "I know very well," 123-4, "full-blown," 124.

40. Barnes, 124; Shlaes, 304-5, "People will say," 305.

41. Leuchtenburg, "Seven Little TVAs," 418, 425, 434-5 and *passim*; *NYT*, March 26, 1938, 28.

42. Holstine, narhist.ewu.edu; Funigiello, 190-3; Myhra, 13.

43. FDR Library, File No. 1081.

44. *NY Times*, Sept. 29, 1937, 22.

45. Lowery, 8; Schwarz 218; Davis, 93; McCraw, 43; "A great river," in "Bonneville Power Administration," https:www.historylink.org/

46. *NY Times*, Sept. 29, 1937, 17.

47. *NY Times*, Oct. 11, 1937; Funigiello, 194-7.

48. "The largest structure," FDR Library, File No. 1085; Daniels, 343-4; Dallek, 313.

49. Northwest Power and Conservation Council, "Fish Passage at Dams." https://www.newcouncil.org/

50. Northwest Power and Conservation Council, "Dams: Impacts on Salmon and Steelhead." https://www.nwcouncil.org/

51. Northwest Power and Conservation Council, "Grand Coulee Dam: Impacts on Fish." https://www.nwcouncil.org/

52. "How Cheap Electricity Pays Its Way," TVA pamphlet, 1937, pp. 4, 7, 29-30, cited in McCraw, 74; "white elephants," Raver, 8; Springer, 34-5; Funigiello, 199-200.

53. Brinkley, 28; Taft & Heys, 145.

54. "For the sake" and "to modify", editorial, *NYT*, Nov. 10, 1937, 24.

55. "One Way to Revive Business," editorial, *NYT*, Nov. 10, 1937 24.

56. Barnard, 118.

57. Andrew E. Busch, Ashbrook Center, "The New Deal Comes to a Screeching Halt in 1938," May, 2006, http://www.ashbrook.org/publicaitons/oped-busch-06-1938.

58. Moore, 21, 32; Krock, *NYT*, Dec. 19, 1937, 65.

59. SEC Historical Society, "Chasing the Devil."

60. Lewis Wood, *NYT*, March 29, 1938, 1, 8; *Electric Bond and Share Co. v. SEC*, 303 U.S. 419, https://caselaw.findlaw.com/us-supreme-court/303/419.html; Barnes, 138; "Even great aggregations," Wood, p. 8.

61. *Electric Bond and Share Co. v. SEC*, 303 U.S. 419.

62. Wood, *NYT*, March 29, 1938, 1.

63. Barnard, 102.

64. Barnes, 125; Taft & Heys, 145; "Mr. Ickes's delight," *NYT*, Jan. 4, 1938, 15.

65. Barnes, 125; Taft & Heys, 123-5; Swidler, "Legal Foundations," 32-3; "as a last resort," Barnard, 119.

66. Barnes, 130; Barnard, 119-20; "just like," Taft & Heys, 125; McCraw, 133.

67. Barnard, 120; McCraw, 134.

68. McCraw, *TVA*, 88-9, 104.

69. Arthur Morgan, *The New Republic*, Dec. 1936, quoted in Barnes, 116.

70. Schwarz, 230.

71. Callahan, 108.

72. Callahan, 109; Taft & Heys, 126; Daniels, 365; "contumacious," Callahan.

73. Taft & Heys, 126; McCraw, 125-31, "you can," 131.

74. Douglas, *Go East, Young Man*, 282-3.

75. Funigiello, 204-6; Springer, 36.

76. Funigiello, 198, 204; "We are certainly," letter, Ross to Norris, Nov. 20, 1937, in Funigiello, 198; Lee, 236; Brinkley, 28.

77. Clemens, 631; Holstine, "Power to the People," narhist.cwu.edu.

78. Daniels, 368-73; Smith, 413; Dallek, 309.

79. "The New Deal," Arthur Krock, *NYT*, Nov. 10, 1938, 15; Smith, 415; "President Roosevelt," Raymond Clapper, "Return of the Two-Party System," *Current History*, December 1938.

80. James E. Davison, speech, annual meeting, Boca Raton, FL, Willkie mss., Jan. 17, 1939, Lilly Library, Indiana University, Bloomington.

81. *NYT*, Jan. 31, 1939, 1.

82. Barnes, 141-2; McCraw, 135-6.

83. Barnard, 122.

84. "We have offered," Taft & Heys, 127; Hellman, 496-7.

85. "Thanks, Dave," and "We sell," *NYT*, Aug. 16, 1939, 1, 33; "(Willkie's) statement," Barnard, 124; "At the SEC," Douglas, 283.

86. *TVA Handbook, 1987*, 171; BPA, *1947 Annual Report*, 2.

Chapter 9—Powering the War Effort

1. J. E. Smith, 425; "We are," FDR Library, File 1168, "the grave hours" and "ordinary rules," File 1177.

2. National Association of Railroad and Utility Commissioners, "Report of the Committee on Generation and Distribution of Electric Power," *Proceedings* (Washington, DC, 1938), 656, in Funigiello, 229.

3. Funigiello, 229-33; "widespread," Federal Power Commission and War Department, "Confidential Memorandum on Shortages of Electric Generating Capacity for War-Time Needs," July 1, 1938, quoted in Funigiello, 230.

4. Funigiello, 233-4.

5. Funigiello, 234-5; "The network" in "Memorandum to the National Defense Power Committee," Aug. 12, 1938, in Funigiello, 234.

6. Funigiello, 235.

7. "Committee to Study Power Supply Facilities for War Emergency," *Electrical World*, Sept. 17, 1938.

8. Funigiello, 235-7; letter, King to Norris, Sept. 8, 1938, Funigiello 236n32.

9. Funigiello, 234-9.

10. Funigiello, 239.

11. "Force a sharp change," *Washington Times*, Sept. 13, 1938; Funigiello, 237-42, "Any plan," 241.

12. Springer, 44-5, "In the hydroelectric," 44.

13. Funigiello, 200; Springer, 37-8.

14. "the disposal," letter, Ross to George O. Muhlfeld, Nov. 1937, in Funigiello, 207.

15. Fischer to Joel D. Wolfsohn, Mar 7, 1938, in Funigiello, 204.

16. Funigiello, 201-2, 206-7.

17. Springer, 44-5; "One of the greatest," *NYT*, March 16, 1939, 28; "It is certain," *Oregonian*, May 26, 1939.

18. Schwarz, 258; "gave ... no quarter," Schlesinger, *Politics of Upheaval*, 384; National Rural Electric Cooperative Association (NRECA), https://www.cooperative.com/content/public/maps/growth/map.html/

19. Coppock, 97-100

20. Funigiello, 164; Carmody, 86.

21. NRECA, https://www.cooperative.com/content/public/maps/growth/map.html/; Funigiello, 164-7; "thrashed about," Schwarz, 262.

22. Doyle, 7; Schwarz, 269-76, "some electric power," 276.

23. Caro, *Path*, 576.

24. NRECA, https://www.cooperative.com/content/public/maps/growth/map.html

25. McCraw, *TVA*, 127-8.

26. McCraw, *TVA*, 128-31.

27. Funigiello, 246-8.

28. Jeffries, 94; Smith, 426; "Hitler would not," John Morton Blum, *From the Morgenthau Diaries* 2:48-9, in J. E. Smith, 428.

29. Funigiello, 248-51; McCraw, 155.

30. Springer, 44-5; Klein, 230; Chandler, 88-90.

31. Taft & Heys, 146-7, "They are shooting" and "We expect," 146.

32. B. Mitchell, 175-6; Taft & Heys, 150-1.

33. George Gallup, "Ebb and Flow of the Third-term Issue," *NYT*, Oct. 13, 1940, 108.

34. *NYT*, Feb. 27, 1938, 1.

35. Jeffries, 89.

36. Jeffries, 82-8.

37. Arthur Krock, "Some Politician's 'Future Book' on 1940," *NYT*, Feb. 23, 1939, 22.

38. Neal, 54.

39. Neal, 69-71; Barnes, 164; Johnson, 76-7, "done enough," 77; "Back home in Indiana," Moscow, 70.

40. Moscow, 64-6; Barnes, 179, 183, "Dewey has," 183; Kluger, 325-7.

41. Lewis, 141-2.

42. Johnson, 102.

43. Freidel, 344.

44. Lewis, "Implausible," 246-7, "sell Czechoslovakia," 247; "On the basis," Barnes, 254.

45. Moscow, 151-6, "Mr. Roosevelt," 151; "This tremendous," *NYT*, Aug. 1, 1940, 1.

46. *NYT*, Nov. 4, 1940, 11.

47. Jeffries, 168-9.

48. Klein, *Call to Arms*, 230; *Electrical World*, June 27, 1940, 52; Taft & Heys, 151-3, "We've got," and "The present," 151.

49. Smeltzer, "Memories," www.sechistorical.org.

50. Callahan, 123.

51. Klein, *Call to Arms*, 200, 230.

52. Klein, *Call to Arms*, 66, 160, 230-1, "there is," and "He's worth," 231.

53. Klein, *Call to Arms*, 161, 230-1, "one of" and "Everything," 161.

54. Klein, *Call to Arms*, 160-3.

55. Billington & Jackson, 192.

56. "represent a reservoir," 20th Century Foundation, *Power*, 196.

57. Springer, 41; Funigiello, 265.

58. *TVA Handbook, 1987*, 171; McCraw, 155; Callahan, 123-6, 161; Wildavsky, 529, 579; *Ashwander v. Tennessee Valley Auth.*, 297 U.S. 288 (1936). www.supreme.justia.com/

59. *1947 Annual Report,* Bonneville Power Administration, 2.
60. Holstine, "BPA Powered the Industry that Helped Win World War II," Oct. 31, 2012. www.narhist.ewu.edu/pnf/articles/s2/i-2/power_people/power.html/
61. Brown, 82; Funigiello, 171-3.
62. Dallek, 403-4, 409-13, "being a true help," 413; Neal, 187-8.
63. Barnes, 254.
64. Neal, 216-7, "It would give me," 216, "We go to war," 217.
65. Lewis, *Improbable,* 281.
66. Frank, "The Willkie What-If." https://www.newyorker.com/news/daily-comment/the-willkie-what-if-f-d-r-s-hybrid-party-plot

Epilogue

1. Taft & Heys, 150-6; Barnard, 102; Hyman, 105.
2. Person, 82; Clemens, 592; National Rural Electric Association Strategic Analysis, March 1999, cited in Lawrence J. Malone, "Rural Electrification Administration," Economic History Association. https://eh.net>encyclopedia>rural-electrification-administration/
3. *TVA Handbook 1956,* 221; *TVA Handbook 1987,* 222.
4. Annmarie Hauck Walsh, *The Public's Business: The Politics and Practices of Government Corporations* (Cambridge, MA: MIT Press, 1978), 32-3, quoted in Chandler, 116.
5. Funigiello, 260.
6. McCraw, 33-4.
7. "develop a plan" and "legislation," Roosevelt, *Public Papers and Addresses, 1934,* 339-40, in Davis, *New Deal Years,* 530.
8. "No company died," quoted in Barnes, 140.
9. Commager, 345.
10. Taft & Heys, 128-9; Schwarz, 234; Commager, 345, quoted in McCraw, 145-6.
11. Emmons, 887-9, data from National Electric Light Association, *Statistical Supplement;* and *Edison Electric Institute,* Historical Statistics, 165; 20th Century Fund, *Power,* 7.
12. Wright, 5.
13. Nye, 317-21; Funigiello, 263.
14. U.S. Bureau of the Census, *Historical Statistics,* and *EEI Pocketbook,* cited in Hyman, 90, 109, 122, 142.

INDEX

Note: Page numbers in italic refer to photos.

ABOUT THE AUTHOR

Author photo courtesy of Swarthmore College

John A. (Jack) Riggs studied history at Swarthmore College before embarking on a career in public policy. Now a Senior Fellow at the Aspen Institute, he was at the center of energy policymaking in Washington, DC, for over thirty years, observing the recent transformation of the electricity industry and helping develop the policies that govern it. He taught a graduate seminar in energy policy for five years at the University of Pennsylvania, moderated energy forums at the Aspen Institute, and testified over a dozen times before Congressional energy committees.

He received a master's degree in public policy at the Princeton School of Public and International Affairs and served five years in Vietnam with the Agency for International Development during the war. As Staff Director of the House Energy and Power Subcommittee, he participated in all the major energy legislation of the 1980s and early 1990s. From 1993 to 1995 he was Deputy Assistant Secretary and then Assistant Secretary for Policy and International Affairs at the U.S. Department of Energy.

As Executive Director of the Aspen Institute Energy and Environment Program and as Senior Fellow, Riggs led the renowned Aspen Energy Policy Forum for nineteen years. He has edited or co-edited several Aspen Institute books and reports.

He served on the Swarthmore College Board of Managers for fourteen years, as chair of the board's Governance Committee, and as president of the college's Alumni Association.

He and his wife live in Washington, DC.